D0097736

The *New*
CAN-OPENER
Cookbook

POPPY CANNON

New York

THOMAS Y. CROWELL COMPANY
Established 1834

The *New*
CAN-OPENER
Cookbook

CONTENTS

❦ 1 ❦

~~~~~~~~~~~~~~~~~~~~~~~~~~~~~~~~~~~

Introduction

A NEW KIND OF COOKING

SOMETHING NEW has been added to the age-old saga of good eating. America, never before gastronomically renowned despite its wealth of excellent ingredients, burgeoning larders, fertile farm lands, herds and flocks, has developed epicurean interests —but with a difference. Our cooking ideas and ideals have their roots in many lands and cultures, but our new way of achieving gourmet food can only happen here—in the land of the mix, the jar, the frozen-food package, and the ubiquitous can opener.

At one time a badge of shame, hallmark of the lazy lady and the careless wife, today the can opener is fast becoming a magic wand, especially in the hands of those brave, young women, nine million of them (give or take a few thousand here and there), who are engaged in frying as well as bringing home the bacon.

There has developed among them a pride in preparing and serving interesting meals. It is no longer considered chic, charming, or "intellectual" to be ignorant in the kitchen, but always there is the problem of time, the crowding of many varied interests.

To the rescue comes the manufacturer of so-called ready-to-serve foods. Actually, at least in gourmet terms, they are not *quite* ready to serve, but they do provide the basis for any number of prideful, even complicated, specialties. The modern cook looks at it this way: other people have the responsibility for the selection of my raw materials, the cleaning and preliminary preparation. When I ply my busy little can opener, I move onto the scene the way a chef comes in after a corps of kitchen helpers has done the scullery chores—the drudgery of cooking. Armed with a can opener, I become the artist-cook, the master, the creative chef.

The use of a can opener may not be news, but the gourmet approach definitely is, for our new-style wielder of the can opener is a perfectionist. Gone are the days when anything quick was considered a triumph and concoctions of tuna fish, cream of mushroom soup, and potato chips flourished among the hurry-up menus. Now we are becoming classicists, and are analyzing the complicated, work-consuming recipes of olden days. We are discovering how the canned stews and chicken fricassees, canned gravy, soup, or consommé can be properly employed in today's living.

Escoffier demands over and over again slowly simmered, painstakingly clarified white or brown stock. On the back of every gourmet range, the stock pot never ceased to simmer—that was in the old days. But now, canned consommé or chicken broth provides an admirable answer. For greater economy, bouillon cubes or meat extract, plus hot water, may be used.

In the canned stew department, there is much that is interesting. Although such stews are notoriously underseasoned to appeal to the *average palate* (that much-maligned and underestimated, unknown quantity which haunts and hog-ties the average manufacturer), they can be transformed with a rinse of red wine, a clove of garlic, parsley, half a bay leaf, and a flicker of mixed herbs to make something delightfully akin to Le Boeuf en Daube as served in France.

Consider a can of beef gravy. There is such a thing put up by one of our largest food manufacturers. No one in his right mind would wax lyrical over it, but it makes a sound and honest beginning or foundation for a dozen excellent sauces.

Or, take the lowly meat ball—not wildly exciting, certainly, but there is inspiration to be found among the Hindus, where cookery is a sacred ceremony, a recipe for Kofta-Ka-Kari (Forcemeat Ball Curries). This is achieved simply by adding to the meat balls and their gravy, the best available curry powder, a well-crushed clove of garlic, dried parsley, thyme, marjoram, and rosemary. Heat and serve inside a ring of cooked rice, decorated prettily with french fried onions (another excellent canned specialty) and pass the chutney, please, and as many other curry accompaniments as are handy: crisp, crushed bacon, coarsely chopped nuts, India relish, grated coconut, chopped hard-cooked eggs, green onion, green pepper.

Jars as well as tins from the ordinary corner store hold gourmet treasure—a jar of real mayonnaise made of whole egg and olive oil, just as any chef would make it, is capable of dozens of interesting variations.

Like the finale in a play, the climax of a meal is the dessert. Far too many meals in this hurried age merely *stop* at a given point—they do not end, they are not climaxed. What a pity, since there are so many uncomplicated yet, thoroughly delightful ways to write a lovely finis to a satisfying menu. To be distinctive, a dessert need not be complicated nor even excessively caloric. Consider the canned fruits and their infinite divertisements. Canned cherries, for instance, made into Cerises au Claret (page 245), chilled very well and served from a frosty glass bowl with lady fingers.

On page 249 you will find Fresh Pineapple Royale, another impressive dessert, cribbed from Escoffier and adapted to present-day hurried techniques.

It's easy to cook like a gourmet though you are a beginner. We want you to believe just as we do that in this miraculous age it is quite possible—and it's fun—to be a "chef" even before you can really cook.

THE RECIPES

We do not suggest or expect that this be your only cookbook, though it might well be your introduction to the art of cooking. So we have made no attempt to cover in our recipes the whole field of cookery. There is, however, a representative collection of recipes in various categories and a sufficient number of each—appetizers, soups, meats, vegetables, salads, desserts, and beverages—to equip you for any occasion. Armed with these recipes and ideas you should achieve with the least possible expenditure of work and tension not only excellent eating but also considerable acclaim.

Every recipe includes a short cut—a canned or quick-frozen food, a mix or a new and simplified way to arrive at a particularly delectable result. In each case we have tried with a few lines of introduction to explain our reasons for including each particular recipe. We have tried also to describe as well as mere words can the appearance and the flavor of the various dishes. Far too many recipes—fine recipes, too—are printed to rest unknown, unnoticed, and untasted within the covers of a book simply because modern authors lack the perspicacity of those old-time ladies who in their handwritten recipes more often than not would title a recipe not merely Veal Loaf, for instance, but Aunt Mame's Special Veal Loaf—very light and fluffy. They might add, "Men of this family have always loved a loaf fixed this way with a hard-boiled egg in the center. . . ."

Not only because of the recipe introductions, but also in the listing of the ingredients you will find this book unorthodox. Only the essential ingredients are listed—not salt, pepper, and water. Also in most recipes the garnishes are included in the ingredients because they are important in making any dish interesting and appetizing.

Because we know that few people outside of home economics classes and TV demonstrations measure before starting to cook we give the amounts along with the recipe directions so that your eye need not do a jumping-jack act from recipe to ingredients and back again to recipe. For instance, a recipe suggests you will need for Sauce Suprême condensed cream of chicken soup, milk, egg, lemon juice. Later when you start to work you learn that 1/4 to 1/2 cup of milk is required, a can of soup, a tablespoon of lemon juice.

The glossary supplies additional information on ingredients, herbs, spices, seasonings, as well as the addresses of many fine mail-order houses.

AT SERVING TIME

A chef does not serve a dish, he *presents* it and his presentation is every bit as important as his preparation. Much of the difference between just cooking and epicurean cooking is the *difference in the way the food is served.* In our effort to lift quickly prepared food to extraordinary heights of appeal we have appended to each recipe a few lines titled "At serving time," which tell you how to serve, how to garnish attractively and with originality, and, in many cases, what to serve with each particular food for an interesting, well-balanced meal.

Present-day menus have become so simple. Individual and family likes and dislikes are so varied that we find it much more helpful to have suggestions for "what goes with what" instead of a full-scale formal menu plan.

YOU WILL NEED

At least half of the social and culinary success of any hurried epicure depends upon a good stock of supplies. The ability to whip up something wonderful with seemingly miraculous speed and ease often depends more on skill in shopping and management than on skill in cooking. In this book we have confined our recipe ingredients to those products which for the most part can be secured in any ordinary grocery store or delicatessen in small as well as big towns and cities. Occasionally an unusual seasoning or a specialty item is mentioned. You have only to consult the alphabetical glossary at the end of the book to get a complete description of anything that seems unfamiliar and information about where you can find it or order it by mail.

Among those products that are called for most frequently in this book and which it would be well to keep on hand—in addition to the ordinary salt, pepper, milk, bread, and butter are: a collection of canned soups, such as cream of chicken, mushroom, consommé, to be used not only as soups but also in the making of sauces; canned meats and fish to suit your fancy; canned or quick-frozen chicken and chicken fricassee and chicken à la king; canned tomatoes, tomato sauce, and tomato paste; your favorite canned or quick-frozen vegetables; oil, vinegar, and prepared salad dressings; cheese, of course; dehydrated vegetable flakes, such as onion flakes, parsley flakes, mixed vegetable flakes; mixes for pastry, rolls, and cookies, as well as cake, pies, and puddings (vanilla-, chocolate-, and custard-flavored puddings are always good to have on hand); "storable" as well as fresh milk—evaporated, dehydrated, or condensed.

And then the core of all epicurean effort is a treasury of seasonings. You will want all the usual spices, herbs, and flavorous seeds such as: salt, pepper, cloves, nutmeg, cinnamon, allspice, ginger, curry, sage, marjoram, thyme, basil, tarragon, savory, rosemary, paprika, and monosodium glutamate (generally known under various trade names, such as Accent, Zest, etc.). And a few of the less usual ones, too, such as cumin, saffron, cardamon, turmeric; condiments, olives, and pickles to be used not only at the table but in preparation of food, extracts over and beyond the usual vanilla. Kitchen Bouquet or some other condiment with a caramelized sugar base adds rich, homemade color to stews and gravies.

Wines also we have employed frequently—red and white table wines, sherry, port, an occasional dash of champagne, rum and brandy for that glorious and ever-so-easy and dramatic trick of serving food flambé (afire).

In this book we have not assumed the presence of anything beyond ordinary stove and refrigerator and have mentioned only a few simple, inexpensive, and helpful hand tools, such as the Mouli grater, the garlic press, and the rotary egg beater.

Although much of your success in contriving the distinguished dish from a ready-to-serve product will depend upon seasoning as well as presentation, it is wise to be light-handed with the spices. A good rule is to add at first when seasoning to taste only about half the amount of seasoning you think will be required, and then, tasting as you go, add bit by bit until the result satisfies you.

Wine is very helpful in glamorizing simple dishes and simple meals, but here too, it is wise to be cautious as to the amounts used and careful also as to the quality. When improvising your own recipes, add half as much wine as you think you'll need. Taste frequently as you add to be sure the wine will not overpower all other flavors.

Remember that wine is flavoring—that the flavoring is very often one of the least expensive ingredients of the dish as well as the most important. Perhaps it would be best to forget the term "cooking wine" or "cooking sherry." The wines you use in cooking need not be expensive but they should be well flavored and well made. The same holds true for other liquors—brandy, rum, liqueurs, and cordials. Cooking with wine need not be expensive when you consider how easy it is to open a bottle beforehand, add wine to the sauce, the soup, the stew or the fish and drink the rest with dinner.

In a number of instances we have suggested the simple drama of serving ordinary foods flambé, or afire. Too many people feel that such theatrics should be confined to the Christmas pudding or an occasional Cherries Jubilee, but a number of famous restaurateurs have led the procession and now all manner of foods from appetizers through soups, meats, fish, puddings, and ices acquire a new attractiveness as well as a definite mellowing and blending of flavors by the addition of some type of spirits, which we suggest should be slightly warmed before being set afire.

❧ 2 ❧

〜〜〜〜〜〜〜〜〜〜〜〜〜〜〜〜〜〜〜〜

The Quick Gourmet Meal

AND HOW TO PLAN IT

I F METHODS OF COOKING have changed in recent years—and they have enormously—this change is slight compared to the revolution in menus. A family dinner as prescribed in the notable *White House Cookbook* in the early nineteen hundreds consisted of approximately a dozen different items, at least four courses, three or four different desserts—not including coffee.

Now even for company three courses are considered lavish. Two-course meals—without an opener—are universally acceptable and in many cases we dine as well at lunch on one main dish, nibbling at the fruit centerpiece for dessert or content with "just coffee, please." The planning of the meal is no longer a problem of "leading up to and away from" the *pièce de rèsistance* as it used to be, but rather it is a question of combining the right flavors, colors, textures, as well as getting the proper amount of nourishment.

Here as in the planning of the most elaborate meals the same basic rules should be observed. First, there must be contrast— contrast in texture, in color, and in flavor. A smooth and creamy dish must be served along with something crisp; chicken à la king, for example, goes well inside a ring of julienne potato sticks. Crunchy rolls, nuts, carrot sticks, all offer interesting texture contrast to soft foods. You would not follow creamed chicken with a creamy dessert. Contrast in color is equally important—green peas, sliced tomato, golden corn—the rich brown of a grilled lamb chop. A bright green sprinkle of parsley and lemon slice and chopped egg on black bean soup. The paleness of pears, a scarlet plum, a vivid apricot, a pale and sunny slice of pineapple in a fruit compote. Such things illustrate the possibilities of color contrasts to provide appetite appeal.

7

Contrast in flavors is even more important. A bland food requires a piquant accompaniment—a pork chop for example or other rich meat such as ham or goose is at its best with something cool and fruity, such as applesauce or pickled peaches. Sometimes flavor contrasts—sweet and sour, bland and spicy are combined in a single dish. More often they accompany or follow each other. A hot curry is ringed with rice and served with a number of sharply contrasted accessories—there's cold beer to sip with a hot curry or chile con carne, followed by fresh fruit.

DRAMA AT THE TABLE

If your food is basically good and if you have contrast in texture, color, and flavor, that's more than half the battle. Add drama and you're sure to make yourself a reputation. All of us in our lifetime have eaten honest, nourishing food that is dull as dishwater.

Drama enters not only in your choice of dishes, silverware, and centerpiece but also in the napkins, the tablecloth or mats, the color of the candles, the color and shape of the water glasses. All these things can add tremendously to the enjoyment of a meal.

Use your color sense, your creative imagination, when you buy table linen or mats. Do not be bound to tradition. Dare to dye an old white damask table cloth a bright shocking pink, a deep leaf green, or a wine red. Have the courage to use a pink plate perhaps on that deep green or red cloth. Consider the possibilities of drapery or curtain material as a tablecloth or runners. If you fear the effect of too much washing on the pattern you might try covering the cloth itself with a clear plastic—but not for formal meals!

Be equally imaginative about the centerpiece. There is no law compelling you to use a brace of candles and a low arrangement of florist flowers. A row of potted geraniums might be far more interesting when you serve a great tureen of party soup. And the centerpiece need not always be dead center. Try the effect of a decorative grouping along one side of the table when there are only three to dinner or place it at the end of a long buffet.

For those times when you particularly want a meal to be "a production" you might plan the menu around some particularly effective dish or accessory in your possession. If you have a huge French casserole make it a point to collect several interesting dishes that can be cooked and served en casserole. Is a beautiful salad bowl a prized possession? Make it a habit to include in your menu a number of main dish salads. Perfect your skill as a salad impresario and mix the dressing at the table.

Have you a chafing dish? a crepe suzette pan? a cut-glass punch bowl? Keep them in mind when you begin to think about "what shall we have to eat?" and don't be self-conscious about repeating your specialties or even your menus. Many a fine restaurant and many a clever hostess have built reputations on a few excellent dishes. If you share the almost universal necessity to be host or hostess as well as cook, learn a few of the tricks of the *métier*. Always allow yourself at least ten minutes alone in the kitchen before dinner is announced. There are various ways whereby guests can be kept happy during this brief interval—with cocktails and canapés or appetizers, television or conversation.

Unless you are exceedingly deft and sure of yourself you may find it wiser to dispense with the first course or to provide one which can properly be set on the table before the guests are called. Make every effort to have by your side either a commodious coffee table or a three-tiered serving table on which extra dishes, accessories, serving spoons, and the like may be set. With a little planning you should be able to arrange matters so that once having sat down to the table you need disappear only once just before the dessert.

Whenever you plan a meal just for yourselves or for company don't attempt too much. Keep it simple—confine your efforts to one or two dishes and make them very, very good.

No matter how simple it is, *never* try out a new dish on a new audience. Even the greatest of chefs has a dress rehearsal before an important dinner.

Serve cold foods cold, chilled foods like salad on plates which have been chilled in the refrigerator, cold drinks preferably in glasses which have been previously filled with ice, frozen desserts on cold plates, too. All this, though it may sound slightly troublesome, is not at all difficult once you become accustomed to the idea. The bowl of salad greens for example all washed, dried and ready for tossing can go into the refrigerator on top of a pile of salad plates. The ice used to chill the glasses can be used later for icing the beverage.

Serve hot foods *hot*. If you have no warming oven (our grandmothers were rather more blessed than we are in this respect what with the old coal range and the warm oven that hung above it) you can use any oven as a warming oven. Keep the temperature somewhere between 150 and 200 degrees—a temperature that should not harm china or silver dishes but will keep plates, serving pieces, coffee and tea cups properly heated. If you are broiling steak or chops and your oven is too hot for the plates, you might use a good-sized top-of-the-stove ovenette such as are sold for baking potatoes, etc. Put an asbestos pad under it and have the heat very low. A steak platter may be warmed on top of the stove on an asbestos pad over a *very* low flame.

To keep your food at its best for second servings it would be wise to invest in some kind of warming equipment. There are a number of inexpensive and attractive warmers on the market on which ordinary serving pieces and casseroles of course may be placed. Most of them use stubby candles—something like votive candles. Ideal, of course, are thermetically controlled electric warming trays, which come in many sizes.

COMPANY DINNERS

One of the most difficult problems about cooking a meal for guests is that of having everything come out on time—all ready and piping hot or perfectly chilled at the one precise moment when dinner is served. In addition to the hazards of the kitchen you must consider the unpredictability of modern lives. To help the hostess retain her poise we suggest planning the meal around food that can *wait*. Nor need this confine you to the inevitable casserole.

Lamb Chops with Elegance

Mexican Guacamole with Crackers and
    Bread Sticks   (in the living room)

Baked Lamb Chops Farci
Broccoli au Gratin
Beet Aspic Salad Ring Filled with Cole
    Slaw

Sliced Quick-Frozen Peaches with Sherry
Petits Fours
Demitasse

Since the lamp chops are stuffed we have omitted from the menu, potatoes or rice. The combination of colors and textures in this menu is particularly interesting, beginning with the pale green and peppery guacamole which is served in avocado shells.

We have with the lamb dark green broccoli and, for contrast, there is the bright ruby of beet aspic ring. As for the dessert, the sliced quick-frozen peaches will be most delicious if they are not entirely thawed, and served with a dash of lemon juice and a bit of sherry or Madeira wine.

Stew with Style

Not merely simple but simply elegant is this menu.

> Smoked Salmon with Trimmings and Canned Sliced Pumpernickel

> Beef Stew with Wine
> Asparagus with Amandine Sauce
> Brown 'n' Serve French Bread
> Red Wine

> Stewed Figs à la Glace
> Demitasse

Italian with Distinction

With so many ready-to-serve Italian specialties—interesting pastas, prepared sauces, canned ravioli, and quick-frozen pizzas available, it is easy to plan, on the spur of the moment, a quick meal which would do honor to a proud Italian cook.

> Antipasto:
> Thin-Sliced Italian Salami
> Pickled Beets
> Pimiento
> Cole Slaw Topped with Anchovy Fillets
> Sardines
> Radishes, Garlicked Olives, Turkish Spiced Mushrooms

Canned Minestrone with Grated Cheese
Green Noodles with Meat Sauce or Al-
    fredo's Noodles or Spaghettini with
    Meat Balls De Luxe
Tossed Green Salad

Baked Peaches Italienne

Sunday Breakfast Buffet

Some people call it brunch and consider it the most modern way
to entertain but actually it has classic forebears in the lavish hunt
breakfasts of other days. There is no gainsaying the fact that it
does offer, especially to the hostess with a weekday job, a unique
opportunity to repay social obligations in a leisurely and graceful
manner.

Here are two menus. For a large crowd you might combine them
—serving two different fruits, hot breads, etc.

I

Large Pitcher of Orange Juice and Melon
    Balls, Sliced Bananas, or Sliced Fresh
    Pears

Kippers
Potato Balls
Hot Rolls
Assorted Preserves
Plenty of Coffee

II

Macédoine of Fruits

Dried Beef and Mushroom Sauce
Grilled Tomatoes
Sure-Pop Popovers, Coffee Cake
Plenty of Coffee

These menus have the virtue of originality because of the omis-
sion of the usual ham or bacon-and-eggs but these favorites could
be added to the buffet or substituted either for kippers or dried

beef. Something sweet for dessert is not generally included in a breakfast plan but we have provided a selection of preserves and/or sweet rolls or coffee cake. Large amounts of coffee will be consumed. Be sure to provide at least 2 1/2 cups per person. Instant coffee is a great boon for occasions like this. Make it strong, keep it fiery hot.

For Immediate Service

Certain dishes which actually involve little effort and comparatively little preparation time are often avoided because so many people dread the hazards involved in a dish that must of necessity be served the instant it is ready. However, once you have learned the technique of planning a meal around such a dish you will find many occasions to show off your ability in making a soufflé, for example, or a puffy omelet, a Swiss fondue or a Baked Alaska.

It is easier to manage a meal around a main course soufflé. Just make certain that your guests are seated a minute or two before the soufflé is ready. If you feel that you must have a first course, serve a hearty appetizer in the living room with a cocktail or tomato juice. Make certain that you have all your other food on hand and ready to serve.

Brandied Liver Pâté with Crusty French
Bread Served Beforehand

Neapolitan Cheese Soufflé
Mixed Green Salad with Fruits

Chocolate Ice Cream Roll (bought) with
Chocolate Sauce (canned)

When you serve a soufflé for dessert, it is much better to time it so that the diners instead of the soufflé will be kept waiting for a few minutes. There are two schools of thought in the baking of soufflés. One, the French method, is the quick method in which the oven is quite hot and the soufflé is cooked 20 to 25 minutes. The other method, variously called English or American, substitutes a moderate oven and, in order to slow the cooking even more, it is suggested that the soufflé be placed inside a pan of water.

In our book, we have advised the French method because of the speed and because the quick soufflé, being crisp on the outside and soft in the center, dispenses with the need of an extra sauce. However, if you find that you need an hour or so to eat your dinner, you can put a dessert soufflé into the oven before you sit down and be quite sure of having it ready when the dessert time comes. When your menu is confined to one or two courses and your guests are fairly fast eaters, the 25 minutes allowed by the French type soufflé should be ample.

In the following menu, we suggest appetizers served in the living room with cocktails.

Ten minutes before the dinner hour excuse yourself and go into the kitchen. It should take you no more than 5 minutes to add the egg whites to a chocolate pudding mixture, which you have already prepared (see page 237), pop the soufflé into the preheated oven. The rest of the menu may include the following:

> Paella à la Valencianna
> Crusty Rolls
> Green Salad with Pimiento Strips
>
> Miracle Chocolate Soufflé with Rum-
>   Flavored Ready-Whipped Cream
> Demitasse

Fish Dinner Menus

Most people feel that planning a fish dinner presents difficulties. There are, of course, superstitions about certain foods which are presumed not to go with fish but most of these ideas have been proved to be nothing more than superstitions. In making a menu that stars a fish dish, abide by the regular rules. If your fish is rich and fatty, like salmon or swordfish, the accompaniments should not be too hearty. If the fish has a sauce, take care not to include in the menu other sauces. If the fish is bland in flavor, provide extra piquancy—lemon sections, pickles, tartare sauce. If the fish has a great deal of flavor like salt mackerel, provide a bland foil in the way of boiled or baked potato. Observe the usual rules as to color—pale white fish should be accompanied by colorful vegetables. Spinach and beets provide this. Strong-flavored vegetables of the cabbage family tend to overpower the delicacy of fish. Peas are fine but almost too popular. Asparagus is an excellent choice.

Here are two menus suitable for days of abstinence, for no meat or meat extracts are used.

I

Claret Consommé with Lime Slices

Fillet of Perch Baked in Cream
Canned Julienne Potatoes
Green Beans with Mushrooms
Cucumbers in Vinegar

Lemon Meringue Pie

II

Canned Vegetarian Vegetable Soup

Shad Roe
Parsleyed Canned Potato Balls
Tossed Green Salad with Diced Beets
    and Chopped Eggs, Tart French
    Dressing

Apple Snow with Cinnamon Sauce

Festive Buffet

Although this menu was originally planned as a New Year's Good Luck Party with a number of traditional New Year's Day delicacies from several different lands, it is easily adapted for any festive occasion, and, except for a little help with the dishwashing, you should find it not at all onerous to prepare. Provide as many or as few hors d'oeuvres and appetizers as you feel are necessary but have them all alone with cocktails or tomato juice in the living-room end of your domain—away from the buffet table which should be entirely devoted to solid food:

Ready-to-Serve Smoked Goose or Turkey
Canned Purée of Chestnuts
Buttered Pumpernickel
Buttered Finger Rolls
Cole Slaw in a Cabbage Shell
Sliced Tomatoes with Parsley
Baked Virginia Ham Garnished with
    Brandied Peaches
Hopping John
Italian Ricotta
Panetone (bought or made from a mix)
Red Wine or St. Louis Glee Wine
Coffee

Thanksgiving Dinner

A friend whose husband is in television wasn't certain until the last minute whether or not they would be able to spend Thanksgiving with her mother in the country. How was she going to prepare for Thanksgiving in their own New York apartment without becoming encumbered with an expensive lot of perishable foods if they went away. They had almost decided to solve the problem by eating Thanksgiving dinner bleakly in a restaurant.

This menu made it possible for them to have on hand everything necessary for a holiday dinner—and precious little which would go to waste.

Raw Vegetable Hors d'Oeuvres
    (celery sticks, raw cauliflower, carrot
    sticks, cucumber fingers, radishes, black
    olives, green olives)

Canned Roast Turkey, Old-Fashioned
    Gravy
Herb Stuffing (packaged)
Brussels Sprouts and Chestnuts in Mush-
    room Sauce
Whole Berry Cranberry Sauce
Sweet Potatoes and Apple en Casserole

Pumpkin Pie and/or Hot Mince Pie
Cold Cider

An enormous plateful of raw, crisp vegetables takes the place of appetizers and salad in this menu. The canned roast turkey and the stuffing require a minimum of preparation. Gravy is made according to the recipe in this book, from the broth in which the turkey is packed. The Brussels sprouts are quick frozen, chestnuts already peeled and cooked in a glass jar—the sauce made from a can of condensed cream of mushroom soup. Old-fashioned cranberry sauce with whole berries in it comes in a can also, as do the sweet potatoes and the sliced apples for the casserole. As for the pie or pies, we suggest buying them at the bakeshop. They will keep admirably in the refrigerator for several days—in the frozen-food compartment of your refrigerator for many weeks.

Wonderful to relate a Thanksgiving dinner such as this one—even with the scraping and cutting of the vegetables, should not take more than an hour's time—including setting the table!

The Salad Meal

Upon occasion a hearty salad served generously can provide the main course for an excellent lunch or supper. When planning a meal around a salad, make certain that your salad includes adequate amounts of some stick-to-the-ribs nourishment—eggs, cheese, meat, poultry, or fish. In other words, if you will forgive the inclusion of a bit of nutritional jargon, make certain that there is sufficient *protein* in your salads as well as greens and vegetables or fruits. When such a salad is served with an oil dressing, and with bread, you need have no fears about having a well-balanced meal. Three salad meals follow:

I

Black Bean Soup with Garnishes

Chicken Salad in Tomato Aspic Ring
Hot Biscuits

Sliced Oranges Mexican with Rum
Cookies

II

Onion Soup or Minestrone with Grated
Cheese

Chef's Salad (made without cheese because there's cheese with the soup)
Hot French Bread

Quick Crème Caramel with Sliced Peaches
Hot or Iced Tea

III

Petite Marmite Henri IV

Fresh Fruit Salad
Brioches

Coeurs à la Crème
Tea or Coffee

Hot Weather Meals

It is generally conceded that even on the hottest day one hot dish
should be included in every meal but the hot food need not necessarily be hearty. It can be a cup of clear hot Madrilène, chicken
broth, or just hot tea or coffee. Hot weather food should include
plenty of protein foods such as egg, cheese, meat, fish, or poultry.
Appearance is particularly important during a hot spell when appetites are inclined to be erratic. When the day is hot serve your
most attractive specialties with your prettiest accessories—chill
plates and glasses, surround the butter dish with chopped ice. Omit
greasy foods. Be careful about candles on the table—they can be
extremely heating. On a breathless day choose cool green leaves
instead of flowers.

I

Hot Clam Broth

Sliced Beef en Gelée
Tossed Green Salad

Hot Bread
Potato Salad with Chives

Strawberries Romanoff
Demitasse

II

Chicken with White Wine and White
  Grapes
Asparagus
Shoestring Potatoes

Fresh Pineapple Royale
Miracle Macaroons
Iced Tea or Coffee

❧ 3 ❧

~~~~~~~~~~~~~~~~~~~~~~~~~~~~~~

EASY AND DRAMATIC

Cocktail Accompaniments

AND APPETIZERS

SHOWCASE—inspiration—source of satisfaction, these party foods, cocktail accompaniments, and before-dinner appetizers are easy to make, delicious, zestfully flavored, and unusual enough to evoke festive feelings, as well as those admiring oh's and ah's and m-m-m's that break the social ice more effectively than many cocktails.

You will find here only a very few canapés or tidbits that are individually concocted and none that require finicky decorating. We suggest rather that your cocktail party guests do most of the work right at the party—and have a fine time doing it!

Any or all of these appetizers may be served before dinner or as party snacks. However, it is a good idea to serve only the simplest appetizers before dinner. The dramatic effects, such as flaming cabbages, and the hot appetizers, are most appropriate for parties.

RECIPES

Brandied Liver Pâté

Pâté of Smithfield Ham

Mexican Guacamole

Raw Vegetable Hors d'Oeuvres

Spiced Carrot Sticks

Cucumber Canapés

Love Apples with Sour Cream

Sherried Mushrooms

Turkish Spiced Mushrooms

Curried Cocktail Meat Balls

Cocktail Kabobs

Melon with Prosciutto

Red Caviar Pantheon

Quick Crab Meat Lorenzo

Oyster or Cherrystone Platter

Smoked Salmon with Trimmings

Cocktail Cabbage Aflame—with Shrimp

Frozen Cheese Alexandra

Liptauer Cheese

International Cheese Board

Deviled Almonds

Fresh-Roasted Chestnuts

Cranberry Juice Cocktail

Tomato Juice Frappé

Brandied Liver Pâté

Tastes for all the world like one of the homemade pâtés of France.

YOU WILL NEED:

liver pâté	butter or margarine
canned chopped mush-rooms	brandy
	parsley or chives

Use equal quantities of canned liver pâté and butter, or margarine: a 3-ounce tin of liver pâté and 3 ounces, or 6 tablespoons, butter or margarine. Melt the butter in a frying pan and in that melted butter, gently brown a 3-ounce tin of chopped mushrooms, well drained. Add the liver pâté to the butter and mushrooms and season with 1 tablespoon good brandy or cognac. Mix well and place the mixture in a small but pretty crock. Smooth the top and cover with a generous layer of parsley or chives, finely cut with scissors. Set in the refrigerator for several hours or overnight to blend the flavors.

AT SERVING TIME:

Place the crock in the center of a decorative plate or small platter. Surround with Melba toast rounds, thinly sliced pumpernickel cut into squares, crisp French rolls cut into half-inch slices, or bread sticks. Provide several butter spreaders and let the guests spread their own.

Smithfield Pâté

YOU WILL NEED:

deviled ham spread, canned Smithfield ham, or minced ham	butter or margarine mustard or mustard pickle India relish or gherkins

With a wooden spoon in a small bowl, combine 1 tin minced ham, Smithfield ham, or deviled ham with an equal quantity of butter or margarine, that is a 3-ounce tin minced ham to 3 ounces or 6 tablespoons butter or margarine, till smooth and very well blended. Taste the butter and ham mixture before adding extra seasonings. Various brands are variously spiced. Most of these ham spreads or mixtures however, will be considerably enhanced by the addition of prepared mustard. We use 1 teaspoon Dijon mustard or other mild mustard to 2 teaspoons chopped mustard chow-chow pickles for the 3-ounce tin of ham. Place the mixture in a small crock or casserole and set in the refrigerator several hours or overnight, to blend and mellow the flavors.

AT SERVING TIME:

Cover the top of the pâté with a thin layer of well-drained chopped India relish or thinly sliced gherkins. Place the crock on a large decorative plate or platter. Surround with finger lengths of whole wheat or rye bread, bread sticks, or crisp French bread or rolls, cut into 1/2-inch slices.

Mexican Guacamole

Originally from Mexico comes the idea for this creamy, unusual, and delicious spread.

YOU WILL NEED:

avocado	chili sauce
small tomato, diced	French dressing
onion	parsley or chives
green pepper or pimiento	

With a silver knife, cut the avocado in half lengthwise. Remove seed. Scoop the flesh carefully from its shell. Save the shell. With a silver fork mash the pulp, then mix in thoroughly diced tomato, 4 tablespoons chili sauce, 2 tablespoons finely chopped onion, 1 tablespoon chopped canned pimiento, or green pepper.

Moisten with French dressing made with 2 parts olive oil and 1 part lime or lemon juice or wine vinegar, and plenty of salt. Put the mixture back into the avocado shell and sprinkle the top with finely cut parsley or chives.

AT SERVING TIME:

Place the guacamole in the shell in the center of a plate. Surround with potato chips, celery sticks, carrot sticks, Melba toast, or tortillas (these come in tins) toasted. Provide spreaders for your guests to serve themselves.

Raw Vegetable Hors d'Oeuvres

These are a boon to all who must watch their calories or their diets. Hors d'oeuvres made of raw vegetables can be a joy to the epicure, and a treat to the eyes as well as the palate. Only the freshest and most perfect vegetables should be used. Always they should be crisp, cold and arranged with an eye to color and design.

For many years a famous New York restaurant has made a specialty of serving raw vegetables in a shiny black bowl filled with crushed ice. A bouquet of celery and finochio is set in the center of the ice; radishes, carrot sticks, black and green olives are set on top of the ice, covering it completely. It is an idea worth copying.

Spiced Carrot Sticks

Once you've tried this recipe you'll never again throw away the spicy liquor from a jar of pickles!

YOU WILL NEED:

raw carrots   liquid from a jar of pickles

Scrape and cut crisp young carrots into strips about 3 inches long and not more than 1/4 of an inch thick. Cover with the spicy vinegar from a jar of pickles and allow to stand overnight in the refrigerator. (If you haven't enough liquid to cover the carrots, stretch it by adding vinegar and water, half and half.)

AT SERVING TIME:

Drain and arrange on a plate or serve in a bowl, with or without crushed ice.

Cucumber Canapés

Almost any spread for bread or a cracker will take on a special zest when piled on top of a crisp slice of cucumber. Unless the cucum-

ber has a tough skin it's better not to peel it. It looks prettier and
the slice has more body.

YOU WILL NEED:

tender young cucumber	paprika
cream cheese or cottage cheese	chives, parsley, or sweet red peppers
horse-radish or Worcestershire sauce	

Cut the cucumber in slices about 1/4 inch thick. Since cucumbers
become limp on standing, it is best not to slice them too far ahead
of time. Top each slice with a cocktail spread of cream cheese, seasoned with horse-radish or Worcestershire sauce, or creamed cottage cheese, mixed with chopped chives or parsley.

AT SERVING TIME:

Arrange on a plate and sprinkle with paprika, chopped chives,
chopped parsley, or finely chopped sweet red peppers.

Love Apples with Sour Cream

Tiny cherry tomatoes and a carton of sour cream make a most interesting first course. However, if these small tomatoes are not
available, any solid, well-flavored tomato cut into chunks may be
served this way.

YOU WILL NEED:

love apples (cherry to-matoes) or any small variety of regular tomatoes	chives
	pepper mill
	salt
sour cream	

If cherry tomatoes are used, no advance preparation is necessary;
they are merely stemmed, washed, dried, and chilled. Ordinary tomatoes should be cut into 1/2-inch chunks just large enough for
eating.

AT SERVING TIME:

Arrange cherry tomatoes or tomato chunks in a wide-mouthed
sherbet or champagne glass, top each portion with 2 or 3 table-

spoons of salted sour cream, sprinkle generously with chopped chives and pass the pepper mill. Eat with small fork or teaspoon, whichever seems easier.

Sherried Mushrooms

YOU WILL NEED:

canned whole mushrooms   Tabasco (optional)
pale dry sherry
almonds, hazel nuts, cream
   cheese (optional)

Drain whole canned mushrooms. Put them into a small bowl and cover with pale dry sherry. Leave them in the refrigerator for several hours or overnight.

AT SERVING TIME:

Bring out the mushrooms in their bowl of wine, provide your guests with toothpicks and allow them to spear the mushrooms.

You may also drain the mushrooms and fill each little cup with a bit of salted almond, a hazel nut, or a tiny ball of cream cheese seasoned with salt, freshly ground black pepper, or a few drops of Tabasco.

Turkish Spiced Mushrooms

This is a Near East specialty made with canned whole mushrooms.

YOU WILL NEED:

canned whole mushrooms   spiced vinegar from a jar of
                              pickles (sweet or sour) or
                              vinegar, water, onion,
                              pickling spices

Drain the liquid from a can of whole mushrooms. Heat the liquid left from a jar of pickles. You may make your own pickling vinegar by simmering together for about five minutes 2/3 cup mild vinegar, 1/2 cup water, 1 small onion, thinly sliced, 1 tablespoon mixed pickling spices. (This makes liquid enough to cover two 3-ounce tins of mushrooms.) Pour the hot spiced liquid over the mushrooms, cool, and set in refrigerator for several hours or preferably overnight.

AT SERVING TIME:
Simply bring the bowl of mushrooms to the table, provide toothpicks, and let the guests spear the mushrooms from the spiced liquid. Or, drain and arrange on a relish tray along with other tidbits.

Haitian Pâtés de Poulet

We first tasted these delightful tidbits at a reception in the presidential palace at Port-au-Prince in Haiti. I have served them to Haitian diplomats in New York who asked for the recipe to take back home to the islands.

While you are at it, why not make up a quantity and pack them for freezing with 2 sheets of waxed paper between the layers.

YOU WILL NEED:

packaged piecrust mix	pimiento-stuffed olives
sliced white bread	parsley
milk	rosemary
minced chicken pâté	ginger
garlic	lemon juice
onion	Tabasco sauce

To make 45 to 50 cocktail pâtés, prepare 2 packages piecrust according to directions. Roll and cut into 2-inch squares.

To make the filling, soften 6 slices white bread momentarily in 1/2 cup milk. Squeeze out and place in a bowl along with two 4-ounce tins minced chicken pâté. Season with 1 clove garlic and 1/4 small onion finely crushed; add 1/4 cup coarsely chopped pimiento-stuffed olives, 1 tablespoon chopped parsley, 1/4 teaspoon powdered rosemary, 1/8 teaspoon ginger, 1 tablespoon lemon juice, 2 or 3 dashes of Tabasco sauce, and salt and pepper to suit your taste. Mix thoroughly. Place a scant teaspoonful of this mixture slightly to one side of each square. Fold into triangles;

crimp edges with a fork. Pack for freezing or bake immediately
about 10 minutes in a moderately hot oven, 375° F. If pâtés are
frozen, the time will be a little longer.

AT SERVING TIME:
The pâtés should be served—and kept—piping hot.

VARIATION: Haitian Rissoles
The same mixture and method can be used to make rissoles or
turnovers that are delicious for luncheon or supper. For rissoles the
pastry should be cut into 4-inch squares. Use a scant tablespoon of
the mixture on each square. For a high glaze, brush pâtés before
baking with a little cream or beaten egg. Recipe makes 15 to 20.

Cocktail Empanadas

Instead of using canned minced chicken pâté as in the above recipe,
use 2 tins of deviled ham pâté and flavor with 2 teaspoons cumin
seed, 1 clove garlic crushed, 1 tablespoon chili sauce.

Melon with Prosciutto

A traditional Italian specialty is adapted to make a modern cocktail snack.

YOU WILL NEED:

honeydew melon or canta- loupe	Italian smoked ham (known as prosciutto) or West- phalian, or Smithfield, ham in paper-thin slices

Scoop the meat of a honeydew melon or cantaloupe into balls or
cut the melon into squares. Wrap each piece in a strip of ham and
secure with a toothpick. Remove some of the ham fat if you think
there is too much.

AT SERVING TIME:
Arrange the ham-wrapped morsels on a large, attractive plate,
decorate with leaves and flowers if you have them. Provide a pep-

per grinder or two so that each guest can add a grind of fresh black pepper to the melon before he plops into his mouth. This appetizer is particularly good with sherry.

Red Caviar Pantheon

At the Pantheon Restaurant near Broadway, New York's theatrical and literary gourmets feast on the culinary glories of Greece. One of the most popular is this appetizer.

YOU WILL NEED:

red caviar	French, or Italian, hearth
onion	bread
olive oil	lemons

To a half-pound jar of red caviar, add 1 finely chopped onion and stir with a wooden spoon till it looks milky. Cut a loaf of crusty French, or Italian, bread into hunks. Remove the soft insides, soften in water, and squeeze dry. Add this and the juice of 3 lemons to the caviar, mash, and stir well. Little by little, add olive oil until the mixture is a pale rose color, light and spreadable. This may be done by hand, or in an electric mixer or blender.

AT SERVING TIME:

Heap into a bowl or pile in the center of a plate and surround with black olives, small wedges of iceberg lettuce, and radishes. Serve small chunks of crisp French bread or rolls in a basket and provide plenty of spreaders for your guests. The crusts of the bread used in making the mixture may be used but be sure to trim them so that they look attractive. Serve them in a pretty bowl or basket.

Quick Crab Meat Lorenzo

Canned, or quick-frozen, cooked crab meat mixed with undiluted cream of mushroom soup makes a quick and easy version of one of the world's most famous canapés.

YOU WILL NEED:

cooked crab meat
lemon juice or sherry wine
cheese
cayenne

condensed cream of mush-
room soup
Melba toast

Flake and separate one cup of crab meat. If there are any large hunks, crumble them. Remove gristle. Moisten with 4 or 5 table-spoons condensed cream of mushroom soup, dipping the soup right out of the tin without diluting it. The mixture should be quite thick—thick enough to drop in blops from a teaspoon. Season with a few grains of cayenne pepper, 1 teaspoon lemon juice or sherry. Brush 1 1/2-inch pieces of Melba toast with melted butter, pile mixture on toast, sprinkle with grated cheese and set in a hot oven, 375° F., just long enough to brown. Makes 20 canapés.

AT SERVING TIME:

Pass the canapés as soon as they are out of the oven. If the browning is done on a heat-proof platter that can go into the oven and to the table, all the better!

Oyster or Cherrystone Platter

Informal, gay, and very tempting is an enormous plate of iced clams or oysters on the half-shell. A fine thing to serve with beer or cocktails.

YOU WILL NEED:

clams or oysters
lemon
oysterette crackers

Tabasco sauce
prepared horse-radish
sea food cocktail sauce

Count on 6 clams or 4 oysters per person. Unless you have special skill and equipment, it's best to cajole your market man into opening the clams or oysters for you. This should not be done too long ahead of time.

AT SERVING TIME:

On a large platter or deep tray with a rim, arrange the clams or oysters in their shells, tuck green leaves or nosegays of water cress here and there and make a border of lemon wedges. Provide a number of cocktail forks for those who want them. Most people will take their clams right out of the shell. Plenty of small paper napkins are necessary. The fixings, i.e., Tabasco sauce, cocktail sauces, etc., should go on a separate tray and there should be several small baskets or bowls of crackers.

Smoked Salmon with Trimmings

Whether it's lox from the corner delicatessen or smoked salmon from Nova Scotia or Sweden, here is an elegant way to serve it— borrowed from 21, New York's notable restaurant.

YOU WILL NEED:

thinly sliced smoked salmon	olive oil
toasted white bread, toasted rye bread, or thin pumpernickel	pepper in a grinder

For each person provide a thin slice of toasted white bread with the crust removed. (Toasted rye bread or thin dark pumpernickel untoasted is preferred by some gourmets.) This is all the advance preparation needed.

AT SERVING TIME:

Place one of your prettiest napkins on a plate, arrange the toast on the napkin, covering it to keep it warm. Pass toast along with a small platter of well-chilled, thinly sliced salmon. Have on the coffee table a pepper grinder and a tiny bottle of the very best olive oil. Each person lays his salmon on the toast, pours on a golden dribble of olive oil, adds a grind of fresh black pepper. This salmon ceremony is most appropriate when you're serving cocktails to a small group around the coffee table.

Cocktail Cabbage Aflame—with Shrimp

If your party falls on Friday or if you would like to have a dramatic cocktail table, try this.

YOU WILL NEED:

red cabbage	lemon, or lime, juice or
canned, or quick-frozen,	vinegar
cooked shrimp	garlic
olive oil	curry powder
	sour cream

Choose the prettiest cabbage you can find, preferably one with large, loose outer leaves. Cut the stem end so that the cabbage will sit firmly on the platter or plate. Turn back the outside leaves like the petals of a great rose. With a very sharp knife, scoop a round hole out of the top of the cabbage just large enough to hold a can of Sterno.

Drain canned, or quick-frozen, cooked shrimp. If the black line around the edge of the shrimp has not been removed, take it out with a sharp paring knife. Cover the shrimp with French dressing made by combining four parts olive oil with one part lemon, or lime, juice, or vinegar; season with plenty of salt and pepper, add 1 clove of garlic thoroughly crushed. Let shrimp stand, covered by the French dressing, for several hours or overnight. Prepare a dipping sauce by adding 1/2 teaspoon curry powder to 1 cup sour cream.

AT SERVING TIME:

Drain shrimp, spear with toothpicks, and stud the cabbage with the shrimp. Light the Sterno and allow guests to heat the shrimp over the flame. Some like the shrimp cold, some like them hot. Everybody will enjoy the curried sour-cream sauce.

Frozen Cheese Alexandra

Unusual and very, very good is a molded frozen cheese served with hot-out-of-the-oven toast—an unforgettable combination.

YOU WILL NEED:

butter	olives
Roquefort or blue cheese	toasted rye bread or whole-
sherry	wheat Melba toast

In a mixer or with a wooden spoon, work 1/2 pound butter or margarine until it is soft and creamy. Crumble into small pieces 1/4 pound Roquefort or blue cheese and work until butter and cheese are well blended. Add 2 tablespoons dry sherry, 2 teaspoons finely cut chives or parsley, press the mixture into a small bowl or mold. Place in the freezing tray of a mechanical refrigerator, or in the frozen-food compartment. Let stand at least 1 hour, or as long as you wish—the longer, the mellower.

AT SERVING TIME:

Loosen the cheese by running a sharp knife around the edges of bowl or mold, then turn it upside down in the center of a serving plate and give it a thump to remove cheese. If it's balky use a thin-bladed knife to loosen. Surround cheese with toasted rye bread cut into finger lengths, or whole-wheat Melba toast warmed in the oven. Provide several spreaders to scoop little hunks of frozen cheese onto the hot toast, eat without spreading.

Liptauer Cheese

This is one of the glories of Budapest, made quickly and easily. Paprika, caraway seeds, and anchovy paste lend color and flavor.

YOU WILL NEED:

cream cheese	paprika
butter or margarine	onion, shallot, or chives
anchovy paste	pumpernickel, whole-wheat
capers	Melba toast, onion, or
caraway seeds	poppy-seed, rolls

With a wooden spoon, combine equal quantities cream cheese and butter or margarine: a 3-ounce package of cream cheese to 3 ounces or 6 tablespoons butter. Add 1 teaspoon capers, 1 teaspoon paprika, 1/2 teaspoon anchovy paste, 1/2 teaspoon caraway seeds, 1 tablespoon very finely chopped onion, shallot, or chives. Salt and pepper to taste. Press into a small bowl or mold, or form into a roll and wrap in waxed paper or aluminum foil. Place in the refrigerator for several hours to mellow and blend.

AT SERVING TIME:

Set the mold or roll in the center of a plate. Surround with thinly sliced pumpernickel, cut into finger lengths or squares, whole-wheat Melba toast, or even more authentically, serve onion rolls or poppy-seed rolls from a foreign bakeshop or delicatessen, cut into small pieces. Provide plenty of spreaders and let each person spread his own.

International Cheese Board

The easiest, most talked about party I ever gave featured cheeses of many lands, set on a cheese board and platters, decorated with green leaves and tiny flags of the countries in which various cheeses originated. Even in a middle-sized town, you will find cheese from a number of different countries, in delicatessens, large markets, or department stores with a food department, or you can order them shipped to you by mail.

YOU WILL NEED:

a selection of cheeses   flags
various breads and crackers

An international cheese board—like any cheese board—should include cheeses of contrasting colors, flavors, textures, for instance, creamy white cheese, yellow cheese, hard and soft cheeses, mellow and sharp.

From France: there is Brie, Camembert, and the more unusual Fromage de Foin (cheese of hay), which is actually ripened in freshly cut hay and retains that wonderful new-mown hay fragrance; Coulommiers, rather like Brie, soft, mellow, and easy to spread.

From Italy: Gorgonzola, Bel Paese, Melfino, and Provoloni.

From Sweden: Kummel cheese, flecked with caraway; Crème Chantilly; Bandost.

From Norway: the famous Gjetost, dark brown goat cheese, made with malt; Nokkelost, a Gouda type, studded surprisingly with whole cloves.

From Denmark: Danish Bleu and Tilsiter.

From Turkey: Kajmak, soft and mellow, and Kasher Penner, a hard, white cheese.

Holland has: Edam, Gouda, and Geheimrath, semi-hard, of a deep, golden yellow color.

Greece has: Pheta, often spelled Fata, a snowy white cheese, with the salt flavor of the brine in which it is packed.

Portugal: famous for Saloi, which comes from Lisbon, a type of hard cheese.

From Brazil: pepper cheese.

From England: Cheddar and Stilton.

And don't forget the famous American Sharp Cheddar Cheese!

AT SERVING TIME: 1814678

Arrange the cheeses on a board or platters—a pastry board will do very well, especially if you cover it with huckleberry leaves, being sure to leave space around the cheese for cutting. Set the appropriate flag in each piece of cheese; and if the cheeses are quite unusual, you might take a moment to write out a card and set it beside the cheese. Be sure to have on hand plenty of knives and spreaders. Provide two or three baskets or plates of bread stuffs. Particularly good with cheeses are: thin, black pumpernickel cut into 2-inch squares; crusty French rolls, cut into 1/2-inch slices; bread sticks, broken into 3-inch pieces; lightly toasted water biscuits; plain, crisp crackers; Melba toast. Bread or crackers should not be too highly or definitely seasoned, but should rather provide a background for the flavors of the cheese.

Deviled Almonds

This recipe, borrowed from the Victorians, transforms ordinary salted almonds from the store into a most unusual spread. Or you can use canned, shredded almonds.

YOU WILL NEED:

salted almonds	Worcestershire sauce, cayenne pepper, or Tabasco sauce
butter	
chutney, India relish, or pickles	Melba toast or crackers

Melt 2 tablespoons butter in a small frying pan. In the butter warm and slightly brown 1 cup coarsely chopped, or shredded, salted almonds. Mix together 2 tablespoons chopped chutney (or 3 tablespoons India relish or chopped pickles) and 2 tablespoons Worcestershire sauce (or a few grains of cayenne pepper or a couple of drops of Tabasco sauce). Pour over the nuts, heat thoroughly. Serve immediately.

AT SERVING TIME:
Place the nut mixture in a small bowl or dish, set in the middle of a tray or plate. Surround with rounds or squares of Melba toast or heated crackers. Provide butter spreaders or coffee spoons so that the guests can dip small scoops of the hot nut mixture onto the Melba toast.

Fresh-Roasted Chestnuts

In many large cities in the autumn and the cold winter months, you can buy roasted chestnuts on the street corners. Take them home and serve them to your guests, or roast them yourself in either of these two ways.

YOU WILL NEED:
    chestnuts   olive oil, salad oil, or
                                           peanut oil

With a sharp knife, cut an X on the top of the nut. Coat with oil, using only about a teaspoonful for each cup of nuts; bake in a very hot oven about 450° F. about 20 minutes. Or place in a heavy frying pan, and shake over the fire about ten minutes.

AT SERVING TIME:
Provide paper napkins and plenty of ashtrays for the shells. Wonderful with any kind of wine, hot punch, or mulled wine.

Cranberry Juice Cocktail

Of all the fruit juice cocktails served before dinner, the cranberry seems to be the least hackneyed. Many people prefer to serve fruit juice cocktails in the living room before dinner rather than at the table.

YOU WILL NEED:

quick-frozen cranberry   lemon, lime, or orange juice
juice concentrate or bot-
tled cranberry juice

Most frozen or bottled cranberry juice is greatly improved by the addition of lemon, lime, or orange. Use at least 2 tablespoons of the citrus fruit juice to 2 cups of cranberry juice.

AT SERVING TIME:

Serve frosty cold in small chilled glasses, garnish with slices of lemon, or lime, or orange, or twists of the peel.

Tomato Juice Frappé

How dull, how dull tomato juice can be! But when interestingly seasoned, frozen and imaginatively served, it becomes one of the best beginnings for a meal.

YOU WILL NEED:

canned, or quick-frozen, to-   cayenne pepper or Tabasco
mato juice   sauce
lemon juice   parsley or water cress
onion or chives   lemon peel

Season 2 cups of tomato juice with 2 tablespoons lemon juice, 2 tablespoons finely grated, or minced, onion or chopped chives (with a Mouli grater it's no trick to mince onions exceedingly fine), a few grains of cayenne pepper or 2 or 3 drops of Tabasco sauce. Pour into the freezing tray of your refrigerator and freeze to a mush, about an hour.

AT SERVING TIME:

Spoon into chilled glasses, a footed cocktail or sherry glass pref-erably, decorate with a topknot of parsley or water cress and a twist of lemon peel. Serve with a demitasse spoon.

❧ 4 ❧

wwwwwwwwwwwwwwwwwwwwww

Delicious and Unusual Soups

E VER SINCE ESAU sold his birthright to his brother Jacob for a
  bowl of savory pottage, which was undoubtedly lentil soup—
soup has been one of the mainstays of good eating.

Today, canned soups are probably the most popular and among
the finest of ready-to-serve foods. According to recent surveys, a
can of soup is America's favorite hot dish for lunch. At the evening
meal, it is not only the introduction but often the main course—
a most satisfying main course, too, when the soup is hearty and
served over toast, crackers, or with rice.

Moreover a fine, thick soup or chowder, served dramatically
from a tureen, bowl, casserole, or chafing dish becomes the *pièce
de résistance* for informal company meals, or even on the buffet.
After years of sampling canned soups in all price ranges, it is a
joy to be able to report that the most readily available popular
priced brands are usually the best soups. Since they are intended
to appeal to millions of people, they cannot be distinctively seasoned. But this allows plenty of leeway for your imagination.

Always correct the seasoning after the soup has been heated, or
just before it goes to the table if it's a cold soup, because heating
or mellowing brings out certain flavors, suppresses others. When
using herbs or spices, don't be too lavish at first—you can always
add more! A quarter of a teaspoon of dried herbs should be enough
to impart a subtle flavoring to a can of soup, 3 or 4 portions. It's
a pretty good rule of thumb to use three times as much of fresh
herbs as dried.

In many of these recipes, wine has been substituted for part of
the required milk or water. Here again, you may step up the proportion of wine, but be sure to taste as you go. You don't want
your soup to taste like an alcoholic beverage!

The manner in which you serve soup is important. In most cases we have suggested that you bring it to the table in a tureen or casserole and ladle the hot soup into *heated* soup plates or bowls. This is no mere conceit. There is all the difference in the world between a really hot, *hot* soup and one that is wanly lukewarm. To heat plates or bowls, place them in the warming oven or a heated and turned-off regular oven, where the temperature is about 150° F. This amount of heat will not harm even the finest china.

In many cases we have suggested that garnishes be added to the soup as it is served at the table. Sometimes a small decanter of wine is passed so it may be added according to individual fancy.

RECIPES

Black Bean Soup Guatemala
Borsch with Boiled Potatoes Polonaise
Cold Borsch Polonaise
Small Town Borsch
Bouillabaisse
Scotch Broth Garni
New Orleans Chicken Gumbo with Rice
Chicken and Water Cress Soup, Mandarin Style
Cream of Chicken Soup Amandine
Cream of Chicken with White Wine and Chestnuts
Clam Broth
Chilled Clam Broth with Cucumbers

Manhattan Clam Chowder
New England Clam Chowder
Old-Fashioned Bacon and Corn Chowder
Old-Fashioned Fish Chowder
Claret Consommé with Lime Slices
Lobster Bisque De Luxe
Minestrone
Onion Soup with Claret
Flaming Onion Soup
Green Pea Soup with Champagne
Split-Pea Garbure
Petite Marmite Henri IV
Vichyssoise I
Vichyssoise II

Black Bean Soup Guatemala

A garnish of avocado slices adds a Latin American look and flavor to a glorified black bean soup.

YOU WILL NEED:

condensed black bean soup
meat extract
Kitchen Bouquet
onion juice
sherry or Madeira wine
avocado

lemon or lime
egg, hard-cooked
chives or parsley
pepper sauce or Tabasco
(optional)

To a can of condensed black bean soup, add 1 can water, 1 teaspoon meat extract, 1 teaspoon Kitchen Bouquet, 1 teaspoon onion juice. Simmer for a few minutes, and just before taking off the fire, add 2 to 4 tablespoons sherry or Madeira wine. Do not boil after adding wine.

AT SERVING TIME:

Serve from a tureen or bowl, ladling the soup into heated bowls or soup plates, pass the garnishes, which should include very thin slices of avocado, slices of lemon or lime, sliced or hard-cooked egg, chopped chives or parsley and, if you like, pass around a tiny bottle of pepper sauce or Tabasco. To keep avocado slices from turning dark, brush or sprinkle with lemon or lime juice.

Borsch with Boiled Potatoes Polonaise

An excellent prepared borsch is available in many parts of the country. Served with boiled potatoes (canned or homemade) this soup makes a fine meal all by itself.

YOU WILL NEED:

canned borsch
onion
rye bread or pumpernickel

potatoes
bay leaf (optional)
sour cream

To a jar or can of borsch, add 1 small finely chopped onion, and a bit of bay leaf if desired. Simmer a few minutes until the onion is very soft.

AT SERVING TIME:

Place a small boiled potato or 2 or 3 well-heated canned Irish potatoes in each plate, ladle the hot borsch over the potatoes and garnish with a large spoonful of sour cream. Heated rye bread or pumpernickel is the ideal accompaniment.

Cold Borsch Polonaise

A jar of prepared borsch can be served in the style of the Polish nobility if a few simple ingredients are added.

YOU WILL NEED:

canned borsch
sour cream
eggs
cucumber or dill pickle

canned shrimp or salmon
(optional)
fresh dill (optional)

To a quart of icy-cold borsch add 1 cup sour cream.

AT SERVING TIME:

Present the soup frosty cold in a tureen or bowl. Have ready a plate on which you have arranged sliced or quartered hard-cooked eggs, sliced cucumber or dill pickles, well-drained canned shrimp or salmon in small hunks. Place a little of each of the garnishes in the soup plate and ladle the soup over the garnishes. A tiny frond of fresh dill adds a pretty look and an excellent flavor. Don't use too much dill; the flavor is *so* definite.

Small Town Borsch

If your own corner store does not carry canned borsch, you can easily make up your own in a few minutes from the most ordinary kind of ingredients.

YOU WILL NEED:

consommé   potatoes
cabbage   canned beets
vinegar or lemon juice   onions
sour cream   sugar

Combine 2 cans consommé, 2 cans water; add 1 cup canned, cut
up or shredded, beets, 4 tablespoons beet juice, 1 cup coarsely
chopped fresh cabbage, 2 onions, sliced or coarsely chopped, 2 tablespoons vinegar or lemon juice, 1 teaspoon sugar. Cook all together until cabbage is just tender. Do not strain.

AT SERVING TIME:

Ladle into bowls, add half of a boiled potato or a couple of canned
whole Irish potatoes to each serving, top with a large spoonful of
thick sour cream.

Russian Tschi

The name is pronounced *chy* to rhyme with try and the soup is
similar to some of the borschs but more cabbagy. Served with
boiled potatoes and sour cream or yogurt and accompanied by
Russian meat pies (see Boats of Beef, page 110), this soup could
be the main event for lunch or supper. This recipe should provide
six big bowlsful.

YOU WILL NEED: *Accompaniments*
sweet and sour cabbage in   potatoes
   jars   yogurt or sour cream
canned tomatoes
canned beets
onion soup
condensed consommé or
   bouillon
bay leaf
butter, chicken or goose fat

Simmer together for 10 to 15 minutes 2 jars sweet and sour red
cabbage, 2 large cans tomatoes, 1 can sliced or julienne beets,
2 packages onion soup (made up according to package directions),
2 cans condensed consommé or bouillon, 2 soup cans water, 1
small bay leaf, and 2 tablespoons butter, chicken or goose fat.

Meanwhile boil 6 potatoes cut in half or heat a can of tiny Irish potatoes along with a bit of onion salt. Drain and shake over fire until they become mealy.

AT SERVING TIME:

Serve soup blazing hot in deep bowls or old-fashioned soup plates. Pass the potatoes, also steaming, in a snowy napkin, and have on hand a bowl of sour cream or yogurt. The potatoes and sour cream or yogurt are added by each person to his portion.

Bouillabaisse

This is a simplified but delicious version of the great fish specialty of Marseilles, which has inspired poets, dazzled gourmets, delighted eaters all over the world. Every single one of the ingredients can be kept on hand on the pantry shelf or in the frozen-food compartment of your refrigerator.

YOU WILL NEED:

quick-frozen flounder, whiting, sole, haddock, perch, whitefish, or a combination	leeks onions garlic canned tomatoes
olive oil	parsley
canned oysters, clams, or mussels	saffron lemon juice or white wine
canned, or quick-frozen, cooked shrimp, crab, or lobster meat, or rock lobster tails	bay leaf canned pimiento (optional) French bread

Cook 2 medium-sized onions, thinly sliced, 1 or 2 crushed garlic cloves, and 2 sliced leeks in 1/2 cup olive oil until golden brown. If you can't get leeks in your market, use more onion. Thaw 3 pounds of quick-frozen fish fillets just enough to cut into serving pieces. Add pieces of fish along with 1 cup canned tomatoes, 1 bay leaf, 2 cups water. Simmer about 15 minutes. Add 1 cup oysters, clams, or mussels (these may be omitted, if desired), and 1 cup shrimp, crab meat, or lobster, 1/2 cup canned pimiento, cut into small pieces. Season with 1/2 teaspoon saffron, salt, pepper, and the juice of 1 lemon and/or 1 cup white table wine. Heat but do not boil.

AT SERVING TIME:
Bring to the table in a tureen or casserole. Some people pour off the broth, arrange the fish on a platter and combine them once again in the serving dish, but this seems like too much trouble. Place a thick slice of French bread in each soup plate or bowl, spoon the bouillabaisse (fish and broth) on top of the bread, and sprinkle with chopped parsley. This makes 8 servings. Served with a salad, fruit and cheese for dessert, it's a magnificent meal.

Scotch Broth Garni

A stout and sturdy pottage, quite unusual.

YOU WILL NEED:

Scotch broth	dry sherry
canned kidney beans	parsley

Combine 1 can Scotch broth, 1 can water, 1 can cooked red kidney beans, liquid and all; simmer for a few minutes, till the flavors are blended, then add 2 or 3 tablespoons dry sherry.

AT SERVING TIME:
Ladle into heated bowls or plates. Sprinkle each portion with about a tablespoonful of coarsely chopped parsley.

New Orleans Chicken Gumbo with Rice

A bit of herb seasoning and a spoonful of rice served in the plate transform a more or less usual soup into a memorable dish.

YOU WILL NEED:

condensed chicken gumbo soup	cayenne pepper or Tabasco sauce (optional)
rice	French bread or bread sticks
parsley	
marjoram	

To a can of condensed chicken gumbo soup, 1 can of water, add 1 tablespoon fresh-chopped parsley, 1/4 teaspoon marjoram, a few grains of cayenne pepper or 1 or 2 drops of Tabasco sauce, salt if needed, and a few grindings of black pepper from the pepper mill. Simmer for a few minutes.

AT SERVING TIME:

Bring to the table in a tureen or bowl. Place a large spoonful of cooked rice—white, wild, or brown rice—in the center of a heated soup plate and ladle the soup over this. French bread or bread sticks are particularly good with this soup.

Chicken and Water Cress Soup, Mandarin Style

A package of dehydrated, or a can of, chicken noodle soup combines with fresh water cress to make a soup with Oriental overtones.

YOU WILL NEED:

canned, or dehydrated, chicken noodle soup	egg
water cress	butter or margarine or chicken bouillon cube

Make up a package of dehydrated chicken noodle soup according to package directions, or use a can of chicken noodle soup. Simmer to blend all flavors. For extra richness add 1 tablespoon butter or margarine or 1 chicken bouillon cube. Take off the fire, add 1 cup (a large handful) of water cress, leaves and tender sprigs, put the cover on the soup and allow to set in a warm place for about a minute or two, just long enough to wilt the water cress.

AT SERVING TIME:

Ladle into bowls or plates and garnish, if desired, with slices or quarters of hard-cooked egg.

Cream of Chicken Soup Amandine

Almonds, sherry, a beaten egg, and a magical touch of mace transform a popular canned soup into a Viennese specialty.

YOU WILL NEED:

condensed cream of chicken soup	dry sherry
milk	almonds
egg	mace
light cream	parsley

To a can of condensed cream of chicken soup add 1 can milk or water, add 1/4 teaspoon mace, heat over a gentle fire for a few minutes. In the bottom of a tureen or serving bowl, which you plan to take to the table, beat 1 raw egg—it's traditional to use a silver fork—add to the egg a tablespoon of light cream and pour the hot soup slowly onto the egg, stirring vigorously so that the egg does not curdle.

AT SERVING TIME:

Add 2 or 3 tablespoons of sherry. Serve in heated soup cups or plates and garnish with salted almonds, coarsely chopped, and a light sprinkle of parsley.

Cream of Chicken with White Wine and Chestnuts

Chestnuts have always been the gourmet cook's delight, but rather troublesome to shell, blanch, and prepare. They are now available in jars, ready to use. Here they are used as a delightful garnish for a chicken soup.

YOU WILL NEED:

condensed cream of chicken soup	white wine
canned cooked chestnuts	paprika (optional)
milk	orange peel

Heat but do not boil 1 can condensed cream of chicken soup, 1/2 can milk or water, 1/2 can white table wine, 1/2 cup canned cooked chestnuts, cut into small pieces. If desired, 1/2 teaspoon paprika may be added to this soup to give it a rosy color.

AT SERVING TIME:

Ladle into heated soup plates and garnish with a twist of orange peel.

Clam Broth

Since such excellent clam broth is now available in jars and bottles, it is surprising that it is served so seldom. A spoonful of tomato ketchup or tomato sauce stirred into the broth gives it an appetizing pink glow.

YOU WILL NEED:

clam broth	whipped cream
ketchup or canned tomato	parsley
sauce	celery salt

Heat clam broth adding 1 tablespoon ketchup or tomato sauce and 1/4 teaspoon celery salt to each cup of clam broth.

AT SERVING TIME:

Ladle into cups, and garnish with slightly salted whipped cream, sprinkle with chopped parsley.

Chilled Clam Broth with Cucumbers

A delightful warm weather soup with an unusual garnish.

YOU WILL NEED:

bottled clam juice	ice
canned vegetable cocktail	Tabasco sauce
cucumber	

Combine equal parts icy cold clam juice and very cold canned vegetable cocktail, season with a little extra salt and pepper, if desired, and a few drops of Tabasco sauce.

AT SERVING TIME:

Serve in a glass or china cup or bowl, adding to each portion a spoonful of crushed ice and a spoonful of finely cut, unpeeled cucumber.

NOTE:

If you have no ice-crushing machine you can crush ice cubes by placing them in a small canvas bag and hitting several times with a hammer or any other heavy object.

Manhattan Clam Chowder

Most of the popular brands of canned clam chowder are made with tomato rather than milk. Hence by definition, they are Manhattan clam chowder. A garnish of green pepper rings and caraway seeds adds distinction to them.

YOU WILL NEED:

clam chowder	green pepper
bacon fat or butter (optional)	onion
	caraway seeds

Add 1 can water to 1 can condensed Manhattan-style clam chowder, 1 tablespoon bacon fat or butter may be added if a richer flavor is desired. Bring to a boil and simmer a few minutes.

AT SERVING TIME:

Ladle into heated bowls or soup plates and garnish with green pepper rings, thinly sliced onion rings, and/or a scatter of caraway seeds.

New England Clam Chowder

When milk is used in place of tomato, the chowder becomes New England style and is much admired down east. White table wine may be substituted for part of the milk.

YOU WILL NEED:

condensed clam chowder
milk
pilot crackers

dry white table wine
paprika, chives, or parsley

To 1 can condensed clam chowder add 1 can milk, or 1/2 can milk and 1/2 can dry (nonsweet) white table wine. Heat but do not boil.

AT SERVING TIME:

Place a pilot cracker in the bottom of a heated bowl or soup plate, ladle the chowder over the cracker and sprinkle with paprika, chopped chives, or parsley.

Old-Fashioned Bacon and Corn Chowder

When you can't think of a thing you want to eat for lunch or supper, this modern version of an old-time favorite will surely tempt you. Modern households are more likely to have bacon on hand than the salt pork called for in older recipes, so we've used bacon.

YOU WILL NEED:

cream-style corn
bacon
potatoes
onion
milk

Worcestershire sauce
crackers
paprika
parsley
butter

With a pair of scissors or sharp knife cut 6 slices of bacon into small pieces and fry. Leave the bacon bits and the fat in the pan, adding to it 1 medium-sized onion, thinly sliced. Cook 5 minutes over a low flame, stirring often so that the onion does not burn. Add 2 cups of boiled potatoes (canned will do very well), cut into 1/4-inch slices; 2 cups boiling water, 1 can cream-style corn, 4 cups milk. Heat to the boiling point, season with salt, pepper, a little Worcestershire sauce.

AT SERVING TIME:

Pour into a heated tureen or casserole, add 2 tablespoons butter and a sprinkle of paprika and/or parsley. Place a cracker (saltine type) in the bottom of a bowl or a soup plate, ladle chowder over the cracker. This makes a generous amount of chowder. 6 to 8 portions.

Old-Fashioned Fish Chowder

If white wine is substituted for 1/4 to 1/2 of the milk the chowder tastes very "French."

YOU WILL NEED:

condensed fish chowder	Worcestershire sauce
milk or milk and light	parsley
cream	chives
butter	paprika
celery seed or celery salt	

To a can of condensed fish chowder add 1 soup can of rich top milk, or 1/2 can milk and 1/2 can light cream (1 soup can of liquid in all), 1/4 teaspoon celery salt or 1/2 teaspoon celery seed, and 1 teaspoon Worcestershire sauce. Bring to boiling point but do not boil.

AT SERVING TIME:

Bring to the table in a tureen, casserole, or bowl. Ladle into heated bowls or soup plates, garnish each portion with a thin pat of butter, sprinkle with chopped parsley, chives, and/or paprika.

Claret Consommé with Lime Slices

A few drops of red coloring add a great deal to the appearance of this clear soup which may be served hot or jellied.

YOU WILL NEED:

condensed consommé	lime, lemon, or orange
claret wine	whole cloves
red vegetable coloring (op-	
tional)	

To a can of condensed consommé add 1/2 can water, 1/2 can claret wine. To give a deep glowing red to soup, add also a couple of drops of red vegetable coloring. Simmer a few minutes to blend the flavors, but do not boil.

AT SERVING TIME:

Serve in heated cups or soup plates and garnish with slices of lime, lemon, or orange, studded with whole cloves. A perfect soup for your company dinner!

Lobster Bisque De Luxe

This bisque of lobster has a heavenly rosy color, a heady aroma and flavor of wine.

YOU WILL NEED:

cooked lobster meat, canned or quick frozen	nutmeg (optional)
cream of chicken soup	paprika
milk or milk-and-cream	parsley, water cress, or green pepper
cayenne pepper	sherry

Heat to the boiling point 1 can cream of chicken soup, 1 can top milk or half milk and half cream. Add 1 cup cooked or canned lobster meat cut into small pieces, 1 teaspoon sweet Hungarian paprika for color and delicate flavor, 2 tablespoons sherry, 1/4 teaspoon nutmeg, and a few grains of cayenne pepper.

AT SERVING TIME:

Bring to the table in a bowl or tureen, ladle into heated soup plates or bowls, and garnish with chopped parsley or water cress, or green pepper rings.

Minestrone

The addition of quick-frozen leaf spinach or chopped cabbage and an extra can of consommé adds a fresh homemade taste to canned minestrone.

YOU WILL NEED:

minestrone
condensed consommé or
    meat extract and water
quick-frozen spinach or
    shredded cabbage

garlic
parsley
bread sticks
Parmesan, Gruyère, or Ro-
    mano cheese

Rub a saucepan with a cut clove of garlic just as you've been accustomed to rub a salad bowl. This will impart to your soup a subtle flavor—just the right amount of garlic. Pour into the pan a can of minestrone, add water if the directions call for it. Add also 1 can condensed consommé, 1 can water or use 2 2/3 cups hot water and 2 large spoonfuls meat extract. When the soup is boiling, add 1 package quick-frozen leaf spinach or 1 1/2 cups shredded cabbage. Heat.

AT SERVING TIME:

Ladle into heated bowls or soup plates. Pass separately a bowl of freshly grated Parmesan, Gruyère, or Romano cheese, and another small bowl of chopped parsley, preferably the broad-leaved Italian parsley. Bread sticks are wonderful with minestrone.

Onion Soup with Claret

Canned, or dehydrated, onion soups can be given great distinction by the addition of claret, Burgundy, or sherry.

YOU WILL NEED:

canned, or dehydrated, on-
    ion soup
claret, Burgundy, or sherry
French bread

garlic
butter or olive oil
Parmesan, Gruyère, or Ro-
    mano cheese

For dehydrated onion soup follow the package directions, but substitute for part of the water, 1/2 cup claret or Burgundy or 1/4 cup sherry. The same amount of wine may be added to canned, ready-to-serve onion soup. The soup should not be allowed to boil vigorously after the wine is added.

AT SERVING TIME:

Serve in individual casseroles or one large casserole. Top with crusts of garlic bread made by rubbing inch-thick slices of French bread with a cut clove of garlic, brush with melted butter or olive oil, and brown in the oven or under the broiler.

There are two ways of serving onion soup. One school insists that the bread crusts be placed on the soup, sprinkled thickly with grated cheese, and set in a hot oven till the cheese melts and browns slightly—about 5 minutes. Others prefer to dip the soup onto the plates over the toast, and pass freshly grated Parmesan, Gruyère, or Romano cheese.

Flaming Onion Soup

This is one of the most dramatic first courses you could serve. It should be served with theater—the toasted bread flambéed on a heatproof platter at the table.

YOU WILL NEED:

canned or dehydrated onion soup	French bread
	garlic
Cognac or brandy	olive oil
water cress or spinach	Parmesan cheese
pine nuts or blanched almonds	

To 2 cans of onion soup or one that you have made from a package add 1/4 cup cognac or brandy. Heat in the usual manner.

Remove from heat, add 1 cup water cress from which the coarse stems have been removed or 1 cup very young spinach torn into bits, and 1/2 cup pine nuts or slivered blanched almonds. (Pine nuts can be bought even in very small towns at Italian grocery stores or in many supermarkets. The almonds already blanched and slivered come in a jar.) In this case the nuts are not toasted.

Cover and allow to steam 1 minute.

Prepare croutes of French bread (about 2 per person), cutting the bread slightly on a slant about 1/2 inch thick. Brush with garlic-flavored olive oil, easily made by adding pressed garlic or instant garlic to the olive oil. Brush bread on all sides and toast or set in the oven until golden color.

AT SERVING TIME:

Arrange the croutes on an attractive heated platter. Have ready 1/4 cup cognac or brandy which should be ever so slightly warmed.

Light the liquor with a match and pour while flaming over the croutes. Place croutes in individual soup dishes and add the soup. Pass a bowl of freshly grated or freshly opened Parmesan cheese.

Green Pea Soup with Champagne

This recipe came from the Grand Hotel, in Stockholm, where the ingredients are wheeled to the table on a silver cart and put together with considerable flourish by the headwaiter in cooperation with the sommelier, who opens the bottle of champagne at just the right moment.

YOU WILL NEED:

condensed cream of green pea soup	champagne
	mace
chicken bouillon cube	dry tarragon, fresh tarragon, or fresh mint
heavy cream	

To a can of condensed cream of green pea soup (or even split-pea soup) add 1/2 can water, and 1 chicken bouillon cube, crumbled and dissolved in a couple of tablespoons of hot water. Add 1/8 teaspoon mace, 1/4 teaspoon dry tarragon, *or* 1 scant teaspoon fresh chopped tarragon. Simmer 5 minutes.

AT SERVING TIME:

Bring the heated pea soup to the table in a chafing dish. Have on hand 1/2 cup heavy cream, slightly beaten, a small bouquet of fresh mint or fresh tarragon sprays, and champagne. Stir the cream into the hot soup, and add at the last minute about 1/2 cup champagne. This will give a delightfully light texture to the soup as well as a delicate winey flavor. Ladle into heated soup plates and garnish with sprigs of fresh tarragon or mint. Serves 3 or 4.

Split-Pea Garbure

The French have a thick and hearty soup made of peas or beans, garnished with sausages and served over garlic-rubbed toast. This is a quick and easy version of that whole-meal soup.

YOU WILL NEED:

dehydrated split-pea soup
onion
thyme or marjoram (op-
 tional)

sausage or frankfurter
French bread for toasting
olive oil
garlic (optional)

Make up a package of dehydrated split-pea soup, according to the package directions, adding to the soup as it simmers, half of a small onion finely chopped, 1/4 teaspoon thyme or marjoram. Drain and brown one small tin of cocktail sausages or Vienna sausage, or frankfurters, cut into 1/2-inch slices. Cut crusty French bread into slices about 1 inch thick, brush with olive oil, and a cut clove of garlic if desired, set in a hot oven 450° F. about 5 minutes, or until golden brown.

AT SERVING TIME:

Bring soup to the table in a tureen or bowl. Have ready on separate plates the browned sausage and the toasted bread. Place a slice of toast in each soup plate, ladle soup over the bread (as for onion soup), and garnish with several slices of sausage or frankfurters.

Petite Marmite Henri IV

A more glamorous fate for leftovers can scarcely be imagined. If you have no leftovers, you can concoct this soup quickly and easily with canned or quick-frozen vegetables and meats from the delicatessen. *Marmite* is a kind of stew but the various ingredients are not cooked together, and the effect gastronomically is different.

YOU WILL NEED:

consommé or bouillon
cooked chicken, turkey,
 beef, or veal
French bread
olive oil

cauliflower, peas, carrots,
 and onions, or cabbage
 and lima beans, or your
 own combination of veg-
 etables
garlic (optional)
Parmesan or Romano
 cheese

Combine 2 cans condensed consommé or bouillon with 2 cans water, 1 cup cooked chicken, turkey, beef, or veal, cut into about

1-inch pieces; add also about 1/2 cup of each of the following: lightly cooked cauliflowerettes, green peas, carrots, tiny onions. Vegetables should all have been cooked separately. Small pieces of cabbage may be substituted for the cauliflower; lima beans may be used instead of the peas, or you may make up your *own* combinations. Simmer meat, consommé, and vegetables about 6 minutes—just long enough to blend the flavors. Too much cooking will toughen leftover meat and cause chicken or turkey to become stringy.

AT SERVING TIME:

Bring to the table in a casserole or tureen. Have ready on the side, toasted French bread, which has been cut into slices about an inch thick, brushed with oil, rubbed with garlic if desired and browned in the oven. At the table, place a piece of toasted French bread in the center of a heated soup plate and ladle the soup over this; sprinkle with Parmesan or Romano cheese. French bread or bread sticks are particularly good with this soup.

Vichyssoise I

Several varieties of canned vichyssoise are quite good, but all need a certain amount of dressing up.

YOU WILL NEED:
canned vichyssoise   chives
heavy cream or sour cream

Follow the directions on the tin. Some types of vichyssoise are condensed and require the addition of milk or cream, others are ready to serve. Chill very well. To save time, place in the freezing compartment of the refrigerator.

AT SERVING TIME:

Stir into the chilled soup, 1/2 cup heavy cream or sour cream. Serve in ice-cold cups, garnish with plenty of chopped chives and pass the pepper grinder.

Vichyssoise II

The simplest of ingredients available at any corner store make up this version of the glamorous vichyssoise. In this recipe we have suggested using a package of quick-frozen mashed potatoes. You can mash your own, or use dehydrated potatoes.

YOU WILL NEED:

quick-frozen mashed potatoes	top milk or light cream
condensed cream of chicken soup	butter
	onion salt
	green onion tops or chives

Defrost potatoes over hot water in a double boiler, you'll need 2 cups. Add 1 tablespoon butter, 1 can condensed cream of chicken soup, 1 teaspoon onion salt, and beat well. Add 1 cup light cream or 1 1/2 cups milk. Chill several hours.

AT SERVING TIME:

Serve in cold soup cups or glass bowls set in crushed ice, if possible. Garnish the ice with green leaves. Garnish each portion with finely cut green onion tops or chopped chives.

❧ 5 ❧

~~~~~~~~~~~~~~~~~~~~~~~~~~~~~~~~~~~~~~~

Eggs

Eggs were probably the original choice of the original "hurried epicure." Being in its natural state so close to perfect eating, the egg remains, as it must have been through history, the favorite recourse of those on the lookout for something good to eat—quick!! Yet despite the fact that speed is the very essence of egg cookery it is not a paradox to insist that the basic principle of egg cookery is slow cooking at low temperature. The difference in time between proper and dreadful egg cookery may be only a few seconds, but the difference in taste and texture is enormous.

RECIPES

Buttered Eggs à la Robert
Eggs Benedict
Eggs Commodore
Eggs Farci in Aspic
Eggs Chasseur
Stuffed Eggs Diavolo
Eggs Farci
Eggs Scrambled New York Style
Lucanian Eggs au Gratin
Eggs with Madeira Sauce
Eggs Mimosa
Mushroom Omelet Flambé

Eggs Oven Poached in White Wine
Eggs Oven Poached in Tomato Sauce
Eggs à la Reine
Scrambled Eggs Creole
Creole Eggs with Cheese
Scotch Woodcock
Eggs Goldenrod
Shirred Eggs Mornay
Shirred Eggs with Sausage Neapolitan

Buttered Eggs à la Robert

Since even for the most skillful of cooks, transferring eggs from pan to platter involves some hazard, it's a good idea to prepare eggs in the dish in which you will serve them. A heat-proof, glass pie-pan, for instance, can be used if you cover the heating unit or flame with an asbestos pad.

YOU WILL NEED:

eggs	butter
Quick Robert Sauce (page 149)	parsley

Melt 1 tablespoon butter in a frying pan or serving dish. Slip egg into hot fat. Do not attempt to cook too many at once. Cook over low heat until edges show a faint line of golden brown.

AT SERVING TIME:

Pour Robert Sauce around rather than over the eggs. Garnish with parsley.

Eggs Benedict

Since the poaching of an egg is a mental as well as a culinary hazard for many not-too-experienced cooks, this recipe calls for eggs that are shirred in the oven rather than poached.

YOU WILL NEED:

eggs	butter
English muffins	Mock Hollandaise Sauce
boiled ham	(page 144)

For each person, provide 1 or 2 halves of English muffins. Tear in half crosswise. Scoop out the soft center so as to leave a good-sized hollow deep enough for an egg to rest comfortably. Toast lightly. Provide for each person a thin slice boiled ham as for a ham sandwich. Place the ham on the toasted muffin, pushing it down in the center so that the egg can be accommodated. Break a raw egg into the nest. Place on a cooky sheet and bake in a moderate oven 350° F. about 6 minutes, or until the white is set.

AT SERVING TIME:

Place the muffins complete with egg on individual plates or on a platter. Cover each egg with Hollandaise Sauce, either canned or Mock Hollandaise. Sprinkle with paprika or parsley. Serve at once, 1 or 2 to a person.

VARIATION: Eggs Commodore

Proceed as for Eggs Benedict but instead of ham, spread English muffin with liver pâté. Serve with canned beef gravy, livened by adding 1/2 teaspoon Worcestershire sauce, 1/2 teaspoon Kitchen Bouquet, a dash of cayenne pepper to each cup of gravy.

Eggs Farci in Aspic

As a first course at a luncheon or dinner or as a main dish at a buffet supper party, eggs in aspic have great elegance.

YOU WILL NEED:

Eggs Farci (page 62)	radishes
consommé	Sauce Ravigote
sherry	(page 148)
water cress	

Set Eggs Farci in a shallow serving dish. Carefully spoon over them a can of condensed consommé to which 1 tablespoon pale dry sherry has been added. Chill. Do not attempt to unmold since the aspic is far too delicate and tender for handling.

AT SERVING TIME:

Garnish the dish with water cress and radishes. Serve from the same dish. Pass separately a bowl of Sauce Ravigote.

Eggs Chasseur

The classic recipe calls for French poached eggs. Our method of oven poaching gives much the same result.

YOU WILL NEED:

eggs	cheese
butter	sherry
condensed cream of	cayenne
chicken soup	onion juice (optional)
canned milk or light cream	

Butter generously 6 individual egg shirrers, tiny casseroles, or custard cups. Break 1 or 2 eggs into each. Set in a moderate oven, 350° F., for about 6 minutes. If you lay a cooky tin or some other cover over the top, the eggs will have the appearance of French poached eggs with the white veil over the yolks. Take from the heat, pour over a sauce made by heating 1 can condensed cream of chicken soup with 1/4 can evaporated milk or light cream, 1 tablespoon sherry, a few grains of cayenne and, if desired, 1/2 teaspoon onion juice. Sprinkle with grated cheese and set back in the oven or under the broiler just long enough to melt the cheese.

AT SERVING TIME:

Bring to the table immediately. A few grinds of fresh black pepper or nutmeg from the grinder point up the flavors. Serves 6.

Stuffed Eggs Diavolo

Prepared yellow mustard takes the place of half a dozen seasonings and spices. This is a very simple deviled egg recipe, and very good.

YOU WILL NEED:

eggs	parsley or mixed fresh herbs
prepared yellow mustard	olives or pimientos

Cut hard-cooked eggs in half, lengthwise. Remove the yolks and put the whites aside in pairs. Mash yolks with a fork, add to each egg yolk 1 teaspoon prepared yellow mustard, salt and pepper, if needed. Refill whites with the mixture.

AT SERVING TIME:

Put together to look like a whole egg and roll in fresh chopped parsley or a mixture of fresh herbs. Or, form the seasoned yolks into little balls. Set a ball inside each egg white and garnish with parsley, sliced olives, or pimiento strips.

VARIATION: **Eggs Farci**

To mashed and seasoned yolks add an equal amount of minced chicken, minced ham, deviled ham, or liver pâté.

Eggs Scrambled New York Style

YOU WILL NEED:

eggs	uncooked ham
milk	onion
butter	canned sliced mushrooms

For this dish you make the garnish first: Cut 1 thin slice of un-cooked ham into matchlike pieces. There should be about 1 cup. Heat the ham in 2 tablespoons melted butter along with 2 table-spoons chopped onion for about 5 minutes. Add one 3-ounce tin sliced mushrooms from which the liquid has been drained and saved. Cook about 3 minutes longer. Serve as a border around or on top of eggs scrambled in the following fashion:

Beat 6 eggs slightly with 1/4 teaspoon salt, 1/8 teaspoon pepper, 1/3 cup milk, and the juice from a 3-ounce tin of mush-rooms. Melt 2 tablespoons butter in a pan, and add egg mixture. Cook over very low heat, stirring constantly until set and creamy.

AT SERVING TIME:

Turn the eggs onto a warm plate and circle with the ham and mushroom garnish. Serves 4.

Lucanian Eggs au Gratin

A combination of canned cooked macaroni and hard-cooked eggs interestingly seasoned makes a fine dish.

YOU WILL NEED:

eggs	cheese
canned macaroni and	onion (optional)
cheese	buttered crumbs

Slice 6 hard-cooked eggs and arrange in layers in a shallow, buttered baking dish along with a can of cooked macaroni and cheese —first a layer of macaroni then eggs and so on. Sprinkle each layer with grated cheese using in all about 3/4 cup. If you like onion, use a medium-sized one, finely chopped. The top layer should be macaroni. The final layer 1/2 cup buttered crumbs. Bake in a moderate oven, 350° F., until sizzling hot and well browned.

AT SERVING TIME:
Serve from the baking dish along with a green salad and a fruit dessert. Serves 4.

Eggs with Madeira Sauce

Serve as a main dish for lunch or a light supper. The demi-glaze Madeira Sauce is nothing more than canned consommé cooked down.

YOU WILL NEED:

eggs	Madeira or sherry
butter	parsley
condensed consommé	

Butter generously the required number of custard cups or small ramekins. Break an egg in each. Don't bother to salt or pepper because the sauce is sufficiently seasoned. Place the custard cups in a shallow pan or frying pan with about an inch of warm water. Cover or not depending on whether you wish the yolks to be veiled with white. Set on a medium fire and allow to cook until whites are set. Serve with Madeira Sauce, made by boiling uncovered a can of condensed consommé until it is boiled down to half its original volume. Add two tablespoons sherry or Madeira wine. Simmer two or three minutes but do not boil.

AT SERVING TIME:
Turn eggs out of the custard cups if you wish, or serve in the custard cups. In either case, spoon 2 or 3 tablespoons of sauce over each egg. Garnish with parsley.

Eggs Mimosa

Stuffed hard-cooked eggs are arranged like the petals of a sunflower, to make a delicious egg salad platter.

YOU WILL NEED:

eggs   cooked poultry, fish, or ham
mayonnaise   olives (optional)

Cut hard-cooked eggs in halves, lengthwise. Remove yolks and
chop with a knife. Into the whites place a spoonful of chopped
cooked chicken, ham, crab meat, lobster, shrimp, or salmon. Cover
with mayonnaise (mixed half and half with sour cream, if you
wish). Sprinkle with the chopped egg yolks.

AT SERVING TIME:

Arrange the stuffed eggs on a plate like the petals of a sunflower.
If the egg halves do not stand solidly, cut a small piece off the
bottom. To add to the illusion of a flower, arrange a center of
chopped black or green olives. Decorate the plate with green
leaves.

Mushroom Omelet Flambé

When guests stay unexpectedly for supper and you've said in all
honesty that you haven't planned a thing you can in a few minutes
appear on the scene bearing this delicate omelet wrapped in fragrant flames.

YOU WILL NEED:

eggs   brandy
canned mushrooms   Worcestershire sauce
butter

Slightly beat 4 eggs just enough to blend yolks and whites. Add
4 tablespoons warm water. Season with 1/2 teaspoon salt, 1/8
teaspoon pepper, 1/2 teaspoon Worcestershire sauce. Melt 2 tablespoons butter in a small frying pan or omelet pan. Add eggs.
Cook over slow heat. Lift edges with a spatula and tip the pan oc-

casionally so that the uncooked part runs underneath. Do not allow to brown but merely to become firm on the outside. The inside should be creamy. In a separate pan heat 2 3-ounce tins of mushrooms in 2 tablespoons of butter.

AT SERVING TIME:

With the spatula turn 1/2 of the omelet over the other and serve on a hot platter. In the center, and around the edges of the omelet, place the heated mushrooms. Slightly warm 4 tablespoons brandy, set a lighted match to the brandy and pour while flaming over the mushrooms. Serves 4.

Eggs Oven Poached in White Wine

Dressy as can be but no trouble at all!

YOU WILL NEED:

eggs	garlic
butter	tarragon, chervil, chives, or
white wine	parsley
Swiss cheese	

Rub individual egg shirrers or custard cups with garlic, butter generously. Break 1 or 2 eggs into each. Sprinkle with salt, freshly ground black pepper, a few grains of cayenne pepper or nutmeg. Pour dry white table wine over the eggs, using about 2 tablespoons of wine to each egg. Sprinkle 1 tablespoon grated Swiss Cheese on each egg. Set in a moderate oven, 350° F., 6 or 8 minutes.

AT SERVING TIME:

Sprinkle with chopped fresh tarragon, chervil, chives, or parsley. Serve at once.

VARIATION: Eggs Oven Poached in Tomato Sauce

Instead of white wine, use canned tomato sauce seasoned to taste with finely chopped parsley, chives, rosemary, orégano, basil, or a combination of herbs. Cheese may be used or not as desired. If dried herbs are used, be very sparing with them.

Eggs à la Reine

YOU WILL NEED:

eggs	cheese
canned mushrooms	toast
heavy cream or cream sauce	sour cream (optional)
butter	parsley or water cress

Butter an individual egg shirrer, oven-proof saucer, or custard cup. Cover the bottom with sliced, drained canned mushrooms that have been slightly browned in butter then moistened with a little cream—sweet or sour. On top of the mushrooms, break 1 or 2 eggs. Cover them with thick cream or canned cream sauce. Sprinkle with 1 or 2 tablespoons grated cheese. Place in a moderate oven, 350° F., about 8 minutes until eggs are set and tops are brown.

AT SERVING TIME:

Garnish with a topknot of parsley or water cress and serve immediately with triangles of toast.

Scrambled Eggs Creole

Scrambled eggs cooked in a double boiler are tender and delicate. Although the cooking time is longer than scrambling in a frying pan, the method appeals greatly to the hurried hostess because the eggs can cook while other chores are being done. Constant stirring is not necessary.

YOU WILL NEED:

eggs	capers (optional)
canned tomatoes or tomato	onion
sauce	Worchestershire sauce (optional)
butter	tional)
mushrooms (optional)	parsley or chives

Slightly cook 1/2 an onion, chopped, in 2 tablespoons butter; add 1 cup canned tomatoes. Season with 1/2 teaspoon salt, 1/8 teaspoon pepper. A few drops of Worcestershire, 1 tablespoon cooked, sliced mushrooms, and 1 tablespoon capers may be added, if you have them on hand. Cook 5 minutes, then add 5 slightly beaten eggs. Cook over slow heat in top of double boiler until creamy.

AT SERVING TIME:

Take eggs from the fire just *before* they begin to look done. They will then be perfect, because the heat of the pan will continue to cook them even as you are removing them. Serve as quickly as possible. Chopped parsley or chives may be stirred in at the last minute or sprinkled over the eggs as a garnish.

VARIATION: Creole Eggs with Cheese

To the tomato mixture and eggs add 1/4 cup grated cheese before cooking.

Scotch Woodcock

Neither Scotch nor a woodcock, this dish of creamed eggs dates back many centuries and is as good today as it ever was.

YOU WILL NEED:

eggs	anchovy fillets
condensed cream of chicken soup	pimiento
	green pepper
anchovy paste	paprika
toast or English muffins	dried celery flakes (optional)
milk or light cream	

To a can of condensed cream of chicken soup, add 1/4 to 1/2 can milk or light cream. Heat. Add 6 coarsely chopped hard-cooked eggs. Season to taste with about 1/2 teaspoon anchovy paste, a little coarsely ground black pepper, and 1 teaspoon dried celery flakes if desired.

AT SERVING TIME:

Serve on toast or toasted English muffins. Garnish with crossed anchovy fillets, strips of pimiento, circles of green pepper, and/or a dash of paprika. Serves 4.

VARIATION: Eggs Goldenrod

Chop whites and yolks separately. Add whites to the sauce and pour over toast. Cut yolks fine or put through a strainer and sprinkle over the top. Instead of anchovy paste, season sauce with a tablespoon of pale dry sherry.

Shirred Eggs Mornay

A shirred egg is an egg to remember when you're entertaining. They need so little attention, look elegant, are easy to serve. If you have no individual egg shirrers, heat-proof, glass custard cups will do very well.

YOU WILL NEED:
eggs
cheese
canned cream sauce or condensed cream of chicken soup

Butter egg shirrers or individual baking dishes. Break an egg or two into each. Sprinkle with salt and pepper. Cover eggs with sauce made by adding 1 slightly beaten egg to 1 can cream sauce or condensed cream of chicken soup. Sprinkle with grated cheese and bake in a moderate oven, 350° F., about 6 minutes. For easy handling it's a good idea to place the individual small dishes on a cooky sheet or broiler pan, then they can all be taken out together.

AT SERVING TIME:
Place the shirred eggs on individual plates or arrange on a large platter and decorate the platter with bouquets of parsley or green leaves.

Shirred Eggs with Sausage Neapolitan

An exciting dish for late breakfast or supper—Sunday or any day.

YOU WILL NEED:
pork sausages
butter
eggs
condensed tomato soup
basil or parsley

Butter 6 individual egg shirrers, oven-proof saucers, or custard cups, break 1 or 2 eggs in each. Around the eggs, arrange 6 small pork sausages that have been cut in 1/2-inch pieces and browned. Cover eggs and sausages with condensed canned tomato soup, undiluted. Sprinkle with finely chopped fresh basil or parsley. Bake in a moderate oven, 350° F., about 8 minutes.

AT SERVING TIME:

Place the shirrers on individual plates or arrange on a large tray or platter. Garnish with bouquets of parsley or green leaves. Serve in baking dishes. Serves 6.

❧ 6 ❧

Main Dishes

STARRING CHEESE, RICE, AND

PASTA

THIS IS A CHAPTER in which we have grouped a number of those dishes which, like many great works of art, are quite unclassifiable. In old-fashioned cookbooks they might have been called entrees. They are for the most part main-course dishes. Several would, with a salad and dessert, constitute one-dish meals.

Among them are such classic dishes as the Welsh rabbit, Swiss fondue, a number of notable pastas—spaghetti in various guises, ravioli, lasagne.

Important rice dishes are here too—pilaf, Spanish rice, Italian risotto.

There are others too, equally indispensable to anyone with an appreciation for good food—polenta for instance, and Philadelphia scrapple.

Each one of these dishes makes use of some short cut—a prepared sauce, a canned product, a quick-cooking rice, a new quick-cooking cereal.

RECIPES

Blushing Bunny
Fondue à la Breakneck Hill
The True Swiss Fondue
Your Own Pizza
Pizza from English Muffins
Ready-Made Pizza
Quiche Lorraine
Quiche Lorraine for Lent
Neapolitan Cheese Soufflé
Welsh Rabbit with Ale and Basil
Welsh Rabbit with Sherry
Macaroni and Ham, Virginia Style
Macaroni Ring
Spring Ring with Buttered Carrots

Green Noodles with Meat Sauce
Ravioli Gratine
Venetian Spaghetti with Clam Sauce
Spaghettini with Meat Balls De Luxe
Gilded Rice
Pilaf Indienne
Ring of Rice
Spanish Rice à la Minute
Risotto Milanese
Italian Polenta
Baked Polenta with Sausage
Scrapple for Brunch

Blushing Bunny

Don't let the whimsical name deceive you—this is a hearty luncheon or supper dish.

YOU WILL NEED:

condensed tomato soup
sharp American cheese
eggs
toast, crackers, or English muffins

milk
mustard

Combine 1 can condensed tomato soup, 1/2 cup milk, 1 cup sharp American cheese finely cut or shredded, 1/2 teaspoon prepared mustard, the yolks of 2 eggs well beaten. Heat over low heat, stirring constantly until cheese is melted and mixture is thickened.

Fold in stiffly beaten whites of 2 eggs.

AT SERVING TIME:

Serve immediately on toast, crackers, or toasted English muffins. Makes 6 servings.

Fondue à la Breakneck Hill

Breakneck Hill is the name of our place in Connecticut, so named they say because the stagecoaches raced down the steep hill toward the Half-Way Inn between Danbury and Norwalk at breakneck speed. Despite our family love of good food, breakneck speed is often necessary in the preparing of it—there is always so much to do.

Chapters have been written about *the true and only way* to prepare, serve, and eat a fondue. The classic recipes call for rather a lot of special cooking equipment. But we, longing for the taste and fun of fondue without fuss, developed one which is completely fail-proof. The knowing ones will raise their eyebrows over the use of a processed Swiss cheese, but therein lies the secret. The

72

processed cheese never gets rubbery. If desired fondue can be reheated; simply add a little more liquid.

YOU WILL NEED:

American processed Swiss cheese
garlic (optional)
nutmeg

French bread or hard rolls
dry white wine
brandy or kirsch (optional)

Rub a chafing dish or top of double boiler with a cut clove of garlic. Toss in a half pound of processed Swiss cheese, cut into small pieces. Add 1/2 cup dry, white table wine. Stir until well blended. Season to taste with salt, freshly ground black pepper, and a touch of grated nutmeg. Two or 3 tablespoons of kirsch or brandy may be stirred in, if desired. All this takes less than 5 minutes.

AT SERVING TIME:

Since this fondue is made so quickly and so easily it is a shame not to do it at the table. It should be served from the chafing dish and the eating of it is a ritual. The fondue must be kept bubbling ever so lightly while the guests alternate in dunking a cube of French bread or hard rolls spiked on a fork.

P.S. A candle warmer and any kind of earthenware or serving pan may be used instead of a chafing dish. The idea is to keep the fondue warm and bubbly. Count on this amount to serve 4.

The True Swiss Fondue

This is a dish famed in song and story. Although the fondue uses no canned or ready-to-serve ingredients, it belongs in the repertoire of the hurried epicure because it requires no previous preparation other than the grating of the cheese and the cuttting of a loaf of bread or crusty rolls into bite-sized pieces. Furthermore, it's so gay, so different, so everlastingly delicious.

YOU WILL NEED:

In the way of equipment:

A quart-size earthenware casserole with handle or a chafing dish
An alcohol stove with a flame that can be adjusted, Sterno, or an electric plate with an asbestos pad

In the way of ingredients:

Switzerland Swiss cheese
flour
garlic

white wine
kirsch or brandy (optional)

Rub your casserole or chafing dish with a cut clove of garlic. To serve 4—pour in 2 cups dry white table wine and set over a very slow fire. When the wine is hot but not boiling, stir with a fork and add, a handful at a time, a pound (4 cups) shredded Swiss cheese, which has been sprinkled with 3 tablespoons flour. Each batch of cheese should be thoroughly incorporated before the other is added. Keep stirring until the mixture starts bubbling. Season with a little salt, freshly ground black pepper from the mill, and a grating of nutmeg if desired. Also 2 or 3 tablespoons of kirsch or brandy may be stirred in.

AT SERVING TIME:

Remove fondue from the fire and set immediately over a small flame or an electric plate with an asbestos pad or a very low alcohol flame—just enough heat to keep the fondue bubbling lightly. Present to each guest a fork spearing a piece of bread complete with a little crust. The idea is for each to stir the fondue with his bread. If he loses the bread off the fork in the fondue according to tradition, the foreit is a kiss—or the drinks. Kirsch, brandy, or white wine is usually served with fondue. Serves 6.

Your Own Pizza

If you would like to make your own pizza there are two ways to do so, both very easy: 1. Use a package of hot roll mix. 2. Use halved English muffins. In both cases, the trimmings are the same.

YOU WILL NEED:

hot roll mix	anchovy fillets
canned tomato sauce	cheese
basil, orégano, or thyme	garlic
olive oil	

Make up a package of hot roll mix according to package directions. When dough has risen spread in large well-greased baking pan about 1/2 inch thick. Allow to rise to twice the height, poke here and there with fingertips. Top with the following: To 2 cups canned tomato sauce add 1 well-crushed clove of garlic, 1/2 teaspoon basil, orégano, or thyme, 8 anchovy fillets cut into small pieces. Pour sauce over dough. Sprinkle liberally with 1/2 cup grated cheese. (Romano cheese is best but other cheese will do.) Dribble 2 tablespoons olive oil over the top. Bake in a hot oven, 450° F., for 1/2 hour. Lower heat to 350° and continue baking 10 minutes more.

AT SERVING TIME:

Cut into sizable squares or wedges and serve piping hot. Serves 4 or 6.

VARIATION: **Pizza from English Muffins**

With a fork tear in half 4 or 5 English muffins. Cover with sauce and cheese as above. Bake in a hot oven, 400° F., about 10 minutes.

Ready-Made Pizza

Quick-frozen Italian pizzas can now be bought in many cities and larger towns. Since they are somewhat thin they seem better suited to appetizer service than use as a main dish. Cut into thin strips or squares. They are excellent with cocktail, soup, or salad.

YOU WILL NEED:

quick-frozen pizza or ready-baked pizza from a pizzeria or Italian restaurant	Parmesan cheese
	olive oil
	orégano or basil (optional)

Brush pizza with olive oil. Sprinkle generously with freshly grated Parmesan cheese. If desired, add a bit of orégano or basil. Reheat in the oven.

AT SERVING TIME:

Cut into small pieces as a cocktail, soup, or salad accompaniment, or cut into good-sized wedges like pie and serve as a main dish with red wine, a green salad, a huge bowl of fruit for desert.

Quiche Lorraine

One of the most famous dishes of Alsace-Lorraine is a kind of cheese custard pie, sprinkled with bits of crisp bacon. It may be made without a crust or you can use a prepared crust.

YOU WILL NEED:

plain pastry	Swiss cheese
eggs	onion juice or extract
bacon	cayenne or Tabasco
milk or light cream	

Fry 6 slices of bacon until crisp and break into small pieces. Mix with 1 cup milk or light cream, 1 cup grated Swiss cheese, 4 slightly beaten eggs, a few drops of onion juice or extract, 1/2 teaspoon salt, 1/8 teaspoon pepper, a few grains of cayenne or a couple of drops of Tabasco sauce.

Line a 9-inch pie plate with plain pastry either quick frozen prepared or made from a packaged mix. Then pour in the cheese and egg mixture. Bake 10 minutes at 450° F. then reduce the heat to 325° and bake until firm or when a silver knife inserted comes out clean. This should take about 30 minutes.

AT SERVING TIME:

Serve neither blazing hot or cold but gently warm. A big bowl of mixed green salad is the traditional accompaniment and with fruit it's all you could possibly want for lunch or supper. Serves 4 to 6.

VARIATION: Quiche Lorraine for Lent

Omit bacon and sprinkle the pie just as it comes from the oven with 1/2 cup canned French fried onions. If you wish, you can put the onions on the custard after it is set but before it is quite ready to come out of the oven so that the onions will be crisp and warm.

Neapolitan Cheese Soufflé

A soufflé sounds, looks, and tastes tremendously complicated. But when you start with a can of condensed soup, it couldn't be easier.

YOU WILL NEED:

condensed cream of tomato soup

eggs

basil, marjoram, or orégano (optional)

sharp cheese

Heat 1 can condensed cream of tomato soup and 3/4 cup grated sharp cheese in the top of a double boiler, stirring until the cheese melts. Take off the stove and stir in 4 egg yolks, one at a time, beating after each addition. Cool, fold in 4 egg whites beaten until stiff but not dry, season, if desired, in the Italian manner by adding 1/2 teaspoon dry basil, marjoram, or orégano. Pour into buttered 1 1/2 quart casserole. Bake in a hot oven, 400° F., 20 to 25 minutes. If you prefer a firmer soufflé, place the casserole in a pan of hot water and bake at 300° F. for 1 to 1 1/2 hours.

AT SERVING TIME:

Rush to the table and serve immediately. This recipe makes 6 portions.

Welsh Rarebit with Ale and Basil

Some call it rarebit because it is a rare and tasty tidbit. Others say the right name is rabbit—that it's the only "rabbit" the hunters ate when they caught no rabbits. Since the making of a perfect rarebit has its hazards, our version makes use of a prepared Welsh rarebit. For this particular occasion, choose the kind that is made with ale or beer.

YOU WILL NEED:

jar of prepared Welsh rarebit

milk, ale, or beer

dry basil

toast, rolls, or English muffins

In the top of a chafing dish or double boiler or over a *low* fire, heat 1 jar Welsh rarebit into which you have stirred 1/4 to 1/2 cup milk, ale, or beer. Sprinkle with dried basil. To get the full flavor of the herb, rub it between the palms of your hands to release the oils and so sprinkle it off your hands into the rarebit.

AT SERVING TIME:

Bring to the table in a chafing dish or spoon the hot rarebit over toast, toasted soft rolls, or toasted English muffins. Foaming mugs of beer or ale are the classic accompaniment. An 8-ounce jar of rarebit serves 2 or 3.

Welsh Rarebit with Sherry

Some brands of prepared Welsh rarebit are flavored with tomato and sherry. This rarebit is delicious when the sherry flavor is slightly heightened and the rarebit combined with thick slices of grilled tomato and crisp bacon.

YOU WILL NEED:

tomato flavored Welsh rarebit with sherry	flour
	butter
sherry	parsley (optional)
cayenne	bacon
tomatoes	

To a 10-ounce jar of tomato-flavored Welsh rarebit, add 4 tablespoons water or sherry, a few grains of cayenne pepper. Heat in the top of a double boiler or chafing dish, stirring occasionally. Slice a large-sized tomato in thick slices, dip in flour, and sprinkle with salt and black pepper, and brown in 2 tablespoons of butter.

AT SERVING TIME:

Spoon the rarebit, while sizzling hot, over hot toast or toasted English muffins. Top each portion with a thick slice of grilled tomato. Garnish, if desired, with parsley and strips of crisp bacon. Serves 3 or 4.

Macaroni and Ham, Virginia Style

A can of macaroni and cream sauce with cheese is the beginning of great wisdom for the hostess in a hurry. Merely sprinkled with cheese and heated in the oven, it is excellent. Dressed up in the manner of old Virginia, it's superb.

YOU WILL NEED:

canned macaroni in cream sauce with cheese	mustard (optional)
	bread crumbs (optional)
ham	butter
cheese	parsley or water cress

Butter a baking dish. Combine 2 cans macaroni and cream sauce (yes, it comes canned with its own sauce) with 1 to 2 cups coarsely chopped or finely cut cooked ham. Season with 2 teaspoons prepared yellow mustard. Place in the buttered baking dish. Sprinkle with 1/2 cup grated cheese and, if desired, 4 tablespoons bread crumbs. Bake at 400° F. or until brown.

AT SERVING TIME:

Set parsley or water cress in the center of the casserole. Serve on hot plates. Serves 6 generously.

Macaroni Ring

An elaborate-looking macaroni ring can be quickly and easily made with canned macaroni.

YOU WILL NEED:

canned macaroni in cream sauce with cheese	milk
	pimiento, green pepper, or
eggs	onion (optional)

Combine a can of macaroni in cream sauce with 1 cup milk, 2 well-beaten eggs. Various additions, such as a chopped pimiento, or green pepper or a tablespoon of chopped onion or onion flakes may be added if desired. Turn the mixture into a buttered ring mold. Set in a pan of hot water. Bake at 350° F., 30 to 40 minutes.

AT SERVING TIME:

Turn out on a warm plate. Fill the center with chicken à la king, creamed mushrooms, or shrimp. Serves 4.

Spring Ring with Buttered Carrots

This attractive ring of noodles and cottage cheese is served traditionally at the Jewish Feast of Weeks which comes usually in May. But it is appropriate, of course, for any season of the year.

YOU WILL NEED:

packaged green noodles	buttered canned carrots
cottage cheese	(optional), water cress,
eggs	spiced crabapples or
buttered bread crumbs	apple rings

Boil contents of an 8-ounce package of green noodles in salted water about 7 minutes. Drain and rinse with hot water. Combine 3 cups cottage cheese, 1 teaspoon salt, 1/4 teaspoon white pepper, and 4 eggs slightly beaten. Add to noodles. Turn into a well-buttered 1-quart ring mold. Sprinkle with buttered bread crumbs, using about 1/4 cup, and bake in a moderate oven, 375° F., for 30 minutes or until browned and lightly crusted.

AT SERVING TIME:

Turn out onto a warm plate. Fill center with buttered canned carrots. Garnish with water cress and spiced crabapples or apple rings. Serves 6.

Green Noodles with Meat Sauce

Green noodles are nothing more than noodles colored with spinach juice. Since the coloring is done by the manufacturer and the noodles are almost as easy to procure as any other type, it's amazing what a sensation they created when they first appeared.

YOU WILL NEED:

green noodles
prepared spaghetti sauce
with or without meat
garlic

basil, orégano, Worcestershire sauce, or red wine
(optional)
parsley (optional)

Cook 2 cups green noodles according to package directions. Be careful not to overcook. Noodles like spaghetti should be cooked *al dente* as the Italians put it—just to the point where it is tender but provides something for the teeth. Drain in a strainer and rinse with hot or cold water to separate the strands.

Meanwhile heat prepared spaghetti sauce. Perk it up by adding a little extra seasoning, basil or orégano or a dash of Worcestershire sauce or a couple of tablespoons of red table wine such as Chianti or Burgundy.

AT SERVING TIME:

Heat a serving dish, rub with garlic, holding the clove with a bit of waxed paper. Pile the drained noodles on the hot plate, make a well in the center and pour the sauce into the well. Sprinkle, if desired, with fresh chopped parsley. Provide a bowl of grated Parmesan or Romano cheese. Crusty bread, green noodles, a green salad, red wine, and a fruit dessert comprise a glorious meal. Serves 4.

Ravioli Gratine

Ravioli, beloved of the Italians, are nothing more or less than square noodles filled with savory meat, chicken, vegetables, or cheese. When homemade, they take hours and hours. But you can buy them complete with tomato sauce in a jar. In most cases the sauce can take a little doctoring, but ready-to-serve ravioli sprinkled with grated cheese and fresh-chopped parsley, heated in a shallow casserole, make a good and filling dish.

YOU WILL NEED:

jar of ravioli in tomato
sauce
parsley, chives, onion tops,
or finochio

cheese
olive oil

In a shallow ovenware casserole or heat-proof, glass pie pan, pour a tablespoon of olive oil. Add the ravioli with sauce. Sprinkle generously with grated cheese, using about 4 tablespoons of cheese to an 8-ounce jar of ravioli. Set in a hot oven, 350° F., for about 20 minutes or until the ravioli are bubbly hot, the cheese melted and delicately brown.

AT SERVING TIME:

Sprinkle with chopped parsley, chives, finely cut green onion tops, or the finely chopped fronds from a bunch of finochio (something like celery with an anise flavor).

Venetian Spaghetti with Clam Sauce

This masterly sauce, formerly a labor of much love and many hours, now cooks in 5 minutes—thanks to a can of minced clams, another can of tomato sauce.

YOU WILL NEED:

vermicelli, spaghetti, or any other type of pasta
canned minced clams
garlic
parsley
olive oil
canned tomato sauce or condensed tomato soup

Start cooking your vermicelli or spaghetti, according to package directions, before you begin the sauce, since spaghetti will take 10 to 15 minutes. Brown 1 or 2 well-crushed cloves of garlic in 4 tablespoons of hot olive oil in a saucepan. Add 1 can tomato sauce or 1 can condensed tomato soup, diluted with 1/2 can water, add 1 tablespoon chopped parsley, a little freshly ground black pepper. Cook about 3 minutes. Add a 7- or 8-ounce can of minced clams with their juice. Cook for only 2 minutes. Too much cooking toughens the clams.

AT SERVING TIME:

Pour hot sauce over cooked spaghetti in a well-heated shallow bowl or platter. Garnish with parsley. Grated cheese is not generally passed with this dish but it is not forbidden!

Spaghettini with Meat Balls De Luxe

For the greatest speed use the thinnest spaghetti the thinner the spaghetti the faster it cooks. Vermicelli and spaghettini, being very thin, cook in about 6 minutes if you like them *al dente* which all connoisseurs insist is the only way.

YOU WILL NEED:

thin spaghetti, spaghettini, or vermicelli	basil
	green olives
canned meat balls in spaghetti sauce	Parmesan or Romano cheese
garlic	capers (optional)

Cook 1 pound spaghetti or its thin cousins, spaghettini or vermicelli, according to package directions. When tender but not soft, drain and arrange on a hot platter.

Meanwhile, open a can of meat balls in spaghetti sauce. Remove the balls and cut in halves. Put back in the sauce and heat along with one well-crushed clove of garlic, 1/2 teaspoon basil, 2 tablespoons chopped green olives, 1 tablespoon capers if desired.

AT SERVING TIME:

Pour hot sauce over spaghetti. Sprinkle with grated cheese— Parmesan or Romano cheese. Serve very hot with green salad, crusty bread, fruit for dessert. Serves 4 to 6.

Gilded Rice

Rice with a golden glow adds a party touch to any meal. Because it's so easy to achieve perfectly cooked rice *every time,* we suggest using quick-cooking rice.

YOU WILL NEED:

quick-cooking rice	curry powder or turmeric
saffron	

Prepare a small package, 1 1/3 cups, quick-cooking rice according to package directions. But add to the water, 1/2 teaspoon saffron, 3/4 teaspoon curry powder *or* turmeric.

AT SERVING TIME:
Fluff with a fork. Makes 3 cups, 4 to 5 servings.

Pilaf Indienne

One of the ladies of the Indian embassy was a guest on my television show when we cooked this pilaf. She asked for the recipe
to give to her chef. That's why we know that though our method
is unorthodox, the flavor must be authentic.

YOU WILL NEED:

quick-cooking rice	raisins
saffron or curry powder	almonds
chicken bouillon cubes	bay leaf
onions	cinnamon
butter	cardamon seeds (optional)
leftover chicken, lamb, beef,	nutmeg
or ham (optional)	garnishes (optional)

To a package of quick-cooking rice, add 1 1/2 cups cold water,
1 teaspoon salt, 3 chicken bouillon cubes, dissolved in 1/4 cup
hot water (this trick of dissolving bouillon cubes in a small
amount of hot water is well worth remembering when a recipe
calls for cool liquid). Add 1/4 to 1/2 teaspoon curry powder or
1/2 to 1 teaspoon saffron. Bring to a full boil, cover and let stand
in a warm place 10 minutes.

In the meantime, fry 2 small, sliced onions in 4 tablespoons
butter to a golden brown. Add 4 tablespoons raisins, 2 tablespoons
coarsely chopped salted almonds, 1/4 teaspoon cinnamon, a bay
leaf, 2 or 3 cardamon seeds if you have them, a dash of nutmeg,
salt, and freshly ground black pepper to taste. (If you wish to serve
this as a main dish rather than as an accompaniment add 1 cup
leftover chicken, beef, lamb, or ham, cut into small pieces.) Mix
with cooked rice. Heat a minute or two.

AT SERVING TIME:

Heap on a heated platter. Garnish in the Oriental manner with
chopped crisp bacon sprinkled over the top, French fried onions
(from a can), chopped chives or parsley, salted almonds, and/or
sliced hard-cooked eggs. Serves 4 to 6.

Ring of Rice

Nothing is dressier than rice molded in a ring—filled with chicken à la king, lobster Newburg, or any creamed vegetable. It is especially easy when you use quick-cooking rice.

YOU WILL NEED:

quick-cooking rice   nutmeg (optional)
butter

Place 3 cups cooked rice (5-ounce package or 1 1/3 cups quick-cooking rice, prepared according to package directions) in a well-greased 8-inch ring mold. Pour on 4 tablespoons melted butter. Set in moderate oven, 350° F., 10 minutes.

AT SERVING TIME:

Loosen the edges of the mold by running a knife blade around it. Place a warm plate over the mold. Turn upside down and shake slightly to loosen the mold. If you wish sprinkle the top with nutmeg. Fill center with any desired creamed mixture. Serves 6.

Spanish Rice à la Minute

YOU WILL NEED:

canned meat balls in to-
  mato sauce
quick-cooking rice
dehydrated onion flakes
dehydrated mixed vegeta-
  ble flakes

butter or olive oil
parsley
chili powder, cayenne, or
  Tabasco
cheese (optional)

To a 5-ounce package of quick-cooking rice (1 1/3 cups), add 1 cup water, 1 can meat balls with their sauce. The balls may be sliced or cut up into pieces so that they "go further." Add 2 tablespoons mixed vegetables flakes, 1 teaspoon salt, 2 tablespoons dehydrated onion flakes. Add 2 tablespoons butter or olive oil. Bring to a full rolling boil, uncovered. Cook 2 minutes. Season to taste with chili powder, cayenne, or Tabasco sauce. Cover and let stand about 10 minutes. If desired, the Spanish rice may be sprinkled with 4 tablespoons grated cheese and set under the broiler for a minute or so until the cheese melts.

AT SERVING TIME:

Garnish with parsley and serve with grated cheese. Serves 4.

Risotto Milanese

Here is a truly delicious variant of Italy's most prized rice dish.

YOU WILL NEED:

quick-cooking rice	chicken livers or giblets
onion	butter
Parmesan cheese	saffron
chicken bouillon cubes	chives or parsley

Cook 1/2 pound chicken livers, which have been cut into small pieces, in 4 tablespoons butter until the red color has disappeared. Or, if you use giblets, cook the giblets of 2 chickens in boiling salted water about 20 minutes or until tender. Drain. Cut up into small pieces.

In a frying pan, melt 4 tablespoons butter and fry 1 large-sized onion finely chopped. The onion should be golden but not dry or dark. Add 1 package (1 1/3 cups) quick-cooking rice and allow the rice to brown a little. Stir to keep it from burning. Now add 1 3/4 cups cold water, 1/4 cup hot water, in which 2 chicken bouillon cubes have been dissolved, 1/2 teaspoon saffron. Bring to a full rolling boil. Add the giblets or liver and 1/2 cup grated Parmesan cheese. Stir with a fork, cover and let stand in a warm place 10 minutes.

AT SERVING TIME:

Serve on heated plates. Pass a bowl of grated Parmesan cheese and also a small bowl of finely cut chives or parsley. This amount makes a main dish for 4 people.

Italian Polenta

Popular brands of packaged yellow corn meal cook in about 1/3 of the time that an old-time Italian cook would have devoted to making one of her country's beloved national dishes. Polenta is nothing more than corn-meal mush combined with grated cheese. Ideal with stews, fish, or meat.

YOU WILL NEED:

yellow corn meal	butter
Parmesan cheese	parsley (optional)

Boil 3 cups water in a saucepan. Mix 1 cup yellow corn meal and 1 teaspoon salt with 1 cup cold water. Pour into the boiling water, stirring constantly. Cook until thickened, stirring frequently. Cover and continue cooking over low heat 10 minutes or longer. Stir in 3 tablespoons butter, 1 cup grated Parmesan cheese. Season with a little freshly ground black pepper, mix thoroughly.

AT SERVING TIME:

Serve very hot. If desired, polenta may be poured into a buttered ring mold. Set in a warm place for 10 minutes, then unmold. The center may be filled with stew, chicken à la king, or any creamed mixture. Garnish or sprinkle with parsley if desired. Or if you'd rather not bother with a mold simply spoon the polenta around the dish making a casual kind of ring.

VARIATION: Baked Polenta with Sausage

Drain and brown canned cocktail or quick-frozen sausages. Place in a shallow oven-proof dish. Cover with polenta prepared as above. Bake 15 minutes in a hot oven, 400° F. If ingredients are already hot, sprinkle with grated cheese and set under the broiler until the cheese melts and browns.

Scrapple for Brunch

Philadelphia scrapple ready for browning can be secured in cans but since it is not universally available, it's good to know about one that can be put together quickly with wheat cereals that cook in 5 minutes or less. The use of minced ham instead of fresh pork may be unorthodox but makes the scrapple taste good.

YOU WILL NEED:

quick-cooking wheat cereal	onion
small can minced ham	thyme or sage

Prepare quick-cooking whole-wheat cereal according to package directions. To 2 cups cooked cereal, add a small jar or tin (3 or 4 ounces) minced ham, 2 tablespoons finely chopped onion, 1/4 teaspoon powdered thyme or sage, salt and pepper to taste. Cook over boiling water about 5 minutes to blend the flavors. Pack into a well-greased refrigerator tray to chill thoroughly and harden.

AT SERVING TIME:

Slice 1/2 inch thick. Fry in butter or bacon fat until crisp and brown on both sides. Serve with syrup or applesauce. Leftover cooked cereal may be utilized very well in this way. Makes about 8 or 10 slices.

Fine Fish Dishes

VIA TIN AND FREEZER

IN THE PAST, what has been difficult for most modern and har-
ried householders has been the primary admonition "first,
catch your fish." Even when you weren't compelled to catch it
yourself there has been the ever present problem of getting the fish
when you wanted it and the even greater problem of cleaning,
boning, skinning, and otherwise preparing it for the pan.

Enter the quick-frozen fillet and the sad tale is ended. Quick-
frozen fish has the advantage of being at least as fresh as the
freshest since the best brands are generally frozen within an hour
or so after being caught. Equally important—such fish comes to
the frozen-food lockers all ready to cook.

The quick-frozen fillet is presented here in a number of interesting classic guises.

Each one of these dishes is achieved with a minimum of effort
in the fewest possible minutes.

In using quick-frozen fish, it is not necessary to thaw beforehand. In several recipes we have suggested thawing only enough to
separate the fillets. By this method the utmost in flavor is achieved
and, furthermore, there is no possibility of deterioration. In case
you should thaw fish completely before cooking, remember that
quick-frozen fish spoils as promptly as fresh.

Never refreeze fish and if you have leftover cooked fish, use
it within twenty-four hours because it does not keep.

In addition to quick-frozen sea food there are of course the
canned varieties, some of which are probably among the best
known and most popular of canned foods. A large number of new
products have within the last few years been added to this category
—shad roe, for example, and prepared fish cakes. Salted, fresh and

dried fish in several forms are now presented so that they no longer require soaking or freshening.

So wide is the choice, so delicate are the flavors that many individuals and families who once insisted "we're not much for fish or sea food," have now completely changed their way of thinking. Whether you are a fish fancier or a nonfancier try some of our short cuts. They may well become some of the most prized and often-repeated dishes of your repertory.

RECITES

RECIPES

Quick Baltimore Deviled Crab
Quick Crab Meat Mornay
Finnan Haddie Delmonico
Fish Poached in White Wine
Fish Soufflé
Norwegian Fish Pudding
Oven-Fried Fillets
Swedish Fish Balls
Seafood Gumbo
Kedgeree
Kippers in Rum
Baked South African Lobster Tails à la Diavolo

Quick Lobster Newburg
Lobster Thermidor
Salt Mackerel, Virginia Breakfast Style
Scalloped Oysters
Fillets of Perch Baked in Cream
Salmon Parisienne
Spiced Salmon
Shad Roe
Shrimp Jambalaya
Fillets of Sole Amandine
Quick Fillets of Sole Marguery

Quick Baltimore Deviled Crab

If this be treason—to concoct Baltimore's own deviled crab from quick-frozen crab meat and cream of mushroom soup—make the best of it, and very good it is!

YOU WILL NEED:

canned or quick-frozen crab
  meat
onion
chili sauce
Worcestershire sauce
parsley
condensed cream of mush-
  room soup

butter or salad oil
egg
dry mustard
lemon juice
bread crumbs

To fill 6 medium-sized crab shells you will need 2 to 2 1/2 cups of crab meat. Combine this amount of crab meat with 1 cup undiluted condensed cream of mushroom soup heated in the top of a double boiler. Season with 1 tablespoon chili sauce, 2 teaspoons Worcestershire sauce, 1 teaspoon chopped parsley, dash of pepper. Place the mixture in 6 crab shells, or individual baking dishes, cover with a paste made of an egg beaten with 1/2 teaspoon dry mustard, 1 teaspoon lemon juice, 1/4 teaspoon salt, and 1/2 cup fine bread crumbs. Brush liberally with melted butter or salad oil and bake until a rich brown.

AT SERVING TIME:

Garnish with a sprig of parsley in the middle of each crab. Serve warm or cold. 6 servings.

Quick Crab Meat Mornay

YOU WILL NEED:

crab meat
condensed cream of chicken
  soup
egg

cheese
milk, water, or white wine
butter
chives or parsley

Heat in the top of the double boiler 1 can condensed cream of chicken soup, 1/4 can milk, water, or white wine. Simmer 2 or 3 minutes, add 1 slightly beaten egg. Butter a shallow casserole or 6 small oven-proof ramekins or custard cups. Place in each a thin layer of crab meat, using about 1 1/4 cups for the 6, cover with sauce, sprinkle with grated cheese, using about 1/2 cup grated cheese. Set under the broiler just long enough to melt the cheese and give a delicate brown.

AT SERVING TIME:

Sprinkle or garnish with chopped chives or parsley and serve immediately. Makes 6 portions.

Finnan Haddie Delmonico

Canned finnan haddie already soaked and cooked is an efficient time saver. Combined with condensed cream of mushroom soup, it makes in double-quick time a delicious variant of one of the famous dishes of the Gay Nineties.

YOU WILL NEED:

canned finnan haddie	eggs
condensed cream of mush-room soup	parsley
	cayenne or Tabasco sauce

Combine cooked finnan haddie, which has been separated into flakes, with 1 can condensed cream of mushroom soup, 4 hard-cooked eggs, thinly sliced. Season with cayenne pepper or a few drops of Tabasco sauce. Heat thoroughly.

AT SERVING TIME:

Serve from a chafing dish or heated bowl. Sprinkle each portion liberally with finely chopped parsley. Boiled or baked potatoes are a must with this. Serves 4.

Fish Poached in White Wine

Any number of different kinds of fish—fillets or sole or flounder, salmon steaks or halibut steaks—may be poached in this fashion.

YOU WILL NEED:

fish fillets, fresh or quick
  frozen
white wine
butter
parsley
peppercorns
cloves

bay leaf
onion
celery (optional)
condensed cream of mush-
  room soup
carrot

Cut 1 pound fillets (2 or 3 fillets) into serving pieces to have them ready to go into hot Court Bouillon.

Court Bouillon

This is the basic and best broth in which to cook most fish. Cut up a medium-sized onion, 1 medium-sized carrot, 2 stalks of celery and cook together in 2 tablespoons of butter with 2 sprigs of parsley for about 3 minutes. Add 4 or 5 peppercorns, 2 cloves, 1/2 bay leaf, 1 teaspoon salt, 2 cups white wine, and 2 cups water. Boil together about 10 minutes. Strain.

Place the fillets in the hot Court Bouillon and simmer but do not boil. Cook about 5 minutes, just long enough for the fish to lose its translucent look.

AT SERVING TIME:

Drain and serve with a sauce made by adding 1/2 cup strained Court Bouillon to a can of condensed cream of mushroom soup. Serves 2 or 3.

Fish Soufflé

A fine main dish for a meatless day, this simple soufflé is made with a canned soup base.

YOU WILL NEED:

flaked, cooked, or canned
  fish
onion, onion juice or ex-
  tract
condensed cream of celery
  soup

eggs
lemon
Worcestershire sauce
Mock Hollandaise Sauce
  (page 144)

Combine 2 cups flaked cooked fish (bass, halibut, flounder, lake trout, or pike, or canned, drained salmon or tuna fish) with 1 can condensed cream of celery soup. Season with 2 teaspoons lemon juice, a little finely chopped onion, onion juice, or onion extract, 1/2 teaspoon Worcestershire sauce. Add one at a time, 3 egg yolks, beating well after each yolk is added. Gently fold in 3 stiffly beaten egg whites. Turn into a buttered, 2-quart baking dish which can go to the table. Bake the quick French way in a hot oven, 450° F., about 25 minutes or if you like a firmer soufflé, bake the American way in a moderate oven, 350° F., for 1 hour or until firm.

AT SERVING TIME:

Rush to the table and serve immediately with Mock Hollandaise Sauce. Makes 6 servings.

Norwegian Fish Pudding

A modernized, quick version of a famous Scandinavian dish— deserving an honored place on your party table.

YOU WILL NEED:

cooked fish	eggs
condensed cream of mush-	cracker meal or flour
room soup	milk
leftovers or canned sole,	butter
halibut, haddock, or	sugar (optional)
perch	lemon juice

Start with 2 cups of cooked fish (canned flaked fish may be used). Chop very fine. Combine with 1 can condensed cream of mushroom soup and add 1/2 can milk. Heat together and simmer a few minutes, stirring occasionally. Set aside to cool. Three-quarters of an hour before eating time add the yolks of 4 eggs, very well beaten, and if you want the true Scandinavian touch, add 1/2 teaspoon sugar. Now gently ease into the mixture the whites of 4 eggs, beaten stiff but not dry. Butter a baking dish or casserole and dust with 2 tablespoons very fine cracker meal or flour. Bake in a medium oven, 350° F., about 30 minutes, until it is puffed and firm and lightly browned.

AT SERVING TIME:

Like any of the soufflés, to which class this pudding belongs, it should be served immediately. Serve with melted butter to which lemon juice has been added. Serves 6.

Oven-Fried Fillets

When you don't want to go to the trouble of deep-fat frying, or when you want to fix quite a few servings all at once, try the quick trick of oven frying. This method is adaptable for all types of fillets and for small fish that are fried whole, such as smelts or porgies.

YOU WILL NEED:

fillets of fish	paprika (optional)
milk	parsley or water cress
soft bread crumbs	lemon or lime
butter or oil	

Thaw a pound box of quick-frozen fillets just enough to separate. Dip in milk, using about 1/4 cup, roll in bread crumbs seasoned with salt and pepper. A little paprika added to the bread crumbs provides an extra pretty brown. Place the fish in a buttered or oiled baking dish, preferably one that can go to the table. Sprinkle with 2 tablespoons melted butter, salad, or olive, oil. Bake in hot oven, 450° F., about 20 minutes or until done.

AT SERVING TIME:

Garnish with parsley or water cress and wedges of lemon or lime. Serves 3.

Swedish Fish Balls

The making of these from scratch is quite a chore, so we suggest that you use several excellent brands that are available either at department store food counters, Swedish delicatessens or by mail order.

YOU WILL NEED:

canned fish balls   butter and lemon juice

Gently heat fish balls in their liquid.

AT SERVING TIME:

Sprinkle liberally with chopped parsley and pass melted butter, seasoned with freshly ground black pepper and lemon juice.

Seafood Gumbo

Although gumbo is quite generally accepted as a Creole invention —part French, part Spanish—its distinctive ingredient, filé powder, was originally made and brought to the New Orleans market by the Choctaw Indians on Bayou Lacombe. This filé powder is nothing more than the tender young leaves of the sassafras bush dried, powdered, and sieved. Nowadays, it can be bought at almost any good food store in various parts of the country—or it's well worth ordering a jar by mail from New Orleans.

Gumbos usually have an alarmingly long list of ingredients. Certainly they have been extravagant as to shopping time and length of simmering. The 5-minute version is a boon, therefore, to the busy cook of today.

YOU WILL NEED:

canned, or quick-frozen,   condensed chicken gumbo
   shrimp, crab meat, lob-   soup
   ster, oysters or cooked,   filé powder
   canned or leftover   rice
   chicken or turkey

To a can of condensed chicken gumbo soup add 1 cup cooked, canned or quick-frozen sea food or chicken or turkey cut into 1-inch pieces. Heat and simmer 3 or 4 minutes. Add 1 teaspoon filé powder—more if you like a very spicy gumbo. Gumbos must never be boiled *after* adding the filé powder, otherwise they will become ropey.

AT SERVING TIME:

Serve with rice in a soup plate, as the main dish for a simple meal which need include nothing more than a salad and a dessert of fruit and cheese or cookies.

Kedgeree

The original of this recipe is said to have been brought by the captains of the clipper ships. Certainly it has an East Indian name and an Oriental flavor. In the Roosevelt family it has been for years a favorite Sunday night dish.

YOU WILL NEED:

rice	parsley
eggs	light cream
cooked, or canned, fish, flaked	curry or Worcestershire sauce

To 2 cups cooked rice add 4 hard-cooked eggs, chopped; 1/4 cup chopped parsley; 2 cups cooked or canned fish (salmon, tuna, codfish, or halibut may be used); 1/2 cup light cream. Season with plenty of salt, pepper, a little curry powder or a tablespoon of Worcestershire sauce. Heat in a double boiler or chafing dish, or place in a buttered casserole, sprinkle with grated cheese and heat in a moderate oven, 350° F., about 20 minutes.

AT SERVING TIME:

Serve from a chafing dish or casserole. Kedgeree, a big green salad, and dessert makes a fine supper menu. Serves 4 to 6.

Kippers in Rum

For brunch at Sunday noon or high tea Sunday at six, nothing is more dramatic than this quick and simple dish of kippers.

YOU WILL NEED:

canned kippered herrings (not the tomato sauce variety)	butter toast lemon or lime
rum	

In a shallow pan, preferably one which can be brought to the table, melt 1 tablespoon of butter, lay kippered herrings side by side in the pan. Sprinkle with freshly ground black pepper. Add enough white or golden rum to half cover. Let stand to warm slightly, then light the rum, and spoon the burning rum over the herrings until it burns out.

AT SERVING TIME:

The burning may be done right at the table, or the dish may be brought blazing into the room. Serve with triangles of fresh buttered toast and be sure to provide sections of lemon or lime.

Baked South African Lobster Tails à la Diavolo

Easier to handle than whole fresh lobster, lobster tails from South Africa are meaty, inexpensive, can be prepared and served exactly like whole live lobsters. Baking in a hot oven is much less trouble than regular broiling and the tails won't curl up.

YOU WILL NEED:

lobster tails
olive oil and/or butter
Diavolo Sauce (page 142)

parsley, water cress, or lemon

Have 1 lobster tail for each person. Cut tails open with a scissors on the soft underside. Brush the lobster tails fore and aft with olive oil and/or butter. Place in a shallow pan and bake 15 minutes in a hot oven, 450° F. While they are baking make the Diavolo Sauce.

AT SERVING TIME:

Place the baked lobsters on individual plates. Pour sauce over and around lobster and garnish with parsley, water cress, or lemon sections.

Quick Lobster Newburg

Lobster à la Newburg has a French sound, but actually it belongs to the New York of Delmonico's and the old Waldorf Peacock

Alley. As the story goes, this dish was composed by one of Delmonico's chefs for an expansive gentleman whose name was Wenburg. Came a parting of the ways between Mr. Wenburg and his erstwhile favorite haunt. The restaurant, still wishing to feature the glorious concoction on their menu, changed the Wen to New and so it has been Lobster Newburg to this day. Our recipe is not the classic version, and it may not be authentic Wen- or Newburg, but it is powerfully good. Furthermore this is not nearly so rich or calorific as the straight cream and butter version.

YOU WILL NEED:

cooked, canned or quick-frozen lobster meat

condensed cream of mushroom soup

egg

sherry or milk and light cream

nutmeg or paprika (optional)

Start with 2 cups cooked lobster meat, canned or quick frozen. The pieces should be good sized, about 3/4 of an inch at least. Combine with 1 can condensed cream of mushroom soup, 1/4 to 1/2 can dry sherry, or you may use equal parts of milk or cream and sherry. Heat but do not boil. Beat 1 egg slightly with a fork. Dip a little of the hot sauce into the egg and stir. This is to prevent the egg from curdling. Add the egg and sauce mixture to the lobster. A touch of paprika may be added, just enough to make the sauce pink.

AT SERVING TIME:

Serve at once, if possible from a chafing dish and add to each portion a few grains of nutmeg. Served with rice or on toast, or garnished with heated julienne potato sticks (canned). Serves 6.

Lobster Thermidor

Theoretically lobster thermidor should be served in lobster shells, but if you should make yours as we make ours, from quick-frozen, already cooked lobster meat, you will find that it tastes very fine indeed when served from a shallow baking dish.

YOU WILL NEED:

cooked lobster meat   condensed cream of mush-
white wine or lemon juice   room soup
mustard   Parmesan cheese

To a can of condensed cream of mushroom soup, add 1/4 can
white table wine or 1/4 can water and 1 tablespoon lemon juice,
4 tablespoons grated Parmesan or Romano cheese, a pinch of dry
mustard or 1/2 teaspoon prepared mustard. Heat in the top of a
double boiler, add 2 to 3 cups lobster meat, cut into good-sized
cubes. Place in a shallow buttered casserole or in lobster shells.
Sprinkle with cheese and bake in a hot oven, 450° F., 15 minutes
or set under the broiler about 5 minutes until cheese melts and
slightly browns.

AT SERVING TIME:
Bring to the table bubbling hot and serve from shells or baking
dish. Serves 4 to 6.

Salt Mackerel, Virginia Breakfast Style

No doubt there are a few underprivileged Northerners who have
never experienced the delight of eating delicate plump fillets of
salt mackerel with tiny boiled potatoes on a lazy Sunday noon!

YOU WILL NEED:

fillets of salt mackerel   parsley (optional)
onions

If your grocery store has never heard of salt mackerel fillets (this
could happen), you may order them in small wooden kegs by mail.
Since the fillets are very salty, it is necessary to soak them in water
overnight, then drain, before cooking. To cook, place the fillets in
the pan, cover with thinly sliced onions, using 1 medium-sized
onion to each pair of fillets. Sprinkle with freshly ground black
pepper. Pour about 1/2 inch of water into the bottom of the pan.
Cover and allow the fillets to steam and heat thoroughly until
done.

AT SERVING TIME:

Sprinkle if you wish with chopped parsley and serve with tiny boiled potatoes and hot biscuits.

Scalloped Oysters

This is a speeded-up version of the old-fashioned New England recipe for scalloped oysters.

YOU WILL NEED:

oysters	prepared herb-flavored stuffing
butter	

Thaw oysters, drain, and reserve liquid. Put a layer of quick-frozen oysters in a shallow buttered baking dish. Mix 1/2 cup of melted butter with 1 1/2 cups prepared stuffing. You may wish to crush the crumbs a little if they seem too coarse. Put a layer of the stuffing in the bottom of the shallow buttered baking dish, cover with oysters, add 3 tablespoons of oyster liquid, repeat and cover top with remaining crumbs. Bake 30 minutes in a hot oven, 450° F. It is best not to have more than 2 layers, for if 3 layers are used the middle layer will be underdone.

AT SERVING TIME:

Serve from the baking dish in which it is baked. Cole slaw is a traditional accompaniment. Serves 4.

Fillets of Perch Baked in Cream

A *plat* comparable to this one is prepared by many a fine chef by first poaching the fish, then preparing a cream sauce, later combining fish and sauce. Here is a short cut using quick-frozen fillets of red perch. Sole or flounder may be substituted.

YOU WILL NEED:

fillets of perch, sole, or flounder	anchovy paste
cream	parsley or water cress

Thaw a pound package of quick-frozen fillets, just enough to separate. With scissors cut the fillets into serving pieces. Arrange on a shallow baking dish which can be brought to the table. Cover with 1 cup light cream which has been delicately flavored with 1/2 teaspoon anchovy essence. (Lacking anchovy essence, use Worcestershire sauce.) Bake 10 to 15 minutes in a hot oven, 450° F., until the fish is done—flakes off readily when touched with a fork.

AT SERVING TIME:

Serve from the dish in which it was baked. Garnish with parsley or water cress. Serves 3.

VARIATION:

Instead of cream, use 1 can condensed cream of mushroom soup. Omit seasonings, but garnish with celery leaves.

Salmon Parisienne

Nothing is more appropriate for a summer lunch or a Sunday Supper in the country than salmon delicately and perfectly poached.

YOU WILL NEED:

quick-frozen salmon steaks	water cress
Court Bouillon (page 94)	lemon or lime

Follow the directions for Court Bouillon, but use 2 tablespoons vinegar and 2 quarts water or 2 cups dry white wine and 6 cups water. Boil about 10 minutes, then place the raw salmon into the broth. Simmer the salmon 6 to 10 minutes per pound according to whether the pieces are thick or thin. Allow the fish to cool in the broth. Chill thoroughly.

AT SERVING TIME:

Drain the fish, garnish with water cress and quartered lemon or lime. In a separate bowl serve Mayonnaise Verte, which is made by adding about 3 drops of green vegetable coloring to 1 cup mayonnaise.

Spiced Salmon

Canned salmon may sound dull. Prepared in this spicy manner, it is anything but! In fact, it is so flavorsome that it may well be used as an appetizer, too.

YOU WILL NEED:

canned salmon	radishes or green pepper
allspice berries	vinegar or white wine
cloves	peppercorns
bay leaf	

Drain a can of salmon and set in a shallow bowl that can be brought to the table. Meanwhile bring to a boiling point 1 cup vinegar or dry white table wine, 1 teaspoon whole cloves, 1/2 teaspoon allspice berries, several peppercorns, a little salt, a bay leaf. Pour over the fish, cover and let stand in the refrigerator several hours, or overnight.

AT SERVING TIME:

Decorate the bowl with crisp romaine, chicory, or green lettuce leaves. Garnish with radishes or green pepper rings, and serve with heated potato chips or julienne potato sticks from a can.

Shad Roe

In other times, this delicacy was reserved only for those few brief weeks in earliest spring when the shad ran and the shad-blow bloomed. Now you can have it any day of the week or year, for excellent shad roe comes in tins.

YOU WILL NEED:

canned shad roe	butter or bacon fat
onion juice or extract	lemon juice
celery or green pepper	bacon (optional)
water cress or parsley	chives (optional)
lime or lemon	

Separate canned roe into pieces but do not break the membrane. Melt 3 tablespoons butter or bacon fat, add roe and cook quickly, first on one side, then on the other. Roe should not be turned more than once, nor should it be cooked too long, or it will become dry. Remove to a warm plate. Add to the fat in the pan a tablespoon of butter, 1/2 cup finely chopped celery or chopped green pepper, a few drops of onion juice or onion extract, a teaspoon lemon juice, salt and pepper. Cook about 4 minutes. Return roe to pan. Reheat 1 minute to blend flavors.

AT SERVING TIME:

Serve if possible in the pan in which the cooking was done. Garnish with water cress or parsley and wedges of lime or lemon. A sprinkle of chopped chives is an excellent addition. Crisp bacon may be used as an accompaniment to the shad roe but it isn't necessary. One pair roe serves 2.

Shrimp Jambalaya

Truly one of the great Creole dishes of Louisiana. Probably the original name was French Jambon à la Riz. Many ingredients such as New Orleans breakfast sausage, oysters, and a large variety of spices can go into a Jambalaya. Our simplified version uses ham, shrimp, and rice.

YOU WILL NEED:

slice of ham	thyme
tomato juice or canned vegetable juice	onions
	butter or bacon fat
shrimp	red pepper or Tabasco
quick-cooking rice	sauce
garlic	parsley or parsley flakes

Brown 2 medium-sized onions, chopped, in 2 tablespoons of butter or bacon fat, add 1 cup ham cut into 1/2-inch squares or into thin julienne strips, 2 cups cooked, canned or quick-frozen shrimp. Allow this mixture to simmer in a covered pan about 5 minutes, then add 1 clove garlic, mashed, 2 cups tomato juice or canned vegetable juice, a few grains of red pepper or 3 or 4 dashes of Tabasco sauce, 1 tablespoon freshly chopped parsley or 1 teaspoon parsley flakes, 1/2 teaspoon thyme, 1 package (1 1/3 cups quick-cooking rice, salt to taste. Bring to a full boil uncovered, allow to cook 2 to 3 minutes. Cover and let stand 10 minutes longer. (Cooked ham may be used, but the flavor is not so rich.)

AT SERVING TIME:

Fluff with a fork. Serve with a tossed green salad and dessert. This makes a full and satisfying meal. Serves 6.

Fillets of Sole Amandine

This is one of the simplest, quickest, and most rewarding ways to deal with fillets of sole, flounder, perch, or any other delicately flavored fish.

YOU WILL NEED:

fillets of sole or flounder	lemon juice
butter or margarine	parsley (optional)
almonds	water cress (optional)

Defrost quick-frozen fillets, enough so that they are easy to separate and handle. With scissors cut into serving pieces. Sprinkle with salt and pepper. Melt 2 or 3 tablespoons butter or margarine in a frying pan. Brown the pieces of fish in the butter, first on one side then the other. Remove from the pan to a warm serving dish, and in the same butter in which you have fried the fish, lightly and quickly brown about 4 tablespoons coarsely chopped salted almonds. Stir in 1 tablespoon lemon juice. Cook for 1 minute. You now have Sauce Amandine.

AT SERVING TIME:

Pour sauce over the fillets of fish, sprinkle with chopped parsley and garnish with nosegays of watercress.

Quick Fillets of Sole Marguery

This unorthodox version of probably the most famous of all French fish specialties is delicious and unbelievably quick. In place of the lemon sole or flounder, any delicately flavored fillets can be used.

YOU WILL NEED:

fillets of lemon sole or flounder	shrimp egg
condensed cream of mushroom soup	paprika Little Neck clams
white wine or water and lemon juice	lobster meat (optional)

Thaw 6 to 8 small fillets (about 3 pounds) just enough to separate and place on a shallow buttered baking dish, perferably one that can go to the table. Sprinkle with salt, pepper, and paprika, and pour over 1/3 cup white wine. Cover with waxed paper, parchment paper, or aluminum foil and bake 10 to 15 minutes in a moderate oven, 350° F. When the fish is done, carefully pour off the liquid in the pan. You will want about 1/2 cup of this liquid. Add it to 1 can condensed cream of mushroom soup. Heat, season with salt and pepper. Beat 1 egg slightly, add a little of the hot sauce to the egg, stirring it well, and then incorporate egg into the sauce. Pour sauce over the fillets. Garnish with canned and drained or quick-frozen cooked shrimp, Little Neck clams, and/or pieces of cooked lobster meat. Sprinkle with grated Parmesan cheese, if desired, and broil 3 minutes, or until thoroughly heated and very lightly browned. Water and lemon juice may be used in place of wine.

AT SERVING TIME:

Serve immediately in the same dish in which it is baked. This makes 6 or 8 servings.

✿ 8 ✿

~~~~~~~~~~~~~~~~~~~~~~~~~~~~~~~~

Double-Quick Meats

BECAUSE THE MEAT of the meal is frequently the most time-consuming as well as the costliest part of the menu, the time and money-saving recipes and suggestions in this chapter will, we hope, be of great help to you. Within this field great strides have been made in the past. Your local chain store or favorite delicatessen has a wide variety of meat specialties—lamb and veal as well as beef stews—beef and kidney already for an English steak and kidney pie—several types of meat balls presented in a variety of sauces—all sorts of meat pies, pot roasts, meats in gravy. If you are careful to select some of the best-known brands you should be agreeably surprised at the good flavor of many canned meats.

In a number of cases manufacturers have been singularly successful in avoiding or disguising a canned flavor. But even the best, in our opinion, may be greatly improved—taste freshened and flavor heightened by herbs, spices, and/or wine or sour cream.

Most canned meats and gravies are not particularly attractive to look at. Too often they have a grayish or drab brick color but this can easily be changed into the deep glossy brown of a French ragout by the addition of widely available bottled gravy darkeners, such as Kitchen Bouquet or Gravy Master. These products contain some spices but the base is caramelized sugar which does not sweeten food. However, if you use too much you might get a slight bitter taste. So add it little by little.

The canned varieties are by no means the whole story. There are the quick-frozen meats too. And also most helpful to the hurried cook with a small family are ready-cooked meats—sliced roasts and baked hams—that are generally available at delicatessens, whose owners always seem to prefer to sell them in sandwiches but can sometimes be persuaded to omit the bread. Buy thick slices and you can embark on a series of dishes that were formerly possible only to those who must first "roast a joint."

May we reiterate that many of the recipes included in this group are economical and need no last-minute fussing.

RECIPES

Beef Stew with Wine
Boats of Beef
Cold Roast Beef Martinique
Dried Beef and Mushroom Sauce
Beef Stroganoff
Sliced Beef en Gelée
Steak and Kidney Pie
California Chile
Frankfurters Paprika
Baked Ham Flambé
Frizzled Ham with Bananas Haitian
Salmi of Ham
Baked Corned-Beef Hash De Luxe

De Luxe Hash with Eggs
Ragout of Kidneys
Baked Lamb Chops Farci
Breaded Lamb Chops aux Fines Herbes
Quick Swedish Meat Balls
Baked Stuffed Pork Chops with Apple
Pan-Broiled Pork Chops
Ragout with Black Olives
Country Sausage with Fried Apples
Shepherd's Pie au Gratin
Hasty Tamale Pie

Beef Stew with Wine

Several good beginnings for beef stew are available in cans. Few are savory enough to serve as is. But the additions suggested here will improve them.

YOU WILL NEED:

canned beef stew	red wine
marjoram or orégano	parsley
garlic (optional)	Kitchen Bouquet

To a can of beef stew, add 1/2 teaspoon Kitchen Bouquet, 1 to 2 tablespoons red wine, or a little more if you wish, 1/2 to 1 clove garlic well crushed, and/or 1/2 teaspoon dried marjoram or orégano. Simmer (do not boil) at least 5 minutes to blend the flavors.

AT SERVING TIME:

Serve in heated casserole. Stew should be bubbling hot. A tablespoon of finely chopped parsley may be sprinkled on the top to give that homemade appearance and a fresh flavor.

Boats of Beef

This is a quick version of piroshki, the boat-shaped meat pies that are made all over eastern Europe. Often they are served as an adjunct to a rich consommé or chicken broth or along with a hearty borsch (see pages 41–43). Or they may be used as an entree for lunch or supper.

YOU WILL NEED:

oven-ready packaged biscuits, regular or buttermilk type	raw egg
	hard-cooked egg
	butter, chicken or goose fat
chopped canned beef	parsley
onion	

To make 10 piroshskis, open a package of unbaked refrigerated biscuits, either plain or made with buttermilk. Flatten the biscuits with your hands or rolling pin until they are only about 1/4 inch thick. Allow to stand at room temperature while you make the filling:

Use 1 cup chopped cooked beef (chopped junior food beef, canned chopped beef, delicatessen beef, or leftovers). Add 1 small onion finely chopped, 1 whole raw egg, 1 chopped hard-cooked egg. Add 1 tablespoon softened butter or chicken or goose fat, season to taste with salt and pepper, and add 1 tablespoon fresh chopped parsley or 2 teaspoons dry parsley.

Place a spoonful of the filling in the center of each biscuit. Bring the edges up together to form a boat shape, open at the top. Brush with beaten egg. Bake in a hot oven, 450° F., 15 or 20 minutes.

AT SERVING TIME:

Serve hot as an accompaniment to soup or as an entree with a leafy green vegetable. Also good cold. A nice change from the usual sandwiches.

Cold Roast Beef Martinique

Leftover or delicatessen roast beef looks and tastes delicious when served like this.

YOU WILL NEED:

cold roast beef   mustard or curry powder
olive oil   parsley or green pepper
vinegar

Arrange 6 slices beef on a platter. Pour over Martinique French dressing made of 1/2 cup olive oil, 1/4 cup vinegar, 1/2 teaspoon salt, 1/4 teaspoon pepper, 1/2 teaspoon dry mustard or curry powder, 1 tablespoon chopped parsley and/or chopped green pepper.

AT SERVING TIME:

Garnish with lettuce or escarole, stuffed olives or pickles, celery sticks and leaves. Serves 4.

Dried Beef and Mushroom Sauce

This is a fine main dish for a late breakfast or a light supper.

YOU WILL NEED:

dried beef
condensed cream of mush-
   room soup
brandy (optional)

water, milk, or light cream
toast or English muffins
parsley, chives, or almonds

Cover 1/4 pound of dried beef with a little cold water and bring
to a boil. Take from the stove and let stand about 5 minutes. This
removes the excess salt from the beef and softens it. Drain the beef
and add it to a can of condensed cream of mushroom soup, that has
been diluted with 1/2 can of water, milk, or light cream. The addition of 1 tablespoon brandy to the sauce will add piquancy for
a particularly elegant effect with no suggestion of a liquor flavor.
Heat slowly, stirring once or twice.

AT SERVING TIME:

Serve on toast or toasted English muffins. Sprinkle with chopped
parsley, chives, or chopped almonds. Serves 4.

Beef Stroganoff

Chip steaks are ideal for the making of this delicious entree.

YOU WILL NEED:

chip steaks
sour cream
tomato juice

onion
canned beef gravy
butter

Cut chip steaks into strips allowing at least 2 steaks for each portion—3 for heartier appetites. To 6 chip steaks allow 1 can beef
gravy. Bring gravy to a boil, stir in 1 tablespoon tomato juice, 2 to
4 tablespoons sour cream and meanwhile lightly brown beef chips
in 1 tablespoon butter with a little chopped onion. This should not
take more than 1 minute. Overcooking toughens the meat. Put the
pieces of meat in the sauce, simmer 5 minutes.

AT SERVING TIME:

Stir well and serve with rice, julienne potato sticks from a can or
noodles.

Sliced Beef en Gelée

This is a quick, easy version of a classic French specialty. It can be made from sliced roast beef (delicatessen beef slices are fine), pot roast or leftovers. This is one aspic that does not require troublesome unmolding. It is served right out of the dish in which it jells.

YOU WILL NEED:

sliced roast beef	carrots
condensed consommé	green peppers
plain gelatin	orégano or thyme
Worcestershire sauce	

Have your beef cut in slices slightly thicker than for sandwiches. Season well with salt, pepper, a little orégano or thyme. Lay 6 slices of beef overlapping in a shallow serving dish. For the aspic combine 2 cans condensed consommé and 1 can water. Soak 2 envelopes plain gelatin in 1/2 cup water and dissolve in 1 cup hot water; add 1 teaspoon Worcestershire sauce and pour over beef. Garnish the top of the dish with circles of thinly sliced carrots and green peppers. You can make a flower using 5 circles of carrots as petals, strips of green pepper as the stem. Put in the refrigerator to jell. This aspic should set in about an hour.

AT SERVING TIME:

Bring the dish to the table, cut into serving pieces. A tossed green salad made with a little tarragon vinegar is particularly good with the beef. Serves 4 to 6.

Steak and Kidney Pie

A lordly dish of old England becomes a quick dish now that we have a canned beef and kidney stew. Other canned stews may also be used.

YOU WILL NEED:

canned beef and kidney stew	Kitchen Bouquet
	packaged pie mix

To a can of beef and kidney stew, add 1/2 teaspoon Kitchen Bouquet. Heat. Make a piecrust from a packaged mix according to the package directions, using only 1/2 of the package, since you will need only one crust. Butter a shallow baking dish or heat-proof glass pie pan. Turn a custard cup upside down in the center of the dish. This is the old-time English trick for keeping the crust high and handsome. Pour the heated stew into the pan. Cover with the piecrust. Make 6 small cuts in the crust to permit the steam to escape. Bake in a moderately hot oven, 375° F., until crust is lightly brown.

AT SERVING TIME:

Serve from the dish in which it was baked. A plate of crisp raw vegetables and relishes go well with this English pie—carrot sticks, cucumber fingers, dill pickles, celery, radishes, olives, gherkins, raw cauliflower. Serves 2.

California Chile

A little extra garlic and paprika, a teaspoon of cumin seed provide authentic flavor for canned chile.

YOU WILL NEED:

canned chile con carne with beans or a can of chile and a can of red kidney beans	garlic paprika cumin seed (optional) parsley or chives

Crush well 2 cloves of garlic and combine with 2 cans of chile con carne with beans *or* 1 can chile (meat) and 1 can cooked red kidney beans. Season with 1 tablespoon paprika, 1 teaspoon cumin seed. Heat, stirring occasionally.

AT SERVING TIME:

Serve with celery, dill pickles, and crackers. Or place the chile mixture inside a ring of cooked rice or cooked yellow corn-meal mush. Sprinkle with chopped parsley or chives.

Frankfurters Paprika

Paprika dishes are the classics of Hungary. When made with a quick-cooking meat, they are swift as well as hearty and savory.

YOU WILL NEED:

frankfurters
paprika
butter or lard
beef bouillon cube
onions

green peppers or tomatoes
(optional)
dill, or caraway, seeds (optional)
fresh dill or parsley (optional)

Cut or chop 2 large-sized onions into small pieces and brown in 2 tablespoons lard or butter until soft and add 1 cup hot water and 1 beef bouillon cube. Sprinkle lavishly with paprika, using at least a teaspoonful for each person. One chopped green pepper and/or 2 tomatoes may be added along with the paprika. Simmer 3 or 4 minutes. Add 4 frankfurters cut into inch lengths. Mix well and cook long enough to heat thoroughly. Season with salt and pepper; a few dill seeds or caraway seeds may be added if desired.

AT SERVING TIME:

Serve with buttered noodles, rice, or mashed potatoes. Garnish if you like with green pepper rings or strips, fresh dill, or parsley. Serves 4.

Baked Ham Flambé

For a buffet supper, nothing is more dramatic than a lordly baked ham ceremoniously flared, if you wish, with rum or brandy. A canned ham is a good stand-by. Whether precooked, home boiled, or canned the procedure for baking is the same.

YOU WILL NEED:

cooked ham
dry mustard
honey

cloves
rum or brandy
brandied or spiced peaches

Use a whole ham or for a smaller group a half or quarter ham. Rub about 1 tablespoon dry mustard into the ham. With a knife, score the rind into diamond shapes. Stud each diamond with a whole clove. Pour over plenty of honey, 1 or 2 cupfuls, depending upon the size of the piece. Bake in a moderate oven, 350° F., long enough to heat through and glaze prettily. Baste 2 or 3 times with the juices from the bottom of the pan.

AT SERVING TIME:

Set on a large platter. In this case, the platter need not be warmed, for ham is best served neither piping hot nor chilled but merely warm. Garnish with brandied or spiced peaches. To Flambé a ham, warm very slightly 1/2 to 1 cup rum or brandy. Set fire to the liquor and pour around the ham. Always serve ham in paper-thin slices.

Frizzled Ham with Bananas Haitian

Cold boiled ham—whether leftover or delicatessen slices—is the basis for an unusual dish for a late supper or an early one.

YOU WILL NEED:

boiled ham	butter
bananas	rum

Cook 8 thin slices boiled ham in butter only a minute or two, just long enough to warm the ham but not long enough to let it become dry or hard. Remove ham from fire. Cut 4 bananas into halves lengthwise. In the same frying pan in which the ham was cooked, delicately brown the bananas, first on one side then on the other.

AT SERVING TIME:

Arrange ham and bananas on a warmed platter or warm plates. Heat 1/2 cup rum slightly. Light with a match. Spoon the flaming liquor over the bananas. Serve with corn muffins and a tossed salad. Serves 4.

Salmi of Ham

When you need something sophisticated in a hurry or have a little cold cooked ham on hand, try this.

YOU WILL NEED:

cold, cooked ham	sherry
currant jelly	cayenne or Tabasco sauce
butter	

Melt 1/2 tablespoon butter and 1/3 cup currant jelly. Add a few grains of cayenne or Tabasco sauce, 1/4 cup pale dry sherry and 1 cup cold cooked ham, cut into small strips. Simmer 5 minutes.

AT SERVING TIME:

Serve from a chafing dish, if you have one. With rice, julienne potatoes, and a green vegetable, this amount will do as a main course for 2 or 3 people. If you wish to serve it with waffles or pancakes it will serve 4 or 5.

Baked Corned-Beef Hash De Luxe

Many and varied are the varieties of corned-beef hash on the market. Shop around for a brand with a low proportion of potato. Dress it up like this.

YOU WILL NEED:

canned corned beef hash	butter
onion	milk, ketchup, or chili sauce
canned beets (optional)	parsley

To a 6- or 8-ounce can of corned-beef hash, add 2 tablespoons finely chopped raw onion, 2 tablespoons milk or ketchup or chili sauce. Add 1/2 cup finely diced cooked beets if desired. Butter generously a shallow casserole or pie pan. Spread hash in the pan. Dot with butter. Bake in a moderate oven, 350° F., until piping hot and crusty underneath, about 20 to 25 minutes.

AT SERVING TIME:

Sprinkle with chopped parsley and serve piping hot from the baking dish. Serves 4.

VARIATION: De Luxe Hash with Eggs

Before putting the hash into the oven, make a number of depressions with a spoon, large enough to hold the required number of eggs—1 or 2 for each person. Bake hash as above for about 15 minutes. Remove from oven. Break an egg into each depression. Cover pan. Bake 8 minutes longer or until egg white is set.

Ragout of Kidneys

Since so many "variety" meats such as kidneys, liver, oxtails, and sweetbreads are quick frozen, it is easy to keep on hand in the freezing compartment of the refrigerator the makings of dishes formerly available only to those who lived near specialty meat shops. This quickly prepared dish is beloved by chafing dish impresarios. It can of course, be cooked equally well in the kitchen. But make sure that it is served very quickly and very hot.

YOU WILL NEED:

lamb, beef, or veal kidneys	parsley or basil
onion	red wine or bouillon cube
butter	

If you use quick-frozen kidneys, all the fat and outer membrane will have been removed properly. If fresh kidneys are used ask the butcher to fix them for you. Cut into 1/2-inch slices. Cover with cold, salty water (1 pint of water, 1 tablespoon salt) and allow to stand for 1/2 hour. Drain.

Sprinkle with salt and pepper. Cook a thinly sliced onion in 4 tablespoons butter until soft and golden. Add sliced kidneys. Cook about 2 or 3 minutes. Pour on 1/2 cup red wine or a bouillon cube dissolved in 1/2 cup hot water. Season with salt and pepper. Simmer 2 or 3 minutes longer, not too long or kidneys will get tough.

AT SERVING TIME:

Bring to the table if possible in the same pan in which they were cooked. A sprinkle of chopped parsley or chopped fresh basil is particularly good as a garnish. The Italians often serve kidneys cooked in this fashion inside a ring of polenta (page 86).

Baked Lamb Chops Farci

Because these chops need no watching while they are baking in the oven, they are a perfect choice for the hostess cook.

YOU WILL NEED:

| thick lamb chops | flour |
| prepared poultry stuffing | egg |

Have chops cut about 1 1/2 inches thick and slit through the lean meat right to the bone. Prepare packaged poultry dressing according to directions reserving about 1/2 cup for coating the chops. Place inside the chop as much as the space will hold. Press together lightly. Skewer with a toothpick if you wish. Dip chops in flour, slightly beaten egg, and poultry dressing. If the crumbs are coarse roll them out. Set chops in a buttered baking dish which can be taken to the table. Bake in a hot oven, 425° F., about 30 minutes, at which time the meat should be sufficiently cooked and the crumbs deliciously browned.

AT SERVING TIME:

Serve plain or with Sauce Jardiniere made by heating 1 can beef gravy with 2 tablespoons dehydrated mixed vegetable flakes. Makes 1 cup sauce—enough for 4 to 6 chops.

Breaded Lamb Chops aux Fines Herbes

An herb-scented prepared poultry stuffing makes a quick and flavorsome coating for lamb chops. If the crumbs are coarse, crush them a little. If fine, use as they are.

YOU WILL NEED:

thin lamb chops	prepared poultry stuffing
flour	salad oil or shortening
egg	

Do not sprinkle lamb chops with salt and pepper. The prepared stuffing is probably seasoned enough. Dip the chops first in flour, then in slightly beaten egg, then in the prepared poultry stuffing. In a heavy frying pan, heat about an inch of salad oil or shortening to 385° F., hot enough to brown an inch cube of bread in 40 seconds. Cook not more than 4 chops at a time from 5 to 8 minutes. Drain on paper towels.

AT SERVING TIME:

Serve on heated platter or plates. Garnish with curly lettuce leaves or escarole.

Quick Swedish Meat Balls

It is possible to transform canned meat balls in spaghetti sauce into a delicious prototype of the famous Swedish köttbullar.

YOU WILL NEED:

canned meat balls in spaghetti sauce	allspice
	heavy cream
Kitchen Bouquet	

To meat balls and their sauce, add 1/4 teaspoon allspice, 1/2 teaspoon Kitchen Bouquet, simmer 5 or 6 minutes.

AT SERVING TIME:

Stir in about 4 tablespoons heavy cream. Serve in true Swedish fashion with boiled potatoes and pass lingonberries or whole berry cranberry sauce. Green beans are the traditional accompaniment to this combination.

Baked Stuffed Pork Chops with Apple

YOU WILL NEED:

pork chops	canned sweet potatoes
onions	canned apples
butter	prepared poultry stuffing
nutmeg or mace (optional)	rum (optional)

Place 4 pork chops on a large oven-proof platter. On top of each chop, place a mound of onion stuffing made by adding 4 boiled and coarsely chopped onions to 1 package prepared poultry stuffing and as much liquid or butter as the package directions indicate. Bake in a moderate oven, 350° F., about 1 1/2 hours or until almost cooked. Take from oven; arrange around the chops canned drained sweet potatoes and canned baked apples. Brush potatoes and apples with melted butter, a very small amount of nutmeg or mace, if desired. Put back into the oven 15 to 20 minutes longer.

AT SERVING TIME:

Serve from the platter on which they were baked. If desired, you can make this dish most dramatic by serving it flambé—simply warm slightly about 1/2 cup rum. Pour over the meat and set fire to the rum.

Pan-Broiled Pork Chops

YOU WILL NEED:

pork chops	parsley, rosemary, or oré-
wine	gano

Have the chops cut about an inch thick. Sprinkle with salt and pepper. Place in a heavy frying pan, brown on both sides. Pour off the fat. Sprinkle with chopped parsley, rosemary, or orégano. Pour around the chops about a tablespoon of wine for each chop. You may use red or white wine, Marsala or sherry. Cover and cook over low heat slowly until tender and richly browned—about 20 minutes. If pan is well covered, the wine and the fat from the chops should keep meat from sticking. However if liquid cooks away add a little hot water.

AT SERVING TIME:

Serve with mashed potatoes, baked sweet potatoes, or saffron rice.

Ragout with Black Olives

This is an interesting and quick dish to make from leftover meats.

YOU WILL NEED:

leftover or delicatessen cooked veal, pork, or lamb	black olives
	cayenne or Tabasco sauce (optional)
canned beef gravy	Worcestershire sauce, claret or Marsala wine
canned mushrooms (optional)	Kitchen Bouquet

To a can of beef gravy, add 1 teaspoon Worcestershire sauce or 2 tablespoons claret or Marsala wine. Season with a few grains of cayenne or a few drops of Tabasco if desired. For a darker, richer color add 1/2 teaspoon Kitchen Bouquet. To the heated sauce add about 2 cups cooked veal, pork, or lamb, cut into 3/4-inch cubes. One 3-ounce can sliced mushrooms may be added if desired. Simmer 2 or 3 minutes.

AT SERVING TIME:

Garnish with black olives and serve with rice.

Country Sausage with Fried Apples

Sausage and apple slices make a combination beloved in old-time plantation kitchens.

YOU WILL NEED:

| pork sausage | nutmeg or cinnamon (op- |
| canned sliced apples | tional) |

Shape sausage meat into flat round cakes at least 1/2-inch thick. They will shrink as they cook. Put into a cold frying pan without grease. Cook slowly about 15 minutes, turning to brown evenly. Pour off fat and save it. Keep sausages warm. Drain canned sliced apples and dry on a paper towel. Put back into the frying pan enough fat to cover the bottom of the pan. Heat the fat and put in the apples. Brown quickly on one side and carefully turn with a pancake turner to brown the other side.

AT SERVING TIME:

Arrange the sausage cakes in the center of a heated platter with the browned apple slices around the edge. The apples may be lightly sprinkled with nutmeg or cinnamon.

Shepherd's Pie au Gratin

A new way to prepare a very old-time dish.

YOU WILL NEED:

canned hash	onion or onion juice
mashed potatoes	cheese
catchup, chili sauce, or	
steak sauce	

Heat a package of quick-frozen mashed potatoes according to package directions. Cover the bottom of a baking dish with half of the potatoes. On top of the potatoes, place a thick layer of hash, well seasoned and moistened with catchup, chili sauce, or steak sauce and onion juice, or you may use 2 tablespoons finely chopped raw onion. Top with the rest of the potatoes. Sprinkle generously with grated cheese and bake in a hot oven, 425° F., about 20 minutes or long enough to heat thoroughly and brown delicately.

AT SERVING TIME:

Serve from the baking dish with a green salad or crisp carrot sticks, celery, and radishes. Serves 6.

Hasty Tamale Pie

Three canned specialties combine happily to make a perfect dish for a supper or buffet. Try to have the ripe olives. They add a lot.

YOU WILL NEED:

canned chile con carne or	canned tamales
canned chile and canned	ripe olives
red kidney beans	garlic
whole kernel canned corn	sharp cheese

Butter a shallow baking dish, rub well with garlic. Put into the dish a can of chile con carne, or 1 can chile (meat) and 1 can red kidney beans, a small can, about 1 1/4 cup whole kernel corn—the kind that comes complete with pimientos and green pepper is particularly good. Sprinkle with 1/2 cup pitted ripe olives. Lay on top canned tamales (with the husks removed if there are husks). Sprinkle with about 3/4 cup grated sharp cheese. Bake in a moderately hot oven, 350° F., until hot and brown—about 20 to 25 minutes. For even greater haste, heat ingredients separately on top of stove. Combine, sprinkle with cheese and set under the broiler just long enough for the cheese to melt and brown.

AT SERVING TIME:

Bring to the table in the dish in which it was cooked. If it's a Mexican dish all the better! We know a man who makes a specialty of tamale pies. He uses a copper pan with handles and ties on two bright colored napkins of different hues. Serves 6 to 8 generously.

❧ 9 ❧

~~~~~~~~~~~~~~~~~~~~~~~~~~~~~~~~

Poultry

SOME OF THE BEST and also some of the worst of the ready-to-serve canned and quick-frozen foods are chicken products. Perhaps one reason for the wide disparity in quality may be the enormous variety of brands, manufacturers, and techniques. Find a good brand and once you have found it never give it up—or at least don't give it up unless it should become evident that there has been a change in management and a consequent change in quality. (Sad to say—this sometimes happens.)

In addition to the ubiquitous canned and quick-frozen chicken à la king, which is so useful in so many guises, you should acquaint yourself with canned chicken fricassee, in which, as in the old-time Sunday dinner, the chicken is left on the bones.

Canned whole chickens and canned turkey are comparative newcomers. Several varieties are well prepared, wrapped in foil and then placed in the can with their own broth, which can be used not only in the making of gravies and sauces but also to serve as soup. Here again as in the canned meat department, the prepared product is often more economical than fresh.

Still another boon to the time-pressed is quick-frozen poultry which is cleaned, cut up and all ready to be thawed and cooked. And blessings on the practical genius who first thought of selling chicken parts!

You no longer need to own a poultry farm or shares in a fancy restaurant in order to be able to enjoy breast of chicken supreme —whenever you have a mind for it.

RECIPES

Barbecued Chicken
Breast of Chicken Supreme
Casserole à la King
Chicken à la Cadillac
Chicken Divan
Chicken Paprika
Chicken Soufflé with Almonds
Chicken à la Terrapin
Chicken Timbales
Chicken with White Wine and
  White Grapes

Paella à la Valencianna
Roast Canned Chicken Flambé
  with Black Cherries
Chicken with Plums
Duck in Aspic au Cointreau
Roast Duck Bigarade
Crisp Brown Turkey
Gravy for Canned Turkey
Chestnut Stuffing
Mushroom Stuffing

Barbecued Chicken

This joy of the Southland is easily made, and a perfect choice for a meal that may have to wait. It can be kept warm for a long time in a very slow oven or reheated when needed.

YOU WILL NEED:

quick-frozen frying chicken
  (about 1 1/2 pounds)
wine vinegar
mustard

Worcestershire sauce, cayenne pepper, or West Indian hot sauce
sugar
butter or olive oil
parsley

Thaw the chicken at room temperature then place it on a shallow oven-proof pan. Rub with dry mustard. Sprinkle with 1 tablespoon Worcestershire sauce, a little cayenne pepper or a few drops of Tabasco sauce or West Indian hot sauce. Pour 1 cup wine vinegar diluted with 1/2 cup water. Bake 30 minutes in moderate oven, basting once or twice. Just before serving, dot with butter or brush with olive oil and set under the broiler just long enough to take on a pretty golden brown.

AT SERVING TIME:

Sprinkle with chopped parsley and serve with fluffy boiled rice. Serves 2.

Breast of Chicken Supreme

Since any part of the chicken can now be secured not only at special shops but at the frozen-food departments of any supermarket, breast of chicken or turkey has ceased to be the extravagant luxury it once was.

YOU WILL NEED:

breasts of chicken
butter
Quick Mousseline Sauce
  (page 147)

nutmeg or mace (optional)
quick-frozen asparagus tips
thin slices boiled, or broiled, ham

126

Sprinkle 4 chicken breasts with salt and freshly ground black pepper and brown slowly and delicately in butter. If breasts are large,
cut in two. If chicken is not thoroughly cooked by the time it is
browned on both sides, place in a pan, cover and set in a moderate
oven, 350° F., about 10 minutes or until tender.

Meanwhile, cook according to package directions 1 package
quick-frozen asparagus cuts and tips. Prepare the Mousseline Sauce
and heat 4 slices of ham in butter.

AT SERVING TIME:

Place on a hot serving tray or platter the hot broiled or boiled ham.
Set the browned chicken breasts on top of the ham. Garnish with
cooked asparagus tips. Surround with Mousseline Sauce. Decorate
with water cress.

Casserole à la King

YOU WILL NEED:

canned chicken à la king
canned macaroni in cream
    sauce with cheese
cheese

bread crumbs
butter
parsley or water cress

Heat separately on top of the stove canned macaroni and canned
chicken à la king. Arrange in layers in a shallow casserole. Top
layer should be macaroni. Sprinkle with 4 tablespoons grated
cheese mixed with 4 tablespoons packaged bread crumbs. Dot with
butter. Set under the broiler just long enough to become bubbly
and brown.

AT SERVING TIME:

Garnish with parsley or water cress. Serve from its own dish.
Serves 4.

Chicken à la Cadillac

Chicken Cadillac probably antedated by some years that car of
class. This version uses canned or quick-frozen chicken à la king.

YOU WILL NEED:
  chicken à la king   bread crumbs
  cooked ham   butter
  asparagus

To an 8-ounce can or a 14-ounce package of quick-frozen chicken
à la king, add 1/2 cup cooked ham cut into small squares. Heat.
Place in a shallow oven-proof casserole or heat-proof, glass pie
dish. Top with lightly cooked asparagus tips. Dot with butter.
Sprinkle with bread crumbs and set under the broiler just long
enough to brown crumbs.

AT SERVING TIME:
Serve bubbling hot from the casserole. This same combination may
also be placed on buttered toast. Serves 4.

Chicken Divan

A certain New York restaurant has become famous for a dish that
is quickly achieved at home. Though it may not be exactly the
same, it is a delicious facsimile.

YOU WILL NEED:
  broccoli or asparagus   cheese
  chicken or turkey   egg white
  mayonnaise

On a buttered heat-proof dish arrange 4 stalks lightly cooked broccoli or 8 stalks cooked asparagus. Cover with 4 thin slices chicken
or turkey (from the delicatessen, if you have no leftovers). Top
with Sauce Divan made by adding 1 stiffly beaten egg white to 1
cup mayonnaise. Sprinkle lightly with 4 tablespoons grated cheese.
Set in a moderate oven, 325° F., just long enough for the dish to
heat thoroughly and the sauce to brown slightly—about 10 minutes.

AT SERVING TIME:
Bring to the table immediately and serve from the same dish.
Serves 2 to 4.

Chicken Paprika

This is an unorthodox but delightfully flavored version of a famous Hungarian specialty.

YOU WILL NEED:

canned chicken fricassee	sour cream
onion	butter
paprika	

Thinly slice and gently fry in butter 1 medium-sized onion. Add 1 flat tablespoon paprika and 4 tablespoons water. Allow the onion to become thoroughly soft, then add 1 can chicken fricassee. Heat thoroughly and stir in carelessly and streakily, 1/4 cup thick sour cream. Do not boil after the cream is in.

AT SERVING TIME:

Serve immediately with buttered wide noodles scattered with poppy seeds or slivered almonds, which are available in tins.

Chicken Soufflé with Almonds

"Something elegant" for a luncheon party. Have guests seated at the table—keep them happy with a chilled soup or other first course—it won't matter if they have to wait a few minutes for the soufflé. It's worth waiting for.

YOU WILL NEED:

condensed cream of chicken soup	eggs
canned chicken	almonds or Brazil nuts

Heat slowly 1 can condensed cream of chicken soup. Add 1 cup finely diced cooked canned chicken. Heat thoroughly. Take from fire. Add 6 well-beaten egg yolks. Cool 5 minutes. Fold in 6 stiffly beaten egg whites. Pour into ungreased 2-quart casserole. Bake in a hot oven, 400° F., for 25 minutes or until soufflé is tall and puffy, firm and golden brown.

AT SERVING TIME:

Sprinkle with 1/2 cup toasted buttered and slivered almonds or Brazil nut chips. Serve immediately. Makes 6 servings.

Chicken à la Terrapin

This is a simple, delicate, and easy approximation of a creamy terrapin stew.

YOU WILL NEED:

canned, or quick-frozen,	cayenne
chicken à la king	eggs
light cream	toast
sherry or Madeira	

Heat chicken à la king and add 1/4 cup light cream, 2 hard-cooked eggs coarsely chopped, 2 tablespoons pale dry sherry or Madeira and enough cayenne to give it a real tang. Heat but do not boil.

AT SERVING TIME:

Serve in a heated dish. Decorate with buttered toast cut into triangles. For true elegance pass small glasses of dry sherry or Madeira.

Chicken Timbales

They sound and look very fancy. Made with canned cooked chicken, they are prepared almost as easily as they are eaten.

YOU WILL NEED:

condensed cream of mush-	parsley
room soup	eggs
cooked chicken	Sauce Suprême (page 150)

To 1 can condensed cream of mushroom soup, add 1 cup finely chopped cooked chicken, 1 tablespoon freshly chopped parsley or 1 teaspoon dried parsley flakes. Heat preferably in the top of a double boiler. Add 3 slightly beaten eggs. Place mixture in 6 custard cups, which have been slightly buttered, filling them about two-thirds full. Place in a pan of hot water and bake 20 minutes in a moderate oven, 350° F., or until firm. Allow to stand in a warm place about 5 minutes.

AT SERVING TIME:
Unmold by running a knife around the edges and turning upside down on a plate. Serve with Sauce Suprême. Serves 6.

Chicken with White Wine and White Grapes

YOU WILL NEED:

canned chicken fricassee	curry or turmeric
dry white table wine	seedless white grapes, fresh or canned

Open and empty a can of chicken fricassee with its gravy into a pan. Rinse the tin with 4 tablespoons dry white table wine such as Riesling, Rhine wine, or Moselle. Add about 1/2 teaspoon curry powder or turmeric. Season with a little extra salt, freshly ground black pepper. Mix thoroughly. Bring to boil, simmer about 2 minutes but do not boil. Add 1/2 cup tiny white seedless grapes. If canned seedless grapes are used, drain them first and heat for a minute in 2 tablespoons of butter.

AT SERVING TIME:
For the utmost in elegance serve with wild rice, which can be bought canned and ready for heating, or saffron rice. Serves 2 or 3.

Paella à la Valencianna

Since this Spanish dish gets its name from the special pan in which it is cooked and served, it seems most appropriate to make it in a pan which can come to the table. Our approximation uses canned chicken fricassee and quick-cooking rice.

YOU WILL NEED:

quick-cooking rice
saffron
canned chicken fricassee
bay leaf
cooked shrimp, crab meat,
   and/or lobster, clams or
   mussels

garlic
Kitchen Bouquet
peas
string beans
artichokes (optional)

To 1 small package (1 1/3 cups quick-cooking rice) add 1 3/4
cups water, 3/4 teaspoon salt, 1/4 teaspoon saffron, 1/8 teaspoon
black pepper, 1/2 bay leaf, 1 clove garlic very finely chopped.
Bring rice quickly to a full rolling boil. Add 1 can chicken fricassee
with its gravy, 1/2 teaspoon Kitchen Bouquet to lend a rich
brown look and flavor, 1 cup cooked shrimp, crab meat, and/or
lobster, clams or mussels, if desired. Also 1/2 cup lightly cooked
peas and green beans. If you have some canned artichokes, cut
them into quarters and add them also. This dish, as you see, can
be as simple or as elaborate as you choose. Heat everything together and simmer 2 or 3 minutes. Cover tightly, let stand in a
warm place 10 minutes longer so that the rice absorbs the varied
flavors.

AT SERVING TIME:

Bring to the table in the pan in which it was cooked. Serve with a
green salad, crusty bread, and cheese for dessert. This serves 3, 4,
or more according to the number and quantity of "trimmings."

Roast Canned Chicken Flambé with Black Cherries

Several brands of canned whole chicken are excellent. Try to find
a brand that has not been overcooked and will not fall apart upon
handling or heating. (Of course, you could roast your own.)

YOU WILL NEED:

whole canned chicken
butter or salad oil
rum or brandy

Kitchen Bouquet
canned black cherries

Take chicken from can where it is generally packed wrapped in foil or parchment. Save chicken broth for gravy or for soup. Remove wrappings. Place chicken on an oven-proof dish, preferably one which can be brought to the table. Combine 4 tablespoons melted butter or salad oil with 2 teaspoons Kitchen Bouquet. Thoroughly brush the bird with this mixture. Sprinkle liberally with freshly ground black pepper, and a tablespoon of rum or brandy. Set in a hot oven, 400° F., or under the broiler just long enough to heat thoroughly—the time depends upon the size of the chicken.

Meanwhile heat and drain a small can of pitted black Bing cherries. A few minutes before serving time arrange cherries around chicken, pour on about 1/4 cup of juice.

AT SERVING TIME:

Have on hand 1/4 to 1/2 cup brandy or golden rum. To ensure a good flambé the liquor should be slightly warm. Pour over the chicken and cherries. Set ablaze and serve as soon as the flames have died down.

VARIATION: Chicken with Plums

Canned red plums or greengage plums may be used instead of black cherries. The plums are generally halved or quartered.

Duck in Aspic au Cointreau

For a summer buffet, this dish is outstanding and very easy to prepare.

YOU WILL NEED:

duckling	consommé
orange	cointreau or sherry
onion	peaches, apples, or pears
cloves	Kitchen Bouquet
honey	cinnamon

Thaw quick-frozen duckling (3 1/2 to 5 pounds). Stuff with 1 orange quartered and 1 onion quartered. Spear each onion quarter with a clove. Roast uncovered in a shallow pan, 1 1/2 to 2 hours at 375° F. About 15 minutes before duck is done, brush with 2 tablespoons honey combined with 1/2 teaspoon Kitchen

Bouquet to give the bird a beautiful golden-brown gloss. Cool to room temperature. Cut with poultry shears into serving pieces.

Arrange in a shallow serving dish about 10 by 6 inches. Pour over duck, 2 cans undiluted condensed consommé to which you have added 3 tablespoons cointreau. If you do not have cointreau, use pale dry sherry. Allow to stand in the refrigerator until consommé has jelled.

AT SERVING TIME:

Bring to the table in the same dish in which it has jelled. Decorate with sliced peaches, apples, or pears. Sprinkle delicately with cinnamon. A bouquet of crisp escarole or water cress looks pretty at one side or in the center.

Roast Duck Bigarade

Since quick-frozen Long Island ducklings have become so widely available, they are an excellent choice for the company dinner.

YOU WILL NEED:

duckling	Kitchen Bouquet
onions	brandy (optional)
orange juice	cayenne
orange marmalade	canned beef gravy
cloves	

Thaw frozen duckling (3 1/2 to 5 pounds). Instead of stuffing the duck, place inside it 2 onions peeled and quartered, each quarter studded with a single clove. Roast uncovered 1 1/2 to 2 hours at 375° F. About 15 minutes before the duck is done, brush lightly with Kitchen Bouquet.

Bigarade Sauce

Meanwhile prepare Bigarade Sauce by beating together 1/4 cup orange juice, 1/2 teaspoon Kitchen Bouquet, a few grains of cayenne, 1 tablespoon Seville orange marmalade, and 1 can prepared beef gravy. If desired, 1 or 2 tablespoons brandy may be added to the sauce. Simmer gently about 4 minutes.

AT SERVING TIME:

Duck Bigarade may be served in either of two ways—brought to the table whole and carved like any poultry or it may be cut into serving pieces beforehand, arranged on the serving dish with the sauce poured around the duck. A bouquet of fresh water cress makes a pretty garnish. Thin slices of unpeeled orange are also used.

Crisp Brown Turkey

In this recipe, canned whole turkey can be given the thick crisp brown crust of the homemade bird, and you can even have old-fashioned gravy to go with it.

YOU WILL NEED:

canned roast turkey	flour
Kitchen Bouquet	onion juice or garlic extract
butter or salad oil	

When you remove the turkey from the can save the broth since it can be used for turkey gravy (see following recipe). Set turkey on a shallow baking pan. Brush with 1/2 cup melted butter or salad oil, mixed with 4 teaspoons Kitchen Bouquet, 1 teaspoon onion juice or a bit of garlic extract. Set in a moderately hot oven, 375° F., just long enough to heat thoroughly and brown. If a thick crust is desired, take bird from the oven about 10 minutes before it is done and sprinkle with 1/4 cup flour. This flour treatment may be repeated 2 or 3 times. Just make sure that you allow enough time for the flour to be thoroughly cooked and browned.

AT SERVING TIME:

Place on a large heated platter—large enough to permit the carver to operate easily. Garnish with orange shells filled with cranberry sauce or relish. Canned drained brandied, or spiced, peaches are another excellent garnish for roast turkey. If parsley or water cress are placed in one large bouquet they will not interfere with carving.

Gravy for Canned Turkey

The broth in which canned turkeys are packed is excellent for making turkey gravy. Instead of fat from the roasting pan, use butter or chicken fat which is available in many delicatessens and some supermarkets.

YOU WILL NEED:
chicken fat or butter   turkey broth
flour   onion
mushrooms, chestnuts,   Kitchen Bouquet
  stuffed, or ripe, olives
  (optional)

Cut 2 slices onion into tiny pieces and brown slightly in 4 tablespoons butter or chicken fat until soft and brown. Sprinkle into
the pan 4 flat tablespoons flour. Brown the flour in the fat, stirring
constantly. Season and darken to suit your taste with 1/2 teaspoon
salt, 1/4 teaspoon pepper, 1/2 teaspoon Kitchen Bouquet.
Chopped mushrooms, chopped chestnuts, chopped stuffed olives,
or chopped ripe olives may be added to the gravy.

AT SERVING TIME:
Gravy must be served and kept very, very hot. If you want to use
an old-fashioned gravy boat be sure that it is heated beforehand.
Even better is a heat-proof bowl kept warm at the table over a
candle flame or an alcohol lamp turned very low.

Chestnut Stuffing

A good packaged poultry stuffing and canned cooked chestnuts
combine to make a delicious turkey dressing. Most poultry stuffing is put up in packages large enough for a chicken. Two packages are generally needed to stuff a turkey. However, if canned
chicken or turkeys are used it is generally better to cook the stuffing in a separate pan.

YOU WILL NEED:
packaged poultry stuffing   cooked chestnuts

To 1 package poultry dressing prepared according to package directions, add 1 cup boiled Italian chestnuts cut into small pieces.

VARIATION: Mushroom Stuffing
Instead of chestnuts drain 2 3-ounce tins broiled-in-butter mushrooms, chopped. Drain and dry mushrooms on a paper towel and
brown in 3 tablespoons butter. Add to 1 package prepared poultry dressing and proceed according to package directions.

10

Sauces for a Gourmet

IN A HURRY

TOP RANK in the hierarchy or culinary artists has always been reserved—and most properly—for the *saucier,* the chef who makes the sauces. The perfect sauce is the zenith, the ne plus ultra of gastronomic accomplishment and appreciation. Up to now the art of sauce-making has always been long and demanding. Formerly a great deal of time was consumed in the reduction, or the boiling down, of liquid necessary for the rich concentration of flavors which is the essence of the fine sauce. More time and skill were consumed in the slow, simmering required for the perfect blending of various ingredients.

The requirements of a good sauce are still the same as they have always been—the methods used in the accomplishment of the *saucier's* aims also remain the same. But in a small and inexpensive can of condensed soup it is possible to find almost the same concentration of flavor, the same blending of ingredients—all done for you!

In addition to the sauces made from various canned condensed soups or from canned beef gravy or canned spaghetti sauce, you will find in this chapter a number of cold sauces with a prepared mayonnaise base. Some of these such as Ravigote, Vinaigrette, and Gloucester are particularly valuable to add an extra note to canned cooked or quick-frozen sea food or to delicatessen cold cuts.

RECIPES

New Allemande Sauce

The name attributes this sauce to Germany but the taste is Parisian.

YOU WILL NEED:

condensed cream of mush-
    room soup
light cream
chicken bouillon cube

Parmesan cheese
egg yolk
lemon juice
nutmeg (optional)

To a can of condensed cream of mushroom soup, add 1/2 can light cream, 1 crumbled chicken bouillon cube. Heat in the top of a double boiler stirring occasionally.

AT SERVING TIME:

Stir in 1 slightly beaten egg yolk diluted with a little hot sauce, add 3/4 teaspoon lemon juice, a few grains of nutmeg, if desired, and 3 tablespoons grated Parmesan cheese.

Amandine Sauce

With sautéed fish or over such vegetables as asparagus, broccoli, and cauliflower, nothing is better than a sauce of almonds. To save yourself the trouble of blanching, soaking, and shredding the nuts, why not buy a small bag of salted almonds? Or a can of sliced, blanched almonds.

YOU WILL NEED:

butter
lemon juice

parsley or chives (optional)
almonds

Use the fat remaining in the pan after frying fish or meat; add enough butter to make about 1/2 cup. Stir until well browned. Add 4 tablespoons coarsely chopped salted almonds, 2 or 3 teaspoons lemon juice, salt and pepper to taste.

AT SERVING TIME:

Pour over or around fried fish, chicken, or cooked asparagus, cauliflower, or broccoli. A sprinkle of chopped parsley or chives may be added if desired.

Béarnaise Sauce

This notable sauce is actually nothing more than a super-seasoned Hollandaise. It is traditional with grilled filet mignon but is equally good with minute steak or a grilled hamburger.

YOU WILL NEED:
prepared or Mock Hollan-   parsley and/or fresh tarra-
  daise Sauce (page 144)   gon onion or chives (op-
tarragon vinegar   tional)

To 1 cup Hollandaise Sauce add 1 tablespoon tarragon vinegar, 1 tablespoon very finely chopped, or scraped, onion or chopped chives. Keep warm over hot water but do not heat or boil.

AT SERVING TIME:
Add 1 teaspoon each finely chopped parsley and fresh tarragon leaves.

Short-Cut Béchamel Sauce

This is one of the classic sauces of the great French cuisine. Formerly the perfect Béchamel Sauce required considerable doing and more than a little skill. But now that we have condensed cream of chicken soup, it couldn't be simpler.

YOU WILL NEED:
condensed cream of chicken   milk or water
  soup

To a can of condensed cream of chicken soup, add 1/4 to 1/2 can of milk or water, depending on how thick a sauce you want. Heat and stir, preferably in the top of a double boiler. Strain if you wish, though actually it isn't necessary.

AT SERVING TIME:
Pass in a separate heated bowl or pour over chicken, fish, or vegetables.

VARIATION: Yellow Béchamel Sauce

To the above sauce add one slightly beaten egg or egg yolk, diluted with a small quantity of the hot sauce. The sauce should not be cooked after the egg is added or it will curdle.

Brown Sauce or Gravy

Many and varied are the methods for preparing this basic sauce. We will leave to the other cookbooks the chore of preparing gravies from scratch and concentrate on the glamorizing of the canned variety.

YOU WILL NEED:
canned beef gravy   red wine or ketchup
Kitchen Bouquet

Canned beef gravy actually needs nothing but heating. However, for a richer color and a more interesting flavor we suggest that you add to a can of beef gravy 1/2 teaspoon Kitchen Bouquet, 1 tablespoon, or more, of red wine, or 1 tablespoon tomato ketchup. Heat thoroughly before using.

AT SERVING TIME:

Serve with or over sliced cooked or roast meats. Especially good with leftovers. A sprinkle of chopped parsley or chives is always attractive.

Chestnut Sauce

With cooked, ready-to-serve chestnuts available, this sauce, formerly long and bothersome to prepare, becomes as quick as it is delectable. A fine sauce for stretching leftover or delicatessen chicken or turkey!

YOU WILL NEED:
canned beef gravy   Kitchen Bouquet
cooked chestnuts   (optional)
sherry or Madeira (op-
tional)

Cut 1/2 cup peeled, cooked chestnuts into small pieces, add to 1 can beef gravy. One-half teaspoon Kitchen Bouquet may be added if desired. Simmer gently 3 or 4 minutes.

AT SERVING TIME:
Add 2 or 3 tablespoons sherry or Madeira wine. Serve with chicken, turkey, or pork.

Curry Sauce

This is admittedly an Anglicized version of this famous East Indian sauce. You can make it as delicate or as fiery as you wish by increasing the amounts of curry powder.

YOU WILL NEED:

condensed cream of chicken soup	butter (optional)
curry powder	apple (optional)
milk or light cream	onion (optional)
ginger or garlic powder (optional)	eggs
	shrimp, crab meat, or chicken

To 1 can condensed cream of chicken soup, add 1 flat tablespoon curry powder. Stir in 1/4 to 1/2 can milk or light cream, 1/4 teaspoon ginger or garlic powder may be added if desired. For an even better flavor you should lightly brown in 2 tablespoons butter, 1 small apple, diced and peeled, and 1 small onion, chopped. Heat everything together and cook for 2 or 3 minutes.

AT SERVING TIME:
Add to this sauce quartered or halved hard-cooked eggs, shrimp, crab meat, or diced cooked chicken. Serve with rice and other curry accompaniments: chutney, salted almonds, India relish, grated coconut, chopped green pepper.

Diavolo Sauce

The Italians usually serve this piquant sauce with lobster. It is excellent, too, with grilled shrimp and very good to dress up leftover sliced beef, lamb, or pork.

YOU WILL NEED:

canned tomato sauce	vinegar
beef bouillon cube or beef	mustard
extract	cayenne or Tabasco sauce

Add to a cup of canned tomato sauce 4 tablespoons vinegar, 1 beef bouillon cube, dissolved in a little hot water, 1/2 teaspoon pepper, a dash of cayenne or a few drops of Tabasco sauce, 1/2 tablespoon prepared mustard. Mix well. Simmer about 10 minutes.

AT SERVING TIME:

Pass in a heated bowl or gravy boat or pour over and around baked or broiled lobster, grilled shrimp, or leftover sliced beef, lamb, or pork.

Estragon Sauce

The haunting flavor of tarragon added to canned beef gravy makes an interesting sauce to serve with meat or broiled chicken.

YOU WILL NEED:

canned beef gravy	fresh, or dried, tarragon or
tarragon vinegar	parsley (optional)

To a can of beef gravy, add 1 tablespoon tarragon vinegar. Heat and simmer 3 or 4 minutes.

AT SERVING TIME:

Sprinkle with 1 tablespoon chopped fresh tarragon leaves or 1 teaspoon dried tarragon. If you have no tarragon, chopped parsley may be used.

Figaro Sauce

The idea of heating mayonnaise may seem startling but it's very easy to do in a double boiler, or small casserole or crock set over hot but not boiling water. This heated mayonnaise forms the basis for a quick version of a well-known classic sauce.

YOU WILL NEED:

mayonnaise   tomato ketchup
parsley   Worcestershire sauce (op-
                                    tional)

To 1 cup mayonnaise add 1 or 2 tablespoons tomato ketchup, 1/2 tablespoon finely chopped parsley, and 1 tablespoon Worcestershire sauce if desired. Warm in a small crock or casserole set over hot water. Do not boil.

AT SERVING TIME:

Pass in a small warm bowl. This is particularly good with baked fish.

Gloucester Sauce

This is one of the "cold English sauces" recommended by Escoffier himself to be served with cold meats. We suggest also that it makes an excellent dressing for egg or fish salads.

YOU WILL NEED:

mayonnaise made from ol-   dill, fennel, parsley, or chives
   ive oil   sour cream
Worcestershire sauce   lemon juice

To 1 cup mayonnaise, add 4 tablespoons sour cream. Stir well and add gradually 1 1/2 tablespoons lemon juice and 1/2 teaspoon Worcestershire sauce.

AT SERVING TIME:

Place in a small bowl in the center of a platter on which you serve sliced cold cuts, or spread over the top of egg or fish salads. In either case, sprinkle the sauce lightly with chopped dill, fennel, parsley, or chives.

Mock Hollandaise

Hollandaise, the most impressive of sauces, terrifies inexperienced cooks—and many experienced ones. There are a number of ways to "mock" the lordly Hollandaise. This one made with prepared mayonnaise tastes and looks very good, but it is less expensive and far less hazardous.

YOU WILL NEED:

mayonnaise made with olive oil	lemon (optional)
lemon juice	butter or margarine
	cayenne (optional)

Pour about 1 inch of hot water into the bottom of a double boiler, set it on the stove over low heat. Put 6 tablespoons butter (3/4 of a quarter-pound stick) into the top of a double boiler. Allow the butter to melt but under no circumstances to get foamy. Take the top pan off the fire. Stir in 1 tablespoon lemon juice, 2 tablespoons mayonnaise, a dash of salt, a few grains of cayenne pepper and, if desired, 1/4 teaspoon grated lemon peel. Stir with the sauce still off the fire until smooth and well blended. Set over the hot water again for half a minute, just long enough to warm slightly. It is not necessary to serve Hollandaise piping hot. It is good when it is lukewarm.

AT SERVING TIME:

Pour over or pass separately with cooked asparagus, broccoli, cauliflower, or Frenched green beans, or use to make Eggs Benedict. Makes about 1/2 cup sauce—4 servings.

Sour Cream "Hollandaise"

Another ingenious way to approximate Hollandaise makes use of commercially soured cream—the kind you buy in cartons.

YOU WILL NEED:

sour cream	**butter**
lemon juice	cayenne

Warm 1/2 cup sour cream in the top of a double boiler but do not allow it to get hot. Stir into it 2 tablespoons softened butter combined with 2 tablespoons lemon juice. Season with a few grains of cayenne pepper, a little extra salt, if desired. This sauce may be made ahead of time. It need not be hot, only lukewarm, since it is served over hot vegetables, chicken, fish, or eggs.

AT SERVING TIME:

Use as a garnish for, or pass separately with, cooked asparagus, broccoli, cauliflower. Can also be used for Eggs Benedict. Makes about 1 cup sauce—serves 6 to 8.

Mint Sauce

Not only with the traditional roast leg of lamb but also with lamb chops, mint sauce is delightful. It is good, too, on a salad of Boston lettuce and sliced tomatoes—a boon to calorie counters.

YOU WILL NEED:
    fresh, or dried, mint leaves   vinegar
    confectioners' sugar

Dissolve 1 tablespoon confectioners' sugar in 1/2 cup vinegar. If the vinegar is very strong dilute it with water. Pour over 1/4 cup finely chopped mint leaves or about 2 tablespoons dried mint flakes. Let stand about 30 minutes in a warm place.

AT SERVING TIME:

Pass in a small pitcher with lamb.

Modern Mornay Sauce

Hundreds of epicurean dishes—fish, vegetables, eggs—call for Mornay Sauce, which is basically a cheese sauce and can be made with almost any kind of cheese.

YOU WILL NEED:
    condensed cream of chicken   milk or white wine
    soup   cheese

Strain a can of condensed cream of chicken soup to remove the bits of chicken and celery. Add 1/2 can milk or dry white wine, 1/2 cup grated cheese. A mixture of Parmesan and Swiss is particularly good. Cook over low heat or in the top of a double boiler until the cheese is melted and the sauce is thick and smooth. Continue cooking and stirring about a minute longer.

AT SERVING TIME:

Pour over or pass separately with cooked vegetables, fish or eggs. Makes about 2 cups of sauce.

Quick Mousseline Sauce

YOU WILL NEED:

condensed cream of chicken soup	egg yolks
white wine or water and lemon juice	nutmeg or mace

To a can of condensed cream of chicken soup, add 1/2 can white wine or 1/2 can water and 1 tablespoon lemon juice. Heat in the top of a double boiler, stirring occasionally.

AT SERVING TIME:

Add to sauce 2 slightly beaten egg yolks diluted with a little of the hot sauce. Season with a few grains of nutmeg or mace.

Sherry Newburg Sauce

The darling of the chafing dish! This sauce was originally composed to adorn lobster. It is equally good with shrimp or crab meat.

YOU WILL NEED:

condensed cream of mushroom soup	nutmeg and paprika (optional)
sherry	milk or light cream (optional)
egg	

To a can of condensed cream of mushroom soup, add 1/4 to 1/2 can dry sherry, or you may use equal parts of milk or cream and sherry. Heat but do not boil.

AT SERVING TIME:

Add the beaten yolk of 1 egg or a whole egg slightly beaten and dilute it with a little of the hot sauce. Season with a dash of nutmeg and a sprinkle of paprika.

Rarebit and Rarebit Sauce

This rarebit, which is also a sauce, is a very good one—so easy, so
quick, so *sure!*

YOU WILL NEED:
  processed American cheese   beer, ale, or milk
  mustard   nutmeg or basil (optional)
  cayenne (optional)

In the top of a double boiler over hot water, melt 1/2 pound (2
cups) processed American cheese, cut into small pieces. Add 1/2
cup beer or milk and stir until well blended. Season to suit your
taste with 1/2 teaspoon of prepared or dry mustard, 1/4 teaspoon
dried basil or a few grains of nutmeg. A little cayenne pepper may
be added if desired.

AT SERVING TIME:
Serve over cooked asparagus, broccoli, cauliflower, green beans, or
lightly grilled tomatoes. Also good with fish and eggs. Makes
about 2 cups of sauce.

Ravigote Sauce

Pickled pigs' feet or lambs' tongues in jars are among the less
usual ready-to-serve meats. They are particularly delicious when
served with this herb-flecked sauce.

YOU WILL NEED:
  olive oil or salad oil   vinegar
  capers   onion
  tarragon or tarragon vinegar   parsley
  chives

Put into a small bowl 1 cup olive oil or salad oil, 1/3 cup vinegar,
a little salt and pepper, 2 tablespoons capers, 1 tablespoon finely
chopped parsley, 1 tablespoon very finely chopped onion, 1 teaspoon each chives and tarragon. If you have no fresh tarragon, 1
tablespoon of tarragon vinegar may be used but do not use all
tarragon vinegar because the flavor is too strong. Mix thoroughly.

AT SERVING TIME:

Pass in a separate bowl or pour around sliced cold cuts such as tongue, meat loaf, etc. If you are serving canned pigs' feet or pickled lambs' tongues, a few tablespoons of liquor from the jar may be stirred into the sauce. Makes 1 1/2 cups sauce.

Quick Robert Sauce

Using canned beef gravy, this piquant and interesting sauce is literally a matter of minutes.

YOU WILL NEED:

canned beef gravy	vinegar
capers	shallot or onion
pickle	cayenne
Kitchen Bouquet	green olives (optional)
mustard (optional)	

To a can of beef gravy, add 1/2 teaspoon Kitchen Bouquet to darken the color and brighten the flavor. Also add 1 tablespoon vinegar, 1 tablespoon finely chopped shallot or onion, 1 tablespoon capers, 1 tablespoon chopped pickle and a few grains of cayenne pepper. A half dozen chopped green olives and 1/2 teaspoon prepared mustard may be added if desired.

AT SERVING TIME:

Pass separately in a heated bowl or pour over beef, lamb, veal, or pork.

Salmi Sauce

A hot and savory sauce redolent of sherry or port—this delicious concoction is said to date back to the Middle Ages. It is particularly good with cubed leftover lamb, ham, or pork.

YOU WILL NEED:

canned beef gravy	currant jelly
cayenne	sherry or port
parsley or chives (optional)	

To a can of beef gravy, add 1/4 glass currant jelly, a dash of cayenne. Heat and stir until jelly is melted.

AT SERVING TIME:
Add 2 tablespoons sherry or port. A little chopped parsley or chives may be used if desired.

Italian Spaghetti Sauce with Meat

There are a number of excellent tomato sauces with meat on the market. But even if you should have nothing on hand but a can of tomato soup and a 1/2 pound of hamburger, this sauce can be put together in a very few minutes.

YOU WILL NEED:

condensed tomato soup	bay leaf
onion	butter, salad, or olive, oil
garlic	chopped beef

Brown 1 medium-sized onion chopped, 1 clove garlic crushed, and 1/2 pound chopped lean beef in 2 tablespoons olive oil, salad oil, or butter for about 8 minutes, or until the meat has lost its red color. Add 1 can condensed tomato soup, 1 bay leaf, 1/4 can water. Simmer 15 minutes to 1/2 hour.

AT SERVING TIME:
Remove bay leaf. Taste and add extra salt and pepper if desired. Serve with spaghetti, macaroni, or rice.

Sauce Suprême

Suprême Sauce is what makes Chicken Suprême and glamorizes many other foods—such as eggs, fish, and vegetables.

YOU WILL NEED:

condensed cream of chicken soup	egg
	nutmeg
milk or light cream	lemon juice

To 1 can of condensed cream of chicken soup, add 1/2 can light cream or top milk. Stir, warm, and strain out bits of chicken and rice. Just before serving stir in 1 or 2 slightly beaten egg yolks or whole egg. Season with a few grains of nutmeg and 2 teaspoons lemon juice.

AT SERVING TIME:

Pour the sauce over and around meat, poultry, or fish. When serving it with vegetables pour it in a wide ribbon over the top of the vegetables and pass a separate bowl of sauce. Makes 2 cups sauce.

Sweet and Sour Sauce

This versatile sauce, made surprisingly from canned consommé and ginger snaps, does miraculous things for delicatessen meats such as sliced tongue, boiled ham, or sliced roast beef.

YOU WILL NEED:

consommé	onion
brown sugar	ginger snaps
vinegar	raisins
allspice	lemon
bay leaf	cayenne

Combine 1 can consommé, 1 can water, 4 tablespoons mild vinegar. Then add 1 small onion sliced thin, 4 tablespoons raisins, 1 small lemon sliced paper thin, 4 tablespoons brown sugar, 1/2 teaspoon whole allspice, a bay leaf, few grains of cayenne pepper. Simmer all together until lemon and onions are tender. Crumble 6 ginger snaps into the sauce. Stir until the sauce is smooth and slightly thickened. Do not strain.

AT SERVING TIME:

Arrange slices of tongue, ham, or beef in a heat-proof serving dish. Pour the sauce over the meat and heat for a minute or so. Garnish with parsley or water cress.

Tartare Sauce

To many people, fried fish, scallops, or oysters would be unthinkable without Tartare Sauce. This is a particularly easy and tasty version.

YOU WILL NEED:
    mayonnaise   India relish
    onion or parsley (optional)

Stir together 1/2 cup mayonnaise and 1/2 cup India relish; 1/2 tablespoon finely chopped onion or parsley may be added. Chill.

AT SERVING TIME:
It's a pretty thought to serve Tartare Sauce in lemon or lime shells as a garnish for a platter of fried fish.

Savory Tomato Sauce

Endless are the uses of this tasty tomato sauce made from a can of condensed tomato soup.

YOU WILL NEED:
    condensed tomato soup   beef bouillon cube or beef
    parsley   extract (optional)
    water or milk   bay leaf
                                    cloves

To 1 can of condensed tomato soup, add 1/2 cup milk or water, 1 bouillon cube or 1/2 teaspoon beef extract, a bit of bay leaf, 1 tablespoon chopped fresh parsley, or 1 teaspoon dried parsley flakes, 4 cloves. Simmer a few minutes.

AT SERVING TIME:
Pass separately in a heated bowl or gravy boat or pour over left-over meats. Serve with fish or hard-cooked eggs, rice, noodles, macaroni, or spaghetti.

Quick Velouté Sauce

Endlessly useful for dozens of dishes, condensed cream of chicken soup provides an admirable short cut to this fine sauce.

YOU WILL NEED:
    condensed cream of chicken   light cream
        soup   nutmeg (optional)

Combine 1 can condensed cream of chicken soup with 1/2 can light cream. Stir, heat in the top of the double boiler, stirring occasionally. Strain to remove any small pieces of chicken or vegetable. Season if desired with a few grains of nutmeg.

AT SERVING TIME:

Pour into a small heated bowl or gravy boat or pour over vegetables, fish, or chicken.

VARIATION: Suprême or Poulette Sauce

Just before serving, stir in 1 slightly beaten egg or 1 slightly beaten egg yolk diluted with a little of the hot sauce. Add 3/4 teaspoon lemon juice. If desired, a 3-ounce can sliced and drained mushrooms may be added to the sauce.

Vinaigrette Sauce

For asparagus, broccoli, cauliflower, green beans, and also for fish, this simplest of sauces may be made from prepared French dressing or from oil and vinegar.

YOU WILL NEED:

French dressing
India relish

parsley or chives (optional)

To 1/2 cup bottled or homemade French dressing, add 3 tablespoons chopped India relish; 1 teaspoon finely chopped parsley and/or 1 teaspoon finely chopped chives may be added if desired. Stir well. Heat if you wish, or serve cold.

AT SERVING TIME:

Stir again just before serving to make sure that the ingredients are well blended. Pass separately or pour over vegetables, fish, or sliced meats such as tongue, ham, or lamb.

11

Vegetables

WITH A DIFFERENCE

STAND-BYS OF the hurried cook are canned and quick-frozen vegetables. Both can, when properly prepared, retain a great deal of the flavor, color, and vitamin value of garden-fresh vegetables. On the other hand, they can be, and very frequently are, ruined by carelessness—too much water, overcooking.

Quick-frozen vegetables are best when they are not allowed to thaw before cooking but are simply placed as a solid-frozen block in a small amount of rapidly boiling water. They should be allowed to cook uncovered, over a moderate heat until completely thawed all the way through, at which time the water should be boiling in the center as well as around the edges of the pan. You may hurry this process along by breaking the block with a fork and turning the vegetable from time to time. But do this carefully so as not to destroy the shape of the vegetable. After the water is boiling, turn down the heat, cover the pan, and cook until just barely tender. Package directions will give you the approximate cooking time for each vegetable. When in doubt, cook *less* rather than longer than advised.

For canned vegetables, the best method is to pour the liquid out of the can, cook it down to half the volume in an uncovered saucepan over a quick fire. Then place the vegetables in a small amount of the juice remaining. Put the cover on the pan and set over medium heat just long enough to heat thoroughly—not a second longer. Serve immediately. Instead of using the cooked-down liquid, you might try the French technique of heating vegetables in butter. Melt butter or margarine in a heavy frying pan or saucepan but do not brown. Place the vegetables in the butter. Cover tightly and heat.

RECIPES

Artichokes with Minced Chicken
Asparagus Amandine
Asparagus with Eggs Parmesan
Broccoli with Eggs Parmesan
Boston Baked Beans Gone to
Heaven
Pickled Beets Flemish Style
Broccoli au Gratin
Red Cabbage Amsterdam
Whole Cauliflower Allemande
Whole Cauliflower with Sauce
Suprême and Walnuts
Old Virginia's Corn Pudding
Eggplant Imam Bayeldi
Eggplant Parmigiana
Mushrooms in Cream under
Glass
French Fried Onions
Peas Parisienne

Peas with Mushrooms
Purée of Peas De Luxe
Quick Hopping John
Broiled Franconia Potatoes
Crusty Potato Pancakes
French Fried Potatoes
Potatoes Chantilly with Cheese
Potatoes Julienne
Fried Sweet Potatoes au Citron
Scalloped Sweet Potatoes with
Apples
Sherried Sweet Potatoes
Sauerkraut Provençal with Red
Wine
Spinach with Sour Cream
Spiced Scalloped Tomatoes with
Herbs
Glazed Scalloped Tomatoes

Artichokes with Minced Chicken

An interesting main dish for luncheon is made from canned French artichokes. Despite its luxurious sound and taste, this "specialty" costs less than lamb chops!

YOU WILL NEED:

canned cooked artichokes
milk
canned minced chicken
condensed cream of mush-
    room soup

butter or cheese
parsley and pimiento (op-
    tional)

Plan to have 3 or 4 artichokes for each person. Set artichoke bottoms in a shallow baking dish or piepan which can come to the table. Hollow slightly at the top and place in each artichoke a small ball of minced chicken—the kind that is generally used for a cocktail spread. Top each with a tiny dab of butter or a bit of grated cheese. Pour around 1 can condensed cream of mushroom soup diluted with 1/2 can milk. Set in a moderate oven, 350° F., about 15 minutes or until thoroughly heated. Baste once or twice with the sauce.

AT SERVING TIME:

Garnish with parsley and strips of pimiento if desired. Serve with hot, crisp French bread or rolls.

Asparagus Amandine

YOU WILL NEED:

quick-frozen asparagus
almonds
butter or margarine

lemon
toast (optional)

Cook 1 package of quick-frozen asparagus. Arrange on a heated serving dish or on 4 slices buttered toast. Meanwhile melt in a frying pan 4 tablespoons butter or margarine. Add 4 tablespoons slivered almonds. Allow almonds to brown slightly in the butter.

AT SERVING TIME:

Pour butter and almonds over asparagus. Serve with lemon quarters. Serves 2 or 3.

Asparagus with Eggs Parmesan

A vegetable entree with an honorable and ancient Italian lineage —perfect for luncheon. Canned green asparagus or quick-frozen stalks make it with ease and speed.

YOU WILL NEED:

canned, or quick-frozen, asparagus	butter
eggs	Parmesan cheese
lemon (optional)	paprika or parsley

Drain canned asparagus tips or cook 1 package quick-frozen asparagus stalks. Asparagus cuts may be used but the dish will then look less attractive. Arrange the cooked asparagus in 4 individual baking dishes or 1 shallow baking dish that can be brought to the table. The baking dish should be generously oiled or buttered. On top of the asparagus break 4 to 6 eggs. Season with salt and pepper. Sprinkle with 1/2 cup grated Parmesan cheese. Set in a moderate oven, 325° F., until eggs are set.

AT SERVING TIME:

Garnish with a flicker of paprika or bit of parsley and provide if you wish, small sections of lemon to be squeezed over the eggs. Serves 4.

VARIATION: Broccoli with Eggs Parmesan

Use lightly cooked quick-frozen broccoli instead of asparagus. The procedure is exactly the same.

Boston Baked Beans Gone to Heaven

Several brands of baked beans with molasses are excellent. Only a little dressing up is needed to give them the appearance as well as the flavor of those beans that are the pride of Boston. If you have no bean pot serve them from a casserole.

YOU WILL NEED:

canned baked beans with	dark molasses
pork and molasses	onion
dry mustard	bacon or salt pork

Place 2 cans Boston baked beans (the kind that is made with pork and molasses) in a bean pot or casserole along with 1 medium-sized whole onion, peeled, 1/2 teaspoon dry mustard, 1/2 cup dark molasses. Cover with sliced bacon or salt pork. Set in a moderate oven, 350° F., and bake 30 to 40 minutes until the beans are piping hot and bubbly and the bacon is crisp and brown.

AT SERVING TIME:

Serve from bean pot along with sliced and heated canned Boston brown bread, cole slaw, sliced tomatoes, and dill pickles. Serves 6.

Pickled Beets Flemish Style

From the old-time Flemish cooks come the tricks of seasoning which makes this recipe unusual and unusually delicious.

YOU WILL NEED:

canned beets	caraway seeds (optional)
vinegar	parsley
allspice berries	brown sugar
bay leaf	

Drain liquid from a No. 2 can of beets. Sliced, diced, julienne, or even tiny whole canned beets may be used. Heat 1/2 cup water with 1/2 cup vinegar, 1/2 bay leaf, 4 allspice berries, 1 tablespoon brown sugar, 1/2 teaspoon salt, dash of pepper. Let stand until well chilled.

AT SERVING TIME:

Sprinkle with caraway seeds and garnish with parsley. Serves 4 to 6.

Broccoli au Gratin

This is a particularly good recipe for leftover broccoli.

YOU WILL NEED:
quick-frozen broccoli in stalks or pieces
condensed cream of celery soup
cheese
bread crumbs

Combine 2 cups lightly cooked broccoli with 1 can condensed cream of celery soup undiluted. Place in shallow baking dish. Sprinkle with 4 tablespoons bread crumbs, 4 tablespoons grated cheese. Bake in a moderate oven, 350° F., 15 or 20 minutes or until hot and lightly brown.

AT SERVING TIME:
Serve from the baking dish. Good for luncheon along with grilled tomatoes and raw carrot strips. Serves 4 or 5.

Red Cabbage Amsterdam

Very popular in Holland is *roodekool,* which combines red cabbage and apples. This is the quick New World version.

YOU WILL NEED:
canned red cabbage
apple sauce
nutmeg
bacon fat
cloves
lemon juice or vinegar
onion

Brown a medium-sized chopped onion in 2 tablespoons bacon fat. Add to 1 16-ounce jar red cabbage along with 1 cup apple sauce, 1/4 teaspoon nutmeg, 2 cloves. Cover, heat slowly over low fire until thoroughly hot and the flavors are well blended, stir occasionally. Taste and add extra salt, pepper, and a little lemon juice or vinegar if needed.

AT SERVING TIME:

Serve in heated dish, garnished with thin slices of lemon stuck with cloves and sprinkled, if desired, with a few gratings of nutmeg. Serves 4 to 6.

Whole Cauliflower Allemande

Since a whole cauliflower is so dramatic and since no one has as yet succeeded in canning or freezing the cauliflower in its entirety, you have no alternative but to cook it yourself. (Do not attempt to use the pressure cooker for this.)

YOU WILL NEED:

cauliflower
condensed cream of mushroom soup

Parmesan cheese
lemon juice or white vinegar
paprika

Select a medium-sized cauliflower the snowiest most unblemished one you can find. Remove outer leaves. Cut off stalk. Soak 30 minutes head down in salted cold water. Cook head down in a deep pan of boiling water to which has been added 1 teaspoon of lemon juice or white vinegar. Do not cover the pan. A medium-sized cauliflower should cook in about 12 minutes. Overcooking makes it soft and mushy.

Drain the cauliflower. Place on a baking dish which can be used for serving. Cover with heated condensed cream of mushroom soup, undiluted. Sprinkle with 1/2 cup grated Parmesan cheese and a little paprika. Bake in a moderate oven, 350° F., until the cheese is melted and lightly browned.

AT SERVING TIME:

Bring to the table on its own baking dish. Garnish with water cress and sections of lemon lightly sprinkled with nutmeg.

VARIATION: Whole Cauliflower with Sauce Suprême and Walnuts

Cook cauliflower as above. Place on baking dish. Cover with Sauce Suprême (page 150). Top with buttered bread crumbs and walnut halves. (These can be secured in tins.) Bake in moderate oven, 350° F., until well heated and lightly browned.

Old Virginia's Corn Pudding

There are sections of this country where it would be considered a sacrilege to serve fried chicken without this wonderful pudding. It is best when made with inexpensive canned cream-style corn.

YOU WILL NEED:

canned cream-style corn	butter
eggs	sugar
milk	onion or onion flakes

Combine 1 No. 2 can (about 2 1/4 cups) cream-style corn with 2 cups milk, 2 slightly beaten eggs, 1 teaspoon sugar, 1 tablespoon butter, 1 teaspoon salt, 1 tablespoon finely chopped onion or 1 teaspoon dried onion flakes. Bake in a buttered casserole in a slow oven, 325° F., about 40 minutes or until firm to the touch.

AT SERVING TIME:

Bring to the table in its own baking dish. Excellent with ham as well as chicken. Serves 6.

Eggplant Imam Bayeldi

Literally translated Imam Bayeldi means "the Imam fainted." In the Middle East they tell this story: Imam, a prominent Moham-medan was very fond of eggplant cooked with meat but his dear wife being a lady who liked to play the Middle Eastern version of bridge in the afternoon forgot to go to the butcher store until it was too late. However, she had in the house a few vegetables and with these she created a dish for her lord and master, a dish with an aroma and flavor so heavenly that Imam swooned with delight. That's why the dish is called Imam Bayeldi—it is the most delicious of all vegetable dinners.

YOU WILL NEED:

eggplant	onions
green pepper	parsley
olive, or salad, oil	canned tomatoes

Cut a large-sized eggplant into quarters. Salt and allow pieces to stand until tiny drops of dark juice appear on the pieces. Meanwhile, brown gently in 1/2 cup olive oil or salad oil 2 sliced onions, 1 large-sized green pepper cut into small pieces. When the vegetables are tender add 1 cup drained solid-packed canned tomatoes, 4 tablespoons chopped parsley, salt and pepper to taste. Cook the mixture about 2 minutes. Wash eggplant. Make a slit down the center of each quarter and stuff with the cooked vegetable combination. Place the quarters in a baking dish and pour a cup of water in the bottom to keep the eggplant from burning and bake in a moderate oven, 325° F., about 40 minutes.

AT SERVING TIME:

Serve a quartered eggplant to each person; or chill, slice, and serve as an appetizer, or a salad. Makes 4 portions, but don't count on it to serve more than 2 people.

Eggplant Parmigiana

Parmigiana, of course, means Parmesan but it seems unfair to refer to this famous dish by any other than its Italian name. This recipe is authentic in every respect except that the tomato sauce comes out of a can.

YOU WILL NEED:

eggplant	basil (optional)
olive oil	orégano (optional)
canned tomato sauce	celery flakes (optional)
Parmesan cheese	garlic or garlic extract
mozzarella or Swiss cheese	

Peel 1 large or 2 small eggplants and cut into thin slices. Brown in 1 cup olive oil and drain on paper. Into a buttered or oiled casserole place a layer of the fried eggplant. Cover with canned tomato sauce whose flavor has been heightened, if you wish, by the addition of basil, orégano, a few dried celery flakes and some crushed fresh garlic or garlic extract. Sprinkle with 3 tablespoons grated Parmesan cheese and cover with a layer of mozzarella or Swiss cheese sliced thin. Repeat. Top layer should be cheese. Bake in a hot oven, 400° F., for 15 minutes.

AT SERVING TIME:

Bring straight from the oven to the table and serve from the same dish in which it was baked. Serves 4.

Mushrooms in Cream under Glass

The French phrase for serving foods under glass is *sous cloche* or "under a bell," and you can get glass covers at specialty shops or department stores. However, heat-proof glass custard cups answer the purpose admirably and look very pretty too.

YOU WILL NEED:

canned whole mushrooms
toast or English muffin
heavy cream or sour cream
parsley

brandy (optional)
lemon juice
butter

Drain whole canned broiled-in-butter mushroom crowns using 8 to 12 mushrooms to serve 2 people—depends on the size of the mushroom and the appetite. Heat mushrooms in 4 tablespoons butter with 1 tablespoon lemon juice, 1/2 teaspoon salt, few grains of pepper, 1 tablespoon chopped parsley. For each serving set a round piece of buttered toast or a halved and toasted English muffin on a heat-proof baking dish. Pile the mushroom caps neatly in a pyramid on top of the toast. Pour 4 tablespoons heavy cream (sweet or sour) over the mushrooms. Cover with glass bell or custard cup and bake in a moderate oven about 20 minutes. Cream will amalgamate deliciously with the toast and mushrooms.

AT SERVING TIME:

If you have classic bells leave them in place and bring the mushrooms to the table. If you are using custard cups remove them and dramatize the service by serving your mushrooms flambé: slightly warm 2 tablespoons brandy over a candle flame. Set alight and pour over mushrooms.

The flame lasts only a fraction of a minute but the effect is lovely and the flavor added by the brandy is considerable.

French Fried Onions

With steak, grilled hamburgers, or liver, as a garnish for creamed dishes, or as an appetizer to serve between meals with cocktails or beer, nothing could be finer than French fried onions. Try the tinned variety dressed up in this manner.

YOU WILL NEED:
  canned French fried onions   cayenne (optional)
  olive oil

Empty a can of French fried onions into a shallow oiled pan. Brush lightly with olive oil. Sprinkle with a few grains of cayenne or freshly ground black pepper. Heat in a moderate oven, 350° F., about 5 minutes.

AT SERVING TIME:
Serve very hot, preferably from the same pan in which they were heated.

Peas Parisienne

YOU WILL NEED:
  quick-frozen peas   lettuce (optional)
  sugar   onions
  parsley   butter

Put 1 12-ounce package solidly frozen green peas into a saucepan with 1/4 cup boiling water, 2 tablespoons butter, 1/2 teaspoon salt, 1 teaspoon sugar, 3 or 4 sprigs parsley, and 2 tiny onions, 2 or 3 leaves of lettuce may be used also if desired. As soon as peas are thawed and water is bubbling, cover closely and cook slowly until peas are tender—about 5 minutes.

AT SERVING TIME:
Remove parsley and onions. Add 1 tablespoon butter, a sprinkle of freshly ground black pepper and serve immediately on heated plates. Serves 3.

Peas with Mushrooms

How to vary the vegetable for a company meal is a constant problem. Here is an unhackneyed combination.

YOU WILL NEED:
canned or quick-frozen peas   butter
canned, sliced or chopped   nutmeg (optional)
  mushrooms

Heat a can or a 12-ounce package quick-frozen peas according to package directions. Drain a 3-ounce tin of chopped or sliced broiled-in-butter mushrooms. Heat mushrooms in 2 tablespoons butter. Combine with peas. Season to taste with a little extra salt, pepper, and, if desired, a few grains of nutmeg.

AT SERVING TIME:
Serve immediately very hot on heated plates or from a heated serving dish. Makes 3 or 4 servings.

Purée of Peas De Luxe

Since only the finest and freshest of green peas are used in the preparation of baby foods, they can be the basis for a specially delicate purée. Remember that one can provides only one adult portion.

YOU WILL NEED:
canned strained green peas   heavy cream
  (baby-food type)   butter

To each can of strained green peas, add a tablespoon of butter and 1 or 2 tablespoons heavy cream, salt and freshly ground black pepper to taste. Heat, stirring constantly to prevent scorching, or use a small double boiler.

AT SERVING TIME:
Serve each portion in a small heated custard cup decorated with a ring of lightly cooked carrots or crossed strips of pimiento.

Quick Hopping John

Variants of Hopping John (very good too!) can be made very quickly from the contents of cans: canned black-eyed peas or canned baked beans and tomato sauce, canned kidney beans—in fact almost any kind of canned bean.

YOU WILL NEED:

quick-cooking rice   cayenne or Tabasco
canned black-eyed peas or   parsley or water cress (op-
   canned beans   tional)
bacon and bacon fat

Start with a package (1 1/2 cups) quick-cooking rice. Drain liquid from a No. 3 can of beans and add sufficient water to this liquid to make 2 cups. Place rice in saucepan together with the 2 cups of liquid. Bring uncovered to a full rolling boil. Add canned beans, 4 slices crisp bacon crumbled, and the bacon fat which came from it. Season to taste with salt, freshly ground black pepper, cayenne or Tabasco. Cook 2 minutes. Take from fire. Cover and let stand in a warm place at least 10 minutes so that the rice will absorb all the flavor.

AT SERVING TIME:

Garnish, if desired, with bacon strips and parsley or water cress. Serve with the traditional accompaniment of sliced tomatoes, thinly sliced onions or scallions, dressed with vinegar, salt, and pepper. Serves 6 to 8.

Broiled Franconia Potatoes

YOU WILL NEED:

canned small potatoes   fine bread crumbs (optional)
butter   Worcestershire sauce

Heat and drain a small buffet tin (about 1 cup) small potatoes. Brush with 2 tablespoons melted butter, which has been mixed with 1/2 teaspoon Worcestershire sauce. Roll in bread crumbs if desired. Set under the broiler until golden brown turning once or twice to brown evenly.

AT SERVING TIME:

Serve with broiled meat or fish. The broiling, as a matter of fact, can be done at the same time as the meat is cooked but the potatoes should not be put under the heat until the meat is almost finished. Serves 2 or 3.

Crusty Potato Pancakes

There was a time when potato pancakes brought visions of knuckles grated along with the raw potatoes. The new packaged or quick-frozen mixes make grating unnecessary, but the mixes can stand extra seasoning.

YOU WILL NEED:

packaged, or quick-frozen, potato pancake mix	cooking oil or shortening milk or light cream
onion	

Make up batter for potato pancakes according to package direction but to enrich the flavor use thin cream or top milk instead of water and add 1 small-sized onion, very finely chopped. For a crisp crust drop by tablespoonfuls into hot shortening or oil, which stands at least an inch deep in the frying pan. Fry on one side then the other. Drain on paper towels.

AT SERVING TIME:

Serve with applesauce and crisp bacon or frizzled ham for late Sunday breakfast or for luncheon. Potato pancakes are traditional with sauerbraten or with goulash.

French Fried Potatoes

Quick-frozen French fried potatoes are a boon. However, many people have discovered that they cannot be made really crisp when they are heated in the oven or by other methods usually recommended on the package. The method described here is an adaptation of one used by fine chefs who keep quantities of French fried potatoes on hand and "finish off" each portion as it is ordered.

YOU WILL NEED:
quick-frozen French fried   salad oil or shortening
   potatoes

In a heavy frying pan place enough shortening or salad oil so that it will stand an inch deep in the pan. Heat to 370° F. If you have no frying thermometer, drop an inch cube of white bread into the fat, if it is golden brown in 20 seconds, the fat is at the proper temperature. Drop solidly frozen French fried potatoes into the hot bath a handful at a time. Cook 40 to 60 seconds. Remove from fat with skimmer. Drain on paper towels. Sprinkle if desired with salt and/or freshly ground black pepper.

AT SERVING TIME:
Place a paper napkin inside a serving dish or bread basket. Place the hot French fried potatoes inside the napkin. Serve immediately.

Potatoes Chantilly with Cheese

Although the potato course rarely gets much attention at a dinner party this one most certainly will. It is a delicious combination of quick-frozen mashed potatoes, cream, and cheese.

YOU WILL NEED:
dehydrated or quick-frozen   heavy cream
   mashed potatoes   cheese
butter   nutmeg (optional)
milk

Prepare about 2 cups dehydrated or quick-frozen mashed potatoes, adding milk and butter according to package directions. Place in a shallow baking dish. Whip 1/2 cup heavy cream, fold in 1/4 cup grated cheese. Season with salt, pepper, a few grains of nutmeg, if desired. Top the potatoes with the cream mixture and bake in a moderate oven, 350° F., until golden brown. If desired, the browning may be done under the broiler.

AT SERVING TIME:

Serve immediately from the baking dish. Serves 4.

Potatoes Julienne

Ready-to-eat canned julienne potato sticks are a joy to have on hand. They are excellent with meats or fish; a fine foil to a creamed dish like chicken à la king; an unusual cocktail snack—particularly when glamorized in this manner.

YOU WILL NEED:

canned julienne potato sticks	cheese or paprika and cayenne
caraway seeds (optional)	butter or salad oil

Place canned julienne potato sticks on an oiled or buttered piepan. Brush with melted butter or salad oil. Sprinkle generously with grated sharp cheese or with paprika and a few grains of cayenne. A scatter of caraway seeds may be used, if desired. Set in a moderate oven, 350° F., just long enough to heat and melt the cheese—about 4 minutes.

AT SERVING TIME:

Serve warm.

Fried Sweet Potatoes au Citron

YOU WILL NEED:

canned sweet potatoes	lemons
butter	rum or brandy (optional)

Drain and cut into small pieces 2 cups canned cooked sweet potatoes. Brown in 4 tablespoons melted butter.

AT SERVING TIME:

Sprinkle with juice and grated rind of 1/2 lemon. Garnish with thin slices of lemon. If desired, pour on 4 tablespoons slightly warmed rum or brandy and set a match to the liquor. Serves 4 to 6.

Scalloped Sweet Potatoes with Apples

YOU WILL NEED:

canned sweet potatoes   brown sugar
canned apple slices   lemon and lemon juice
butter   mace, nutmeg, or allspice

Cut 2 cups canned drained sweet potatoes into slices about 1/4 of an inch thick. Arrange in layers in a buttered baking dish along with an equal quantity of canned apple slices, also drained. Sprinkle layers with 1/4 cup dark brown sugar, 4 tablespoons butter, 2 teaspoons lemon juice, 1/2 teaspoon nutmeg, mace, or allspice. The top layer should be potatoes. Bake in a hot oven, 400° F., about 20 minutes or until thoroughly heated and browned on top. If the casserole seems dry, pour over about 1/2 cup of the juice from the can of apples.

AT SERVING TIME:

Decorate the top with thin slivers of lemon rind. Particularly delicious with chicken in any form, ham, or pork. Serves 6.

Sherried Sweet Potatoes

Cooked sweet potatoes of good quality are available in cans. Some are plain, others are already candied or glazed. Either type may be used for this recipe. If you use the candied sweet potatoes, omit the browning and sugaring.

YOU WILL NEED:

canned sweet potatoes   sherry
butter and brown sugar (if
  unglazed potatoes are
  used)

Potatoes should be cut in halves lengthwise. Drain. Heat in 1/4 cup butter with 1/3 cup brown sugar in a heavy frying pan. Turn and brown on both sides.

AT SERVING TIME:

Place on heated plates. Pass a small decanter of sherry and let each person pour a little on his sweet potatoes.

Sauerkraut Provençal with Red Wine

Canned sauerkraut is most versatile—it can be chilled, drained, and served raw in place of a salad or vegetable. However, one of the dressiest ways, is French in origin.

YOU WILL NEED:

canned sauerkraut	consommé or beef bouillon
onion	cube
red wine	

Drain a No. 2 can of sauerkraut. Add 1 thinly sliced onion, 1 cup red wine, 1/2 cup condensed canned consommé or 1/2 cup hot water in which 1 beef bouillon cube has been dissolved. Cover and cook slowly about 20 minutes. Do not drain.

AT SERVING TIME:

Since the juice is so delicious it is best to serve this sauerkraut in a deep sauce dish or saucer. Garnish, if you like, with sour cream and add a sprinkle of caraway, or poppy, seeds. Serves 4.

Spinach with Sour Cream

Quick-frozen chopped spinach is one of the quickest and easiest vegetables to prepare. Blanketed with paprika-pink sour cream it is also a delight to look at and to taste.

YOU WILL NEED:

quick-frozen chopped spin-ach	paprika
sour cream	tarragon vinegar (optional)

Cook a package of quick-frozen chopped spinach according to package directions. Be careful not to overcook. (Only about 1 minute of cooking is necessary after the vegetable is completely thawed and the water boiling.) Drain if necessary. Place in a heated serving dish. Cover with 1 cup sour cream to which has been added 1 teaspoon paprika and if desired 1 tablespoon tarragon vinegar.

AT SERVING TIME:
Bring to the table immediately and serve carefully so that each portion has its topping intact. The combination of hot vegetable and chilled sour cream is exceedingly good. Serves 3 to 4.

Spiced Scalloped Tomatoes with Herbs

Old-fashioned favorites like this should not be tampered with. Although this recipe uses canned tomatoes and baker's bread, the flavor is the traditional one.

YOU WILL NEED:

canned tomatoes	onion or onion flakes
toast	allspice
butter	brown sugar
bread crumbs	

Butter a casserole and sprinkle with bread crumbs. Pour in 1 No. 2 can (about 2 1/2 cups) solidly packed canned tomatoes, 1 tablespoon finely chopped onion or dried onion flakes, 1 tablespoon brown sugar, 1/2 teaspoon powdered allspice, salt and freshly ground black pepper to taste. Cover top with inch squares of buttered toast. Bake in a hot oven, 400° F., until thoroughly heated all the way through and golden brown on top.

AT SERVING TIME:
Serve from baking dish. 6 portions.

VARIATION: Glazed Scalloped Tomatoes
Omit allspice from the seasonings; add 4 tablespoons dark brown sugar to the tomatoes and scatter sugar on top of toast. Dot with bits of butter. The casserole will then acquire a delicious glaze.

❧ 12 ❧

~~~~~~~~~~~~~~~~~~~~~~~~~~~~~~~

Salads

HEARTY AND OTHERWISE

THE SALAD is the dream of the hurried gourmet, since preparation is reduced to a minimum and the most dramatic effects can be secured with the least possible effort. There is one point, however, at which you must not skimp or hurry and that is in the careful washing of the greens. Formerly we were told that salad greens should be washed as soon as they came from the garden or market but now we are assured by the experts that it's best to wash them as you need them. Salting the water is helpful and in cold weather it is not necessary to freeze your hands—adding a bit of warm water does no harm.

Careful drying with a clean soft towel or paper towel is just about as important as thorough washing, for wet greens mean a watery dressing. Salad greens should be crisp and well chilled.

So much for the mundane requirements of a good salad. The rest is art. Fantasy and imagination play a large part in successful salads but nowadays it is well to remember that the most effective salads are casual. Ornate and overdecorated salads are no longer smart.

RECIPES

The Classic Salad

To those who follow the French tradition this is the only salad worthy of the name. Always it should be "tossed" at the table— the well-washed greens cut or torn into pieces and brought to the table in a large bowl. This bowl need not always be wooden. You can use china, glass, or pottery. But it should be *big*.

Fine vinegar and the best of oil are the heart and soul of a proper salad. Many sticklers insist that nothing but pure olive oil is permissible—and certainly the finest olive oil imparts a flavor that can be secured in no other way. However, some people prefer the flavor of dressing made of corn oil, peanut oil, or an oil that combines one of these and varying amounts of olive oil.

As to the vinegar, there is much difference of opinion. Some insist upon cider or wine vinegar; others prefer the stout flavor of malt vinegar. A large and ever widening group is devoted to tarragon and other herb-flavored vinegars. Even more numerous are those who combine a small amount of herbal vinegars with other types.

Without attempting to enter into the age-old controversies on whether oil and vinegar should be combined beforehand to make the dressing or whether oil and vinegar should be added first or last when a salad is dressed at the table, we offer directions reduced to ultimate simplicity.

Tossed Green Salad

Combine several different kinds of greens—romaine as well as iceberg lettuce, escarole, chicory, water cress. Whenever possible include the less usual types of greens—dandelion greens in season, corn salad, Boston lettuce, peppergrass, endive, and tender young leaves of spinach.

YOU WILL NEED:

salad greens	vinegar or lemon juice
olive oil	garlic (optional)

Rub a large salad bowl with a cut clove of garlic. Place in the bowl about 2 cups well-washed and dried, crisp and chilled salad greens.

AT SERVING TIME:

Sprinkle greens with 3/4 teaspoon salt, a liberal sprinkling of freshly ground black pepper from the mill. Very slowly add 4 tablespoons olive oil tossing the greens lightly with fork and spoon until every leaf glistens. Then sprinkle with 1 tablespoon vinegar or lemon juice. Toss again—but not enough to wilt the salad. Taste a leaf and if necessary correct the seasoning. Serve immediately on chilled plates. Serves 3 to 4.

VARIATIONS:

Tossed Green Salad with Fruit

One of the most delightful fruit salads is nothing more than a tossed green salad to which is added 1/2 to 1 cup well-drained, quick-frozen fruit salad or sections of oranges, tangerines, pineapple wedges, or grapefruit sections. Omit garlic. Lemon juice is often preferred to vinegar for fruit salads.

Tossed Green Salad with Chapon

Instead of rubbing the salad bowl with garlic, cut the heel off a loaf of French bread or a crusty French roll, rub well with garlic or insert a half clove of garlic into the bread. Toss this bit of bread with the salad to impart a delicate flavor of garlic. Remove the crust of bread, *chapon,* or leave it for those who love it.

Tossed Green Salad with Vegetables

To classic tossed green salad add 1/2 to 1 cup well-drained and chilled, cooked or canned vegetables, or raw vegetables, cut into thin slivers or slices.

Tossed Green Salad aux Fines Herbes

Sprinkle salad greens with 2 tablespoons finely chopped fresh parsley or chives, or use 1 tablespoon chopped fresh basil, chevril, mint, or tarragon. If you wish, you may use a combination of these various herbs. It is possible to use dried herbs for salad, but they should first be allowed to stand at least 10 minutes in a little of the vinegar or olive oil you are using in your salad. Don't forget that 1 teaspoon of dried herbs is equivalent to a tablespoon of fresh herbs.

Beet Aspic Ring

A nice change from the ever-present tomato aspic.

YOU WILL NEED:

beet juice	lemon-flavored gelatin
vinegar	horse-radish

Make up a package of lemon-flavored gelatin according to package directions using instead of water, juice from canned beets, 3 tablespoons vinegar, 1 tablespoon horse-radish, salt and pepper to taste. Chill until firm in small ring mold, which has been lightly oiled with olive oil.

AT SERVING TIME:

Unmold. This can be done most effectively by running a knife blade around the edges of the mold. Place a chilled plate over the mold. Turn upside down so that mold is now on top of plate. Shake the mold slightly in order to loosen the gelatin. It is quite all right to unmold salad 1/2 hour before using. But be sure to put it into the refrigerator. Garnish with crisp lettuce leaves and fill center of the mold with cole slaw or sliced cucumbers covered with sour cream. Serves 4.

Carrot Salad Italienne

The Italians serve this delectable dish either warm or cold, as a salad or a side dish. It's an attractive way to dress up canned carrots.

YOU WILL NEED:

canned carrots   wine vinegar
garlic   lettuce (optional)
olive oil   parsley (optional)

Heat 1 can carrots, drain, and while they are still hot, add 2 tablespoons olive oil, 1 tablespoon vinegar (red wine vinegar preferably), and 1 clove garlic. Season with salt and pepper. Cover and
let stand at least half an hour.

AT SERVING TIME:

Serve either warm or cold, as a side dish or salad. If served as a
salad, chill, place on lettuce leaves, and garnish with chopped parsley. Serves 4 to 6.

Chef's Salad

Practically anything in the way of meat, cheese, and salad greens
can go into a chef's salad. It is basically a mixed green salad made
hearty—and hence much more acceptable to men—by the addition
of solid food usually cut into julienne strips.

YOU WILL NEED:

cooked chicken or tongue   eggs
chives or parsley (optional)   mustard (optional)
salad greens   anchovies (optional)
Swiss cheese   French dressing or oil and
boiled ham, salami or bo-   vinegar
  logna

To serve 4 put about 4 cups of crisp chilled salad greens into a
garlic-rubbed bowl. Arrange on top of the greens in small heaps
the following ingredients or any desired combination (everything
should be in pieces shaped like match sticks) 1/4 pound Swiss
cheese, 1 cup boiled ham, salami, or bologna, 1 cup cooked chicken
or tongue. Slice a hard-cooked egg and use that along with 8 anchovies to decorate the heaps. Sprinkle if desired with chopped
chives or parsley.

AT SERVING TIME:

At the table add 1/2 cup French dressing or "dress" at the table in
the French manner by slowly pouring on 6 tablespoons olive oil

or salad oil, mix until the greens glisten, sprinkle with 2 tablespoons vinegar, season to taste with salt, freshly ground black
pepper, a bit of mustard if desired. Serve immediately.

Chicken and Almond Mousse

YOU WILL NEED:

chicken bouillon cube	gelatin
egg yolks	almonds
cooked chicken	cayenne
heavy cream	celery of fennel

Beat slightly 3 egg yolks. Gradually and slowly add to them 1 cup
hot chicken broth made from a bouillon cube. Cook this over hot
water until mixture thickens. Add 1 tablespoon granulated gelatin
soaked in 1 tablespoon cold water. Stir well until gelatin dissolves.
Add 1/2 cup diced cooked chicken and 1/2 cup salted almonds
finely chopped. Season to taste with salt and a few grains of cayenne. Set in the refrigerator until mixture begins to thicken. Then
fold in 1 cup heavy cream beaten until stiff. Turn into a mold
and chill or into a bowl which can be brought to the table.

AT SERVING TIME:

Garnish with crisp leaves of celery or fennel, and celery or fennel
sticks. Serve with small hot rolls. Serves 6.

VARIATION: Chicken Mousse with Sherry

Two tablespoons of sherry may be added to the mousse.

Chicken Salad with White Grapes

YOU WILL NEED:

cooked or canned chicken	lime, or lemon, juice
mayonnaise or salad dress- ing	lettuce or escarole
white grapes	heavy cream

Cut 2 cups chicken into pieces—not too small. Sprinkle with
3 tablespoons lime, or lemon, juice. Make a foamy salad dressing

by adding to 3/4 cup prepared mayonnaise or salad dressing, 1/2 cup heavy cream whipped.

Add half of this dressing to the chicken. Mix thoroughly. Pack into oiled bowl or 4 custard cups and allow to stand in the refrigerator until thoroughly chilled.

AT SERVING TIME:

Unmold on lettuce leaves on chilled individual plates or small platter. Cover salad with remaining dressing as if you were frosting a cake. Garnish with seedless white grapes. Serve with tiny hot cheese biscuits.

Crab Meat and Avocado Salad with Gloucester Sauce

This is a pretty—and delicious—main dish at lunch or supper.

YOU WILL NEED:

avocados   Gloucester Sauce (page 144)
cooked crab meat   parsley or chives

Cut 2 medium-sized avocados in half crosswise. Scoop out and cut avocado into cubes. Combine with 2 cups cooked canned or quick-frozen crab meat, which has been carefully picked over and separated into large flakes. Mix lightly with 1 cup Gloucester Sauce. Place mixture into avocado shells. Cover thickly with finely chopped parsley or chives. Serve immediately.

AT SERVING TIME:

Pass extra Gloucester Sauce in a small bowl if desired. Serves 4.

Crab Meat Ravigote

Canned crab meat from Japan or Alaska is particularly good. It's nice to have shell-shaped dishes—real crab shells or those of glass or plastic. But they aren't really necessary.

YOU WILL NEED:

canned crab meat	parsley
eggs	Ravigote Sauce (page 148)
French dressing	

To 2 cups of canned crab meat, which has been carefully picked over and separated into large flakes, add 4 tablespoons highly seasoned French dressing and 2 finely chopped hard-cooked eggs. Mix thoroughly. Place in 4 shell-shaped dishes or lettuce cups. Pour over Ravigote Sauce.

AT SERVING TIME:

Sprinkle liberally with finely chopped parsley, using about 1 tablespoon parsley on each portion. Serve 1 shell per person. Serves 4.

Eggs in Aspic

Stuffed hard-cooked eggs may not sound too exciting, but try them in this fashion—either as an appetizer or for a salad entree.

YOU WILL NEED:

eggs	Worcestershire sauce
deviled ham	lemon juice
Madrilène Aspic (page 182)	water cress
mayonnaise	green pepper

Cut 6 hard-cooked eggs in halves lengthwise. Remove yolks and mash with 1 3-ounce tin deviled ham. If a little extra moistening is needed, use a bit of cream or mayonnaise. Make balls of this mixture and place inside the whites as for deviled eggs. Place in a shallow serving dish which can be brought to the table. Carefully spoon over the eggs Madrilène Aspic. Chill.

AT SERVING TIME:

Garnish the dish with water cress and strips of green pepper. Pass separately a bowl of mayonnaise highly seasoned with Worcestershire sauce thinned with lemon juice. As an appetizer, serve 1/2 egg with aspic per person. As a main dish salad, 2 halves.

Molded Fruit Salad in Wine

Fruit-flavored gelatin desserts in which wine is substituted for part of the liquid, offer quick wine jellies to be served as desserts. Various combinations may be used. We suggest below the flavors which combine most happily with different types of wines and various fruits.

YOU WILL NEED:

canned drained fruit or   red wine
  fruit salad   Mock Devonshire Cream
strawberry, raspberry, or   Dressing
  cherry gelatin dessert   lettuce

Make up a package of cherry, raspberry, or strawberry gelatin dessert according to package directions but use 1 1/2 cups water and 1/2 cup red wine. Allow the gelatin to chill and thicken slightly. Then add 1 cup drained canned fruit or fruit salad. Raw apples, pears, or oranges may be combined with the canned fruit. The only type of fresh fruit you must not use is pineapple because it prevents gelatin from stiffening. Pour into a mold or bowl, place in refrigerator until firm.

AT SERVING TIME:

Pass separately a bowl of Mock Devonshire Cream made by combining 1 cup creamed cottage cheese with 1 cup sour cream, 1 teaspoon sugar, and few grains of allspice. Stir until very smooth. Serves 6.

Madrilène Aspic

Canned consommé madrilène reinforced with a little gelatin, a dash of wine, and a bit of extra seasoning makes a delicate and different molded salad.

YOU WILL NEED:

canned jellied madrilène   gelatin
pale dry sherry or vermouth   marjoram
cayenne

Although the canned jellied madrilènes on the market already have gelatin in them it is necessary to add more if you want a firm, easily handled mold. This recipe makes a quart of aspic, enough for a standard 8-inch ring mold.

Use 2 cans madrilène. Soak 2 tablespoons plain gelatin in 1/2 cup cold water about 5 minutes until softened. Heat madrilène to boiling point and add enough water to make 4 cups of liquid. Dissolve gelatin in the hot broth. Add 1/4 cup pale dry sherry or dry vermouth, 1/4 teaspoon cayenne, and a pinch of marjoram. Pour into the mold. Chill for several hours or over night.

AT SERVING TIME:

Remove the aspic from the mold and fill the center with cold mixed vegetables that have been marinated in French dressing.

Neo-Caesar's Salad

The original Caesar's salad is an invention from California to which tremendous drama is attached, mainly because it is mixed at the table with a raw egg plopped on top of the greens. Don't worry about any raw egg taste because the lemon juice used in the dressing and the tossing take care of that. This version is called Neo-Caesar because bread sticks have been substituted for the original croutons, because the whole procedure has been considerably simplified.

YOU WILL NEED:

assorted salad greens	egg
olive, or salad, oil	lemon juice
Parmesan, Cheddar, or blue cheese	bread sticks
garlic	Worcestershire sauce (optional)

To serve 4 as a main course, use 6 cups crisp chilled salad greens such as lettuce, romaine, escarole, and chicory all broken into bits. Place in a bowl well rubbed with garlic. Scatter over the greens 1/2 cup freshly grated hard cheese such as Parmesan, Cheddar, or blue cheese.

AT SERVING TIME:

Start the ceremony by breaking a raw egg on top of the greens. Sprinkle upon the egg and over the greens, 6 tablespoons canned or fresh lemon juice (2 average-sized lemons). Toss lightly and add gradually 3 tablespoons olive, or salad, oil. Season to taste with salt, freshly ground black pepper and, if desired, 2 teaspoons Worcestershire sauce. At the last minute add 1 cup (4 to 6) Italian bread sticks broken into pieces. Serve immediately.

Tomato Aspic au Moment

Tomato aspic already jelled and ready to slice and serve comes in convenient cans. Since it is actually a pectin jelly rather than a gelatin product the shape of the aspic does not depend upon chilling so that you could take it right off the shelves, open the can and serve. Chilling, however does improve the flavor.

YOU WILL NEED:

canned tomato aspic	celery, fennel, or spring on-
lettuce or romaine	ions
mayonnaise or sour cream	curry powder

Chill. Open both ends of the can and push the aspic onto a chilled plate. Cut into 4 or 6 slices. Garnish with lettuce or romaine, and crisp little circles of celery, fennel, or spring onions.

AT SERVING TIME:

Pass separately a bowl of curry-flavored mayonnaise or sour cream, made by adding 1/2 teaspoon curry powder to 1/2 cup dressing or sour cream. Serves 4 to 6.

VARIATION: Tomato and Cucumber Aspic in Cucumber Boats

Cut 2 medium-sized cucumbers in half lengthwise. Scoop out the center and cut into 1/2-inch cubes. Cut or break chilled canned tomato aspic into pieces. Combine with diced cucumber and place in cucumber shells. Garnish with parsley or water cress. Serves 4.

Tomato and Sliced Egg Ravigote

Equally good either as an appetizer or a main dish luncheon salad. If you serve it as an appetizer, portions may be half as large.

YOU WILL NEED:
tomatoes   Ravigote Sauce (page 148)
eggs

Arrange 4 small-sized, thinly sliced tomatoes around the edge of a round platter. Arrange sliced eggs in strips to make an attractive design overlapping them slightly. Garnish with Ravigote Sauce.

AT SERVING TIME:
Pass a separate bowl of sauce and crusty hot French or rye bread and sweet butter.

White Wine Aspic

This aspic is endlessly useful for any number of delicious salads— tongue, fish, salmon, chicken, and vegetable.

YOU WILL NEED:
condensed chicken con-   white wine
sommé or chicken bouil-   gelatin
lon cubes

Heat but do not boil, 1 can condensed chicken consommé with 1/2 can dry white table wine and 1/2 can water. Soak 2 envelopes (2 tablespoons) gelatin in 1/2 cup water, dissolve in hot consommé. Chill until firm.

AT SERVING TIME:
In addition to its many uses in molded salads, this aspic may also be used as a garnish for cold meats or fish. Simply mold in a shallow pan. Cut or break into small pieces and place in mounds upon crisp lettuce leaves as a garnish. Makes 1 pint.

❧ 13 ❧

wwwwwwwwwwwwwwwwwwwww

QUICK BREADS

Biscuits, Waffles, and Griddle
Cakes

MOSTLY FROM MIXES

FOR BREAKFAST, lunch, or supper—with appetizers, soups, salads, main dishes—as a dessert or a dessert accompaniment, a hot bread adds interest and variety. Often it makes all the difference between a mere snack and a real meal.

In this chapter we have collected a number of suggestions for transforming bakeshop breads and rolls quickly and easily into hot breads with homemade fragrance and just-baked flavor.

In addition to many recipes describing new and interesting uses of mixes there are recipes that show how partially baked goods— brown'n'serve breads, rolls and cinnamon buns as well as quick-frozen waffles and canned griddle cake batters may be served in ways that are essentially new and exciting but which hark back to the days of long and lavish feasting.

Since various brands of mixes are packed in different-sized packages they often vary in proportions and ingredients. We have suggested in each case that the basic recipe on the package be followed for mixing and baking. Our recipes suggest additions and variations applicable to a large number of the most popular brands. We have also included a number of helpful tricks that do not generally find space on labels.

RECIPES

Herb Loaves
Ready-Baked Bread with Herbs
Boston Brown Bread
Butterscotch Rolls
Butterscotch Pecan Rolls
Drop Biscuits
Cheese Drop Biscuits
Orange Drop Biscuits
Blueberry Squares
Cheese Straws
Spiced Coffee Cake
Date-Nut Muffins with Sherry
Honeyed Cinnamon Crisps
Hush Puppies
Cinnamon Toast Logs
Brown Sugar Logs
Louisiana Pain Perdu
Buttermilk Batter Cakes

Bacon Batter Cakes
Ham Batter Cakes
Pancakes or Griddle Cakes
Apple Pancakes
French Pancakes
Maple Pancakes
Old-Fashioned Buckwheat Cakes
Patty Shells from Bread
Poor Knights (*Arme Ritters*)
Popovers from a Mix
Sure-Pop Popovers
Yorkshire Pudding
Quick Sally Lunns
Angel Sally
Quick-Frozen Waffles
Nut Waffles
Wonders or Doughboys

Herb Loaves

A crusty French or Italian loaf of bread may be used in this fashion. But even better are the brown'n'serve loaves which are partially baked and may be stored in the refrigerator for a couple of weeks or kept in the frozen-food locker for months. Bread heated and flavored in this fashion is a welcome change from the popular garlic bread.

YOU WILL NEED:

brown'n'serve French bread dried, or fresh, chervil, tarragon, or basil	olive oil or butter

Brush loaf with olive oil or melted butter. Sprinkle over the top dried or fresh herbs, rubbing them between the fingers in order to release the oils. Bake in a hot oven, 450° F., about 10 minutes or until lightly browned. These loaves need not be set on a pan but can be cooked directly on the shelf of the oven. However, if you use a pan, or cooky tin, it need not be greased.

AT SERVING TIME:

Bring the loaf whole and hot to the table, preferably in a basket lined with a napkin.

VARIATION: Ready-Baked Bread with Herbs

A French or Italian loaf from the bakeshop may be brushed with oil and sprinkled with herbs as above, but the oven should not be hot, only about 325° F., and the time required should be cut to about 5 minutes.

Boston Brown Bread

Boston brown bread is now available in tins. Canned brown bread, however, should always be served steamy hot, unless of course it is sliced thin for sandwiches. On most tins of brown bread you will find directions telling you to immerse the can in hot water. This method of heating takes a long time, and what is more important, the hot can is difficult to handle. The method suggested here is much simpler.

YOU WILL NEED:
canned Boston brown bread

Open a can of brown bread at both ends and push the bread out of the can. Place in the top of a double boiler. Cover and heat over boiling water.

AT SERVING TIME:
Bring to the table in one piece and slice about 1/2 inch thick; or slice in the kitchen and serve in a bowl or basket lined with a napkin, with Boston baked beans, of course, cole slaw, and apple pie for dessert. Serves 4.

Butterscotch Rolls

Partially baked brown'n'serve rolls can be easily transformed into all manner of specialty breads. Sometime when you long for a touch of sweet and have nothing but plain rolls in the house, try this.

YOU WILL NEED:
brown'n'serve rolls   brown sugar
butter or margarine

Soften and mix 1/2 cup butter or margarine with 3/4 cup light brown sugar. Put half of the mixture in the bottom of a shallow pan. Place the rolls flat side down in the pan. Cover the top with the rest of the butter-sugar mixture. Bake in a hot oven, 400° F., 5 to 7 minutes. Remove rolls from pan immediately before syrup hardens.

AT SERVING TIME:
Serve warm with tea or coffee.

VARIATION: Butterscotch Pecan Rolls
Mix with the butter and sugar 1/4 to 1/2 cup coarsely chopped pecans or walnuts.

Drop Biscuits

Now that such biscuit mixes are available, the only time-consuming operation is the rolling and cutting of the biscuits. On most packages you will find a recipe for making biscuits that are dropped from a spoon. These, of course, are quickest of all.

YOU WILL NEED:
  biscuit mix

Make according to package directions but use twice as much liquid as required in the regular rolled biscuit recipe. Drop by teaspoonfuls in small, buttered muffin tins or on a buttered cooky sheet. Bake about 10 minutes in a hot oven, 450° F.

AT SERVING TIME:

Have everybody at the table ready and waiting. Rush the biscuits from the oven and serve them hot.

VARIATIONS:

Cheese Drop Biscuits

To 2 cups biscuit mix add 1/2 cup grated sharp cheese.

Orange Drop Biscuits

Drop batter into very small, buttered muffin tins or a buttered cooky sheet and on the top of each biscuit place a small lump of sugar which has been dipped for just a moment in orange juice. Fine for tea.

Blueberry Squares

Sometimes the berries may cause a muffin to become a little heavy or soggy, so we use a white cake mix, and place the berries on top of the batter. The squares may be baked in muffin tins but it is easier to use a square pan.

YOU WILL NEED:
> white cake mix
> blueberries

> sugar and cinnamon (optional)
> butter

Make up a package of white cake mix according to directions. Pour into a buttered square pan. Cover with 1/2 to 1 cup blueberries either fresh, canned, or quick frozen. If canned or frozen berries are used they should be well drained. Sprinkle very lightly with 1 tablespoon sugar mixed with 1/2 teaspoon cinnamon, if desired.

AT SERVING TIME:
Bring to the table in the pan in which it was baked. Cut in squares and serve warm with sweet butter.

Cheese Straws

Those crusts of bread which are ordinarily thrown away make delicious salad or soup accompaniments. They may also be served with cocktails.

YOU WILL NEED:
> crusts of bread
> butter or salad oil
> sharp cheese

> paprika
> caraway seeds (optional)

Arrange bread crusts on a piepan or cooky sheet. Brush with melted butter or salad oil. Sprinkle generously with sharp cheese, grated, and with salt, pepper, and paprika. A few caraway seeds may be used if desired. Set in a moderate oven, 350° F., just long enough to melt the cheese.

AT SERVING TIME:
These are best when served warm.

Spiced Coffee Cake

A yeast type of coffee cake mix is on the market but far more widely distributed are hot roll mixes and biscuit mixes from which excellent coffee cake can be made with a minimum of effort. Full directions will usually be found on the package. Here is a recipe for a delectable, crunchy, an spicy topping.

YOU WILL NEED:

hot roll mix or biscuit mix · milk · eggs · sugar · allspice or cloves, cinnamon, and nutmeg · brown sugar · bread crumbs · butter · canned chopped walnuts

Follow package directions for making coffee cake from biscuit or hot roll mix using milk, eggs, and sugar as directed. Add also 1/2 teaspoon powdered allspice or 1/4 teaspoon cloves, cinnamon, nutmeg. For a spicy topping, sprinkle over the top of the batter before it goes into the oven the following mixture: 1/2 cup old-fashioned dark brown sugar, 2 tablespoons bread crumbs, 2 teaspoons cinnamon, 5 tablespoons melted butter, and 1/2 cup chopped walnuts. Bake according to package directions, preferably in a pan that can be brought to the table.

Date-Nut Muffins with Sherry

YOU WILL NEED:

date-nut muffin mix · sherry or brandy · milk · nutmeg

Follow package directions for date-nut muffins but substitute for part of the milk 1/4 cup sherry or brandy and add a few grains of nutmeg. Bake in muffin tins according to directions.

AT SERVING TIME:

These muffins make a delicious dessert when served warm with mock Devonshire cream, made by combining equal quantities of sour cream and creamed cottage cheese.

Honeyed Cinnamon Crisps

Packaged Ry-Crisps, never before noted for their taste appeal, take on zest with these trimmings.

YOU WILL NEED:

Ry-Crisps	honey
butter	cinnamon

Set Ry-Crisps on a cooky sheet, and place on each a teaspoon of honey, a dab of butter, and a sprinkle of cinnamon. Set under the broiler to heat and toast.

AT SERVING TIME:

Serve very hot—with tea, coffee, or chocolate.

Hush Puppies

Hush puppy mix is on the market. Add to the mix a little extra something in the way of seasoning and you have an excellent quick crisp bread to serve with soups or salads or with cocktails.

YOU WILL NEED:

hush puppy mix	parsley
cayenne or Tabasco sauce	

Make up mix according to package directions but add 2 table-spoons very finely chopped parsley and a few grains of cayenne or 3 or 4 drops of Tabasco sauce. Bake on top of the stove on a griddle or in the oven according to package directions.

AT SERVING TIME:

Serve hot as can be!

Cinnamon Toast Logs

The vogue for ready-sliced bread has made certain old-fashioned specialties difficult to prepare. Lacking whole bread, these cinnamon logs may be made even with sliced bread.

YOU WILL NEED:

bread	butter
cinnamon	sugar

Butter 3 thin slices of bread. Lay one on top of the other. Remove crust and cut into 3 strips. Brush with melted butter, roll in a mixture of cinnamon and sugar, using 1 teaspoon cinnamon to 3 tablespoons sugar. Place in a moderate oven until sugar has melted.

AT SERVING TIME:
Bring directly from the oven to the table and serve with tea.

VARIATION: Brown Sugar Logs
Use light brown or old fashioned dark brown sugar instead of white.

Louisiana Pain Perdu

Literally translated, *pain perdu* means "lost bread"—the bread that would have been lost or wasted if a clever Creole cook did not transform it.

YOU WILL NEED:

French bread	eggs
milk	sugar and cinnamon or ma-
sherry (optional)	ple syrup, honey, pre-
butter	serves, or marmalade

Beat together in a shallow bowl or deep soup plate 2 eggs, 1 cup milk, 1/2 teaspoon salt, 1 tablespoon sherry, if desired. Soak in milk and egg mixture 8 slices of crusty French bread cut about 1/2 inch thick. Bread should be soaked until soft but still shapely. Brown on hot well-greased griddle or in butter in a frying pan, browning first one side and then the other.

AT SERVING TIME:
Serve on heated plates sprinkled with sugar and cinnamon or pass maple syrup, honey, preserves, or marmalade.

Buttermilk Batter Cakes

These are made with a ready-made batter, sealed under pressure in a container with a valve which permits you to squirt out of the can the exact amount you need for each cake—a great convenience for the small family or the lone-eater because the unused portion may be kept for several days in the refrigerator.

YOU WILL NEED:

canned buttermilk pancake batter	cooking oil or butter syrup, honey, or maple sugar

Cakes may be baked on a heavy frying pan, a soapstone, or an aluminum griddle. Test to be sure that the griddle or frying pan is hot enough for baking by dropping on the surface a bit of cold water. If it sputters and boils rapidly, the correct baking temperature has been reached. Usually it is not necessary to grease a griddle after an initial rubbing with unsalted fat or oil when it is new, but if you feel the need of greasing use a bit of bacon fat or a cut potato.

Release the valve and pour onto the griddle 3 or 4 tablespoons of batter for a medium-sized cake. Direct the liquid to the center of the cake and it will spread to the edges. Bake until the surface is dotted with tiny bubbles but not long enough for the cake to be dry on top. Turn once.

AT SERVING TIME:

Serve hot off the griddle on heated plates with melted butter, syrup, honey, or maple sugar.

VARIATIONS:

Bacon Batter Cakes

Sprinkle over the surface of each cake before it is turned 1 crisp slice of bacon coarsely crumbled.

Ham Batter Cakes

Cut boiled or baked ham into tiny cubes and sprinkle 2 tablespoons over each cake before turning.

Pancakes or Griddle Cakes

The terms pancakes and griddle cakes are used interchangeably in many sections of the country, and the mixes from which the popular griddle cake is made are usually sold as pancake mix or pancake flour. These are self-rising preparations to which only liquid —and sometimes a little melted butter is added. Many mixes contain in addition to wheat flour one or more other kinds such as corn, rye, rice, buckwheat, and soya flour.

YOU WILL NEED:

pancake mix
milk
butter

butter or margarine (optional)
honey, syrup, or molasses
egg

Make up batter according to package directions. Griddle cakes taste better if the milk is at room temperature and if it is stirred with melted butter or margarine into a slightly beaten egg. For hearty cakes, batter should be just thin enough to pour. If more liquid is added the cakes will be thinner and more delicate. Be careful not to overbeat. This is one time when lumps do no harm. Heat griddle or frying pan. (Many griddles do not require greasing but if necessary grease with a piece of bacon or rub with a cut potato.) Drop batter by spoonfuls or pour from a pitcher. To make sure that all the cakes are the same size, measure the batter by using 3 or 4 tablespoons or 1/4 cup each time. When a pancake is dotted all over with little air bubbles it is usually ready to turn. Use a spatula or pancake turner. Flip over and brown the other side. Try not to turn pancakes more than once or they may become heavy.

AT SERVING TIME:

If possible, make your pancakes at the table on a table grill, or set the table close enough to the stove so that cakes may be served "right off the griddle" on heated plates. Provide butter and honey, syrup, or molasses. It's a good idea to heat together equal parts butter or margarine and syrup. In this way the butter goes further and is more evenly distributed.

VARIATION: Apple Pancakes

Peel and core a sour juicy apple. Slice as thin as possible and add 1 apple to batter made from 2 cups pancake mix. Drop by spoonfuls onto hot griddle or greased frying pan. These cakes are most attractive when made small. Use only about 1 tablespoon of batter to each pancake. Serve 4 to each person with sugar or honey.

French Pancakes

These are very different from griddle cakes—much thinner and of a different texture. Pancake mixes do not work very well for this type of cake although you will find recipes listed on many packages. It is very simple to make the batter yourself and, incidentally, this is one place where you need not bother sifting the flour. Use it as it comes.

YOU WILL NEED:

all-purpose flour	sugar
milk	salad oil
eggs	cinnamon (optional)

Put 3/4 cup flour and 1/2 teaspoon salt into a bowl. Make a well in the center and pour in 1 cup milk and 2 eggs. Stir and beat until perfectly smooth. Batter should be thin as coffee cream. If necessary, add a little extra milk. Heat a five-inch frying pan. Pour in a few *drops* of salad oil and tip so that the bottom of the pan glistens with a thin film of oil. Pour in 2 or 3 tablespoons batter—just enough to cover the pan thinly. Tilt so that mixture spreads evenly. Cook on one side. Turn and cook on the other side.

AT SERVING TIME:

Sprinkle with sugar or sugar and cinnamon. Roll up or fold in quarters and arrange on hot platter. Makes about 18 pancakes.

VARIATION: Maple Pancakes

Brush the pancakes with melted butter. Sprinkle with maple sugar. Roll and serve 2 or 3 per portion on a heated plate with a section of lemon which can be squeezed on the pancake.

Old-Fashioned Buckwheat Cakes

When sour milk or buttermilk and molasses or dark brown sugar are added to a buckwheat pancake mix, the result is like the old-fashioned buckwheat cakes which so delighted our New England ancestors.

YOU WILL NEED:

buckwheat pancake mix   egg
maple sugar or molasses   butter
sour milk or buttermilk   molasses or brown sugar

To 2 cups dry pancake mix, add 1 cup sour milk or buttermilk, 1 egg beaten until light, 3 tablespoons melted butter, 1 tablespoon dark molasses or brown sugar. If batter is too thick add more buttermilk. Bake on a greased griddle or frying pan until tiny bubbles appear on top, turn only once.

AT SERVING TIME:

Serve hot from the griddle on heated plates with butter and maple sugar or molasses. Country sausage is a perfect accompaniment.

Patty Shells from Bread

Canned or quick-frozen chicken à la king and almost any kind of creamed or sauced entree tastes better when served in a shell. Regular patty shells can, of course, be bought or ordered from bakeries but they can also be made very quickly.

YOU WILL NEED:

thinly sliced white bread   paprika (optional)
butter

Butter the thin slices of bread with melted butter. Remove the crusts. Fit slices into well-buttered muffin tins or custard cups. Set in a moderate oven, 350° F., about 7 minutes, just long enough to take on a delicate brown.

AT SERVING TIME:

Patties may be used warm or at room temperature. If you would like to have a frill of pink around the edge, cover the bottom of a saucer with paprika and dip the rim of the patty into the paprika. Fill with creamed mixture. Serve immediately so that the bread will not become soaked.

Poor Knights (Arme Ritters)

This is a German version of what we call French toast. As the name would imply it is thrifty but aristocratic.

YOU WILL NEED:

stale bread	nutmeg
butter	milk
jam, marmalade, or pre-	eggs
serves	almond, or vanilla, extract

Spread 3 slices (1/4 inch thick) stale white bread with jam, marmalade, or preserves. Top each with a slice of bread. Cut each sandwich in half diagonally. Do not remove crusts.

In a shallow dish or soup plate, beat 2 eggs with 1 cup milk, 1/2 teaspoon salt, 1/2 teaspoon almond, or vanilla, extract. Soak sandwiches in mixture until softened but not mushy, turning them first on one side then on the other so that the bread will absorb all the egg and milk.

Brown first on one side then on the other in butter in a frying pan.

AT SERVING TIME:

Serve piping hot on warm plates and have on hand a nutmeg grater so that each person may add a little freshly grated nutmeg as desired.

Popovers from a Mix

For popovers there is a mix which, if you follow the baking directions carefully, will assure you tall handsome popovers—crisp and toast-brown on the outside, tender and moist on the inside. Since it is not beating but steam which causes a popover to pop, we suggest that you get your oven as hot as you possibly can—at least 500° F. to start. Later, after the popovers have risen, you can turn down the oven to finish the baking. Many cookbooks suggest preheating the muffin pans but when the oven is hot enough this is not necessary. There is one thing to remember: *if your popovers don't pop the oven was not hot enough.*

YOU WILL NEED:
popover mix   honey, jam, or preserves
butter

Follow the package directions. Make certain that the oven is hot enough. You may find that popovers bake in less time than the directions suggest. Turn oven heat down about 100 degrees after the popovers have risen very high. To make certain that popovers are thoroughly baked, it is often necessary to remove one from the oven, break it open and make sure that the inside is not raw.

AT SERVING TIME:
Serve hot with sweet butter, if you have it, and honey, jam, or preserves. Good for breakfast but also excellent with a luncheon salad or a hearty supper soup.

Sure-Pop Popovers

Even without a mix, popovers are not at all difficult to make and they're so rewarding—if they pop! This recipe is considerably "speed-up": it eliminates the sifting of flour, the melting of shortening and it adds for those who want further insurance a bit of baking powder.

YOU WILL NEED:
flour   salad oil
eggs   baking powder (optional)
milk

Beat 2 eggs until light. Add 1 cup milk, 1 tablespoon salad oil (not olive oil). Beat together with a rotary egg beater. Add 7/8 cup all-purpose flour. Sifting is not necessary but if you wish to sift the flour then use 1 cup flour measured after sifting. The reason for the difference is quite obvious for sifting aerate flour, makes it less bulky. With the flour add 1/4 teaspoon salt, 1/4 teaspoon baking powder, if you have it. Beat until smooth with the egg beater. The mixture should be heavy as whipping cream. If too thick, add a little more milk.

Heavy iron muffin pans are generally used for popovers but they are not necessary. You may use aluminum pans if you wish, or oven-proof custard cups. Grease thoroughly bottom and sides. Fill 1/2 full with mixture. Have the oven preheated to at least 500° F. When the popovers have popped, that is in about 15 minutes, turn down the oven to 400° F. and continue baking 10 to 15 minutes longer or until done. The crust should sound crackly-crisp when tapped with your finger nail, the inside staying pleasantly moist—almost doughy but not wet. To be really sure you must break one open.

AT SERVING TIME:

Serve hot with plenty of butter for breakfast with jam, honey, or preserves, with a luncheon salad, or a hearty supper soup. Makes 8 popovers.

VARIATION: Yorkshire Pudding

Use the popover batter, or popover mix but bake in a 10-inch pan in which there must be fat—1/4 inch deep hot beef drippings, bacon or sausage fat will do. Yorkshire pudding is best baked in a dish which can be brought to the table right from the oven. Cut in squares and serve with roast beef and gravy. By serving Yorkshire pudding you can transform sliced delicatessen beef and a can of beef gravy into an old-fashioned roast beef dinner.

Quick Sally Lunns

Who was Sally—where she lived—or how her name happened to be given to this popular Southern tea bread, we have never discovered. Sally appears in many guises, in different regions of the country. Risen Sally Lunn is made from a yeast dough but Quick Sally is made with baking powder.

YOU WILL NEED:

biscuit mix	eggs
sugar	milk
butter	

To 2 cups biscuit mix add 3/4 cup milk, 3 eggs well beaten, 1/4 cup sugar, and 2 tablespoons melted butter. Pour batter into well-greased muffin tins and bake in a hot oven, 400° F., about 15 minutes.

AT SERVING TIME:

The old recipes say "run with Sally Lunn to the table" for this tea bread must be served so hot that the butter melts into the feathery bread instantly. Makes 12 Sally Lunns.

VARIATION: Angel Sally

Sally Lunn is often baked in an angel-cake pan or a ring mold. The pans should be well greased with butter and the cake baked at 350° F. about 40 minutes.

Quick-Frozen Waffles

The ultimate in speed and ease is the quick-frozen waffle which makes a waffle iron unnecessary. They may be heated in a toaster, under the broiler or in a hot oven. Although many brands are well made these waffles are not usually as tender as home-baked. For this reason it is a good idea to pour over them immediately a combination of butter and honey or syrup mixed together.

YOU WILL NEED:

quick-frozen waffles	cinnamon, nutmeg, or all-
butter or margarine	spice (optional)
maple syrup or honey	

Heat according to package directions. It is not necessary to thaw beforehand.

AT SERVING TIME:

Serve hot on heated plates and pour on immediately equal parts butter or margarine and maple syrup or honey. A dash of cinnamon, nutmeg, or allspice may be added to the syrup mixture if desired.

Nut Waffles

YOU WILL NEED:

quick-frozen waffles	honey or syrup
butter or margarine	pecans, almonds, or walnuts

Brush quick-frozen waffles with melted butter or margarine. Sprinkle with coarsely chopped toasted pecans, almonds or walnuts. Set in a hot oven just long enough to heat thoroughly.

AT SERVING TIME:

Serve hot with honey or syrup or with whipped cream or vanilla ice cream as a dessert.

Wonders or Doughboys

YOU WILL NEED:

hot roll, or bread mix   vegetable shortening or lard

Make up dough and allow to rise according to package directions for plain bread or rolls. Form dough into small balls about the size of a golf ball, or if you prefer, roll out dough 1/8 inch thick. Cut into strips and then into 2-inch squares or diamonds. Cover and let stand 10 or 15 minutes. Fry like doughnuts, dropping into deep hot fat, 375° F. (hot enough to brown an inch cube of bread in 40 seconds). Drain on paper towels.

AT SERVING TIME:

Serve hot as a bread, particularly with a hearty vegetable soup. Or shake in a paper bag with 1/2 cup sugar, 1 tablespoon cinnamon and serve with coffee or tea in the afternoon.

❧ 14 ❧

~~~~~~~~~~~~~~~~~~~~~~~~~~~~~~~~~~~~

Cakes, Pies, and Cookies

WITHOUT FUSS

Mixes make child's play of baking. But one thing is certain, you must follow to the letter the directions on the package. Then, and only then, will you have perfect cakes, pies, cookies, and cupcakes—with a minimum of time, effort, and expense. Curiously enough, the novice often has better luck with mixes than the experienced baker, probably because she is less likely to improvise or use older and unsuitable methods.

Here are a few warnings and suggestions that will make baking with mixes easier, faster, surer—and more fun.

Do not sift any kind of mix. It is not necessary, for all ingredients have already been thoroughly combined in the manufacturing.

Do not undermix or overmix. If you have a hand beater, count your strokes. If you use an electric mixer, watch the second hand of your clock or use an egg timer.

All you need is paper to prepare your pans when baking a cake. Almost any kind of paper will do—waxed, brown, or plain white. No greasing is necessary. Cut a circle a little smaller than the bottom of the pan and be certain that the paper does not touch the edge of the pan or the cake will crack. For most cakes all that is needed is a small square of paper in the center of the pan. This is a good trick to remember when you're in a hurry.

Although there is some disagreement even among the experts about the necessity of preheating the oven, you are always on the safe side if you do light the oven about 10 minutes beforehand. An oven thermometer is almost a necessity, but if you have none, or if yours is untrustworthy look in the glossary for old-fashioned ways in which to judge the heat of the oven. Opening the oven door lowers the oven temperature, so do this as little as possible.

Do not overbake either cakes, cookies, or pastries made from mixes. For the perfect cake, leave it in the oven the minimum time suggested on the package or maybe a few minutes less. If the cake shows just a sign of pulling away from the sides of the pan, it is done. Or place your finger lightly on the cake. If it makes no depression, the cake is done. Or insert a wire cake tester or a clean broom straw. If it comes out clean, the cake is done.

What you do to your cake after you take it from the oven is most important. Set the cake—pan and all—on a wire rack to cool for 5 to 10 minutes. The wire rack allows the air to get under the cake as well as around it. Loosen the cake around edges. Turn upside down and peel off the paper carefully. Then turn right side up again on the rack to finish cooling. If a topping is to be baked on, place topping on hot cake. For a boiled or 4-minute frosting, cool cake about 30 minutes before frosting. Buttery frostings should be put on the cake when it is thoroughly cool so that the heat of the cake will not melt the frosting.

A package of cake mix generally makes 2 8-inch layers. For a small half-size cake use half a package of mix. Mix in a small mixing bowl with half the amount of milk called for on the package. Beating and baking times remain the same.

Unless you are very sure of yourself and have had a great deal of experience not only in baking but in baking with mixes, it is wisest not to improvise too much on the basic ingredients: Do not add eggs unless your particular cake mix calls for them; do not use water instead of milk; do not vary the amounts of liquid. There are, however, a number of flavoring and glamorizing tricks that you can safely use. One to 3 teaspoons grated orange rind may be used. Buttermilk may be substituted for sweet milk in devil's food or chocolate cake mix. One-fourth to 1/2 teaspoon of extract (orange, lemon, almond, or peppermint) may be added to white or yellow cake. For pistachio flavor use half and half vanilla and almond extracts. When spices are added, it is best not to use more than a teaspoon in all. Chopped nuts and/or chopped fruits are good in ginger bread, devil's food, chocolate, or spice cake mix, but be careful about adding too much of them to a white cake batter or they will sink to the bottom because this batter is usually thinner.

RECIPES

Angel Cake à la Glace
Applesauce Cake
Cherry Upside-Down Cake
Pineapple, Apricot, Peach, Loganberry Upside-Down Cake
Chocolate Praline Cake
Gateau au Citron
Tropical Coconut Cake with Orange Coconut Frosting
Election Cake
Lady Baltimore Cake
Miracle Fruit Cake
Ring Cake for Anniversaries
Fluffy Uncooked Frosting

Pink Peppermint Frosting
Pistachio Frosting
Orange Frosting
Quick Fudge Frosting
Devonshire Cream Tarts
Glazed Strawberry Tarts
Miracle Macaroons
Old-Fashioned Sour Cream Cookies
Crumb Pie Shell
Crumb Tart Shells
Apple Pie with Cheese
Lemon Meringue Pie
Lord Marlborough Pie

Angel Cake à la Glace

A bought or mix-made angel cake has many glamorous possibilities. Here it is combined with ice cream.

YOU WILL NEED:

bought angel cake
vanilla ice cream

shredded coconut or
chopped nuts
chocolate sauce

Fill the center of an angel cake with 1 pint vanilla ice cream. Sprinkle over both the cake and ice cream either shredded coconut or chopped nuts. Have on hand a can of prepared chocolate sauce to which may be added additional flavoring: To 1 cup of sauce add 1 tablespoon undiluted concentrated quick-frozen orange juice or 1 tablespoon Grand Marnier liqueur.

AT SERVING TIME:

Serve immediately so that the ice cream cannot melt and soak into the cake. Pass sauce separately. Sauce may be either hot or cold.

Applesauce Cake

A spice cake mix and canned applesauce make a quick modern version of this wonderful old-fashioned cake which can also be served warm as a pudding.

YOU WILL NEED:

spice cake mix
baking soda
powdered cloves
ready-whipped cream or
sweetened sour cream

canned unsweetened apple-
sauce
raisins and/or nuts
butter
flour

Make up a package of spice cake mix according to the package recipe. Add 1/2 teaspoon baking soda, 1/4 teaspoon powdered cloves, 1 cup unsweetened applesauce, 1 cup raisins and/or nuts, cut into small pieces. Bake in 2 buttered and floured rectangular pans like bread pans. Baking time is slightly longer than cake without applesauce—about 40 minutes in a moderate oven, 350° F., or until done.

AT SERVING TIME:

Cut into slices about 1/2 inch thick. Serve cold or, if desired, cut in squares and serve warm with ready-whipped cream or slightly sweetened sour cream.

Cherry Upside-Down Cake

YOU WILL NEED:

canned pitted red sour cherries	butter or margarine
white cake mix	brown sugar
	almond extract (optional)

Drain syrup from a No. 2 can of pitted red sour cherries and save for sauce. Melt 4 tablespoons butter or margarine in a heavy frying pan or a cake pan and add 1/2 cup brown sugar. Place cherries in the pan close together. Pour on batter made from a package of white cake mix. Bake at 350° F. about 25 minutes. Cool cake 5 minutes. Invert the pan on a plate and let stand 1 minute before removing pan.

AT SERVING TIME:

At the table cut into squares and pass separately a sauce made by cooking the syrup down to half the original quantity. A bit of almond extract may be added to the syrup if desired.

VARIATION: Pineapple, Apricot, Peach, Loganberry Upside-Down Cake

Any of the above fruits either canned or quick-frozen may be used instead of cherries. They should be well drained. Pecans may be placed on top of the butter-sugar mixture before the fruit is added.

Chocolate Praline Cake

YOU WILL NEED:

chocolate cake mix	light cream
brown sugar	vanilla
butter	coconut

Bake a chocolate cake from a mix in a square or loaf pan.

Praline Frosting

While the cake is still hot, spread over the top the following mixture: 1/3 cup butter melted, 1/2 cup dark brown sugar, 4 tablespoons light cream, a dash of salt, 1/2 teaspoon vanilla, 1 cup shredded coconut. Place under broiler about 5 minutes or until golden brown and bubbly—or bake in a moderate oven, 350° F., about 10 minutes.

AT SERVING TIME:
Cake may be served warm in squares directly from the baking pan, or cold, taken from the pan and served in slices with vanilla ice cream on the side.

Gateau au Citron

YOU WILL NEED:

spice or chocolate cake mix
walnuts or other nut meats

citron peel or mixed candied fruits and peels

Make up a package of chocolate or spice cake mix according to directions. Fold into the batter 1/2 cup diced candied citron peel or mixed candied fruits and peels, and 1/2 cup chopped walnuts or other nut meats. Bake according to package directions, preferably in a long narrow pan.

AT SERVING TIME:
Turn out on a platter. Dust lightly with confectioners' sugar and decorate with nut meats and candied cherries.

Tropical Coconut Cake with Orange Coconut Frosting

YOU WILL NEED:

angel food cake
confectioners' sugar
lemon juice

orange juice
orange coloring
shredded coconut

Buy an angel food cake and spread with orange coconut frosting made without cooking.

Orange Coconut Frosting

Combine 3 cups sifted confectioners' sugar with a dash of salt, 1 tablespoon lemon juice, and enough orange juice to give a spreading consistency, about 3 to 4 tablespoons. Tint delicately with 3 drops orange coloring. Frost top and sides of cake and sprinkle thickly with 1 1/2 cups shredded coconut while frosting is still soft. The moist southern-style coconut, which is packed in tins, is particularly good.

AT SERVING TIME:

This is most delicious when served together with orange sherbet. Cut cake at the table and pass the bowl of sherbet separately.

Election Cake

According to the Browns, learned commentators on culinary matters, the Connecticut Election Cake has always been dedicated to the feasting of both winners and losers. The recipe for this cake was invariably found "sandwiched between household accounts and directions for cough cures in old farm wives' note books." The cake is found under various names and with many different ingredients in many of the 48 states. Sometimes the recipe "was recognizable only by the fact that it was raised with yeast and had fruit in it." Here is an unorthodox version, prepared from a package of hot roll mix.

YOU WILL NEED:

hot roll mix	brandy or rum
white frosting mix	cinnamon
lemon	nutmeg or mace
seedless raisins	

Make up a package of hot roll mix according to package recipe for coffee cake. *But* for 1/2 cup of the liquid substitute 1/2 cup brandy or rum. Add to batter 1 teaspoon lemon juice, 1 teaspoon grated lemon rind, 1 teaspoon cinnamon, 1/2 teaspoon nutmeg or mace. When dough has risen to double its bulk, punch it down, and add 1 cup seedless raisins. Bake in greased bread tins according to package directions. When cold cover with white frosting made from a mix.

AT SERVING TIME:

Slice as you would bread and serve with coffee. In the old days this cake always ended the veal dinner, which was as essential to Election Day as turkey and pie for Thanksgiving.

Lady Baltimore Cake

One of the great glories of the table in Maryland and other parts of the South has been the Lady Baltimore cake. A facsimile of this cake can be made from a package of white cake mix and the Fluffy Uncooked Frosting. Since Lady Baltimore has always been a queenly cake in size as well as delicacy, we suggest using 2 packages of white cake mix.

YOU WILL NEED:

white cake mix	almond extract
Fluffy Uncooked Frosting	pecans
(page 213)	figs
rose flavoring (optional)	seeded raisins

Make up 2 packages white cake mix according to directions. Add 1/2 teaspoon almond extract or 1 teaspoon rose flavoring. Bake in 3 8-inch round layer pans in a moderate oven, 375° F., 25 to 30 minutes or until done. Put together with Lady Baltimore Filling and top with Lady Baltimore Frosting.

Lady Baltimore Frosting and Filling

Double the recipe for Fluffy Uncooked Frosting. Save half the frosting for the top and sides of the cake and to the other half add 1/2 cup chopped pecan nuts, 3 dried figs cut into thin strips, 1/2 cup seeded raisins cut up, 1/2 teaspoon almond extract.

AT SERVING TIME:

This is a large cake which deserves your prettiest plate or platter and a garland of fresh blossoms and green leaves.

Miracle Fruit Cake

YOU WILL NEED:

spice cake mix
pitted dates
ready-to-use candied fruits
and peels
nut meats

baking soda
seedless raisins
sherry, rum, or brandy (optional)
egg white

Make up a package of spice cake mix according to package directions adding 1/2 teaspoon baking soda. If desired, up to 1/4 tablespoon sherry, rum, or brandy may be substituted for an equal
quantity of liquid.

Combine 1 cup sliced pitted dates with 3/4 cup seedless raisins,
1 cup ready-to-use diced candied fruits and peels.

Line a casserole with greased heavy waxed paper. Put in a layer
of batter. Sprinkle with a layer of fruit, then with batter, alter-
nating fruit and batter till dish is 3/4 full. The last layer should
be batter. Bake in a slow oven, 375° F., about 1 hour or until done.
Decorate as follows: 15 minutes before the cake is done brush with
a slightly beaten egg white; quickly arrange on the cake in a pattern bits of candied fruit, maraschino cherries, and/or chopped
nuts. Return to the oven. Finish baking.

AT SERVING TIME:

A fruit cake may be brought to the table and served as well as
stored in its own casserole. For a gala appearance, pin a napkin
around the casserole and decorate with a spray of leaves. To serve
fruit cake flambé, slightly warm 1/4 cup brandy or rum, set ablaze
and pour over the fruit cake. If possible, serve a little flame on each
slice. If you store your fruit cake, pour a little brandy over it from
time to time to keep it moist. Keep tightly covered in a cool place.

Ring Cake for Anniversaries

For a wedding anniversary nothing could be prettier than a white
cake baked in a ring mold topped with a "golden frosting" and
served with flaming brandy set in a cup inside the ring.

YOU WILL NEED:

white cake mix   Orange Frosting (page 214)
almond extract   orange (optional)

Make up a package of white cake mix according to directions but add 1/4 teaspoon almond extract and 1 to 3 teaspoons grated orange rind. Bake according to recipe on package.

When cake is cool, frost with Orange Frosting.

AT SERVING TIME:

Set on an attractive plate. Decorate with rose leaves or huckleberry leaves, if desired. Set inside the ring a heat-proof glass custard cup. When the Moment arrives, turn down the lights. Pour into the cup some slightly warmed rum or brandy. Set it ablaze with a match. Add a bit of the warmed liquor to each slice.

Fluffy Uncooked Frosting

This frosting has the look and flavor of real old-fashioned boiled frosting but there is no cooking involved—only a few minutes of beating.

YOU WILL NEED:

egg white   sugar
cream of tartar   vanilla

Combine 1 unbeaten egg white with 3/4 cup sugar, 1/4 teaspoon cream of tartar, and 1 teaspoon vanilla in a small deep bowl and mix well. Add 1/4 cup boiling water and beat with a rotary egg beater or at the high speed of an electric mixer until the frosting will stand in stiff little peaks. This should take about 4 minutes. Makes 3 cups of frosting—enough to cover the top and sides of 2 8-inch layers. A cake with this frosting should be kept uncovered at room temperature. Don't put it in the refrigerator.

VARIATION:

Pink Peppermint Frosting

Use above recipe substituting for the vanilla 1/4 teaspoon peppermint extract. Add a few drops of red pure-food coloring to tint delicately. Especially delicious on devil's food cake.

Pistachio Frosting

Use above recipe and decrease the vanilla to 1/2 teaspoon. Add 1/4 teaspoon almond extract. If desired, tint a delicate green with pure-food coloring and garnish with pistachio nuts.

Orange Frosting

Use the above recipe but substitute for the boiling water 1/4 cup heated canned orange juice. Omit vanilla.

Quick Fudge Frosting

Several frosting mixes are on the market. To most of these nothing but water and butter need be added. Variations in flavor may be achieved by substituting for part of the water, a little rum, sherry, brandy, or orange juice. Sweetened condensed milk makes an excellent quick fudge frosting if you should find yourself without a mix on hand:

YOU WILL NEED:
    unsweetened cooking choc-   vanilla and/or almond ex-
      olate   tract
    sweetened condensed milk

Put 2 squares of unsweetened cooking chocolate into the top of a double boiler along with 1 can sweetened condensed milk. Stir until melted. Add 1 teaspoon vanilla and a few grains of salt or 1/2 teaspoon vanilla and 1/2 teaspoon almond extract. Then, little by little, add about a tablespoon of hot water, just enough to make the frosting thin enough to spread.

Be sure that cake or cupcakes are cool. Brush off loose crumbs. To frost a layer cake, place a little frosting on the bottom layer, spreading it almost to the edge. Set second layer on top, centering it evenly. Then smooth the frosting on outside of cake in sweeping strokes over top edge and down sides. Pile remaining frosting on top, spreading lightly to edges. If you have any difficulty, dip your knife into warm water.

Devonshire Cream Tarts

YOU WILL NEED:

Crumb Tart Shells (page 217)
sour cream
rum (optional)

creamed cottage cheese
sugar
cinnamon

Add to a cup of creamed cottage cheese, 1/2 cup thick sour cream, 2 tablespoons sugar, and 1 tablespoon rum, if desired. Place mixture in 6 or 8 tart shells, or a baked or cracker-crumb pie shell. Cover with drained sliced quick-frozen peaches or halved apricots.

AT SERVING TIME:

Garnish with slightly sweetened thick sour cream and dust lightly with cinnamon. Serves 6 or 8.

Glazed Strawberry Tarts

Many bakeshops will, if you ask them, make up for you either puff paste or piecrust shells for tarts. In some specialty food shops you can buy already baked tart shells. For this delicious dessert and many others your own cracker-crumb crust, may be used. The rest is wonderfully easy. You will note that a professional-looking glaze is given to the fruit by the simple expedient of melting bought currant jelly.

YOU WILL NEED:

tart shells
strawberries

ready-whipped cream
currant jelly

Into the bottom of 6 small or 4 large tart shells place a tablespoon of ready-whipped cream. On top of the cream, arrange large fresh or drained whole quick-frozen strawberries. Melt gently over a very low heat, 1/2 cup currant jelly and pour carefully over the berries. Chill.

AT SERVING TIME:

Arrange tarts on a serving plate. Garnish with green leaves. A pint of fresh strawberries or a 12-ounce package of quick-frozen strawberries will make 6 tarts.

Miracle Coconut Macaroons

YOU WILL NEED:
flake coconut	sugar
egg	almond extract

Combine 1 1/2 cups packaged flake coconut with 1/2 cup sugar. Mix well. Add 1 well-beaten egg and 1 teaspoon almond extract. Let stand about 5 minutes so that the ingredients will stick together. Drop by teaspoons on a greased cooky sheet and bake in a moderate oven, 350° F., about 15 minutes.

AT SERVING TIME:
Serve warm or cold with fruit or ice cream. Delightful when used to top a pudding such as Viennese Chocolate Mousse. Makes 1 dozen macaroons.

Old-Fashioned Sour Cream Cookies

There are special cooky mixes on the market but one may also use almost any of the packaged cake mixes. Recipes for baking cookies from cake mixes will be found on most packages.

YOU WILL NEED:
cooky or white cake mix	sour cream or buttermilk

Use cooky or white cake mix. Follow recipe for drop cookies but substitute sour cream or buttermilk for the liquid required. Drop from teaspoon onto greased cooky sheet. Bake in a moderate oven, 375° F., 10 or 12 minutes or until delicately browned around the edges.

AT SERVING TIME:
Since these cookies are not very rich they are infinitely better when served fresh—right out of the oven whenever possible. From the average package of cooky or cake mix you should get about 2 dozen cookies.

Crumb Pie Shell

Packaged bread crumbs or finely crushed graham crackers, ginger snaps, or zwiebacks may be used to make Crumb Pie Shell. To an inexperienced cook or one who does not care to bother about pastry, this type of crust is most useful.

YOU WILL NEED:

fine crumbs   butter or margarine
sugar

To 1 1/2 cups crumbs, add 1/4 cup sugar, 1/2 cup melted butter or margarine. Save 1/2 cup of this mixture and use the rest to line a 9-inch piepan, patting it firmly against the bottom and the sides with the back of a spoon. Better still, do it with your fingers. Chill until firm in the refrigerator, or bake 8 minutes at 375° F. and then chill until you want to use it.

AT SERVING TIME:

Fill with mixture for whipped cream pie: cover the bottom with whipped cream and top with drained canned sweetened fruit, drained quick-frozen fruit, or fresh fruit. Sprinkle with reserved crumbs.

VARIATION: Crumb Tart Shells

Instead of using a piepan, line custard cups with crumbs, and firmly press them in. Bake or chill as above and use as the shell for any kind of tarts.

Apple Pie with Cheese

This is no place for a discussion of the immemorial rites and "rights" of making a proper American apple pie. Not only the great Henry Ward Beecher but many others have recorded their views on this topic. However, as an example of how tradition may work hand in hand with modern convenience, we suggest this recipe:

YOU WILL NEED:

apple pie   butter or margarine
American cheese   nutmeg

Buy the best apple pie you can find. Brush the top lightly with
melted butter or margarine. Slice American cheese or buy the
sliced variety. Cut the slices into strips about an inch wide and arrange on top of the pie like spokes of a wheel or in a lattice pattern. Sprinkle lightly with grated nutmeg, and set in a moderate
oven, 350° F., about 10 minutes, or until the pie is warm and the
cheese soft and lightly browned.

AT SERVING TIME:

The pie should be brought warm to the table and served with large
cups of coffee.

Lemon Meringue Pie

YOU WILL NEED:

lemon pie filling mix   cream of tartar
egg whites   sugar
piecrust mix or Crumb Pie   butter
   Shell (page 217)

Make up pie filling according to package directions but for extra
flavor stir into the filling, just after you take it off the stove, a tablespoon of butter. Mix well, turn into a baked 8-inch pie shell,
made from prepared mix or use a crumb crust. To make the meringue, beat until frothy 2 egg whites, 1/8 teaspoon salt, 1/4 teaspoon cream of tartar. Then gradually add 4 tablespoons of sugar,
a little at a time, beating constantly. Continue beating until the
meringue is stiff. Top the pie filling with the meringue and bake
in a hot oven, 400° F., 8 to 10 minutes.

AT SERVING TIME:

If pie is baked in an attractive piepan, or one which can be set into
a basket, it's a good idea not to try to remove it from the pan because there is always the danger of breaking the pie. Pie will cut
better and look more attractive if it is allowed to chill thoroughly
before you try to cut it.

Lord Marlborough Pie

YOU WILL NEED:

Crumb Pie Shell (page 217)　　canned cubed apples
apple jelly　　　　　　　　　　port wine or brandy (op-
custard pudding mix　　　　　　　tional)

Prepare custard pudding from a mix according to package directions. Cool slightly until custard is firm—about 15 minutes, stirring occasionally to keep smooth. Pour into 8-inch pie shell. Cover
with canned well-drained cubed and ready-cooked apples (called
pommettes). Sprinkle apples with 1 or 2 tablespoons port wine or
brandy. Melt 1/2 cup apple or crab apple jelly and when melted
spoon carefully over the apples. Chill immediately.

~~~~~~

Desserts

PUDDINGS AND PUDDING SAUCES,

Soufflés, Frozen Desserts

A DRESSED-UP DESSERT goes a long way toward transforming a quick and simple meal into an occasion. Such desserts need not be fattening and, with all the help available at the grocery store and bakeshop, even elaborate desserts are quick and easy.

On grocers' shelves today are dozens of mixes for puddings, pie fillings, ice creams, and sherbets; there are a multitude of canned and quick-frozen fruits, cakes, and cookies, ready-to-eat ice cream often in convenient storable cartons that fit into your ice trays, dessert sauces, ready-whipped and sweetened cream as well as a low calorie, high protein, quick-frozen topping, which looks and tastes quite a lot like whipped cream and is perfect for the calorie-counter.

One that is particularly useful is a custard flavor dessert mix. It contains no eggs, cooks in about 7 minutes, looks and tastes remarkably like old-fashioned baked custard. Many contain some arrowroot for finer texture and to prevent lumping. In addition to the usual flavors—vanilla, butterscotch, and chocolate—there is also a caramel. Several pie fillings are equally fine for puddings: These include lemon, coconut, orange, and coconut-cream.

Instant pudding mixes are prepared with starch cooked under pressure at high temperatures. They make a finished pudding in only 30 seconds—need no cooking whatsoever and are merely beaten with cold milk. By increasing the amount of milk—using 1 1/2 times as much as the recipe calls for—you can make creamy sauces for instant, as well as regular, pudding mixes. Since most of the puddings are on the sweet side it is usually unnecessary to add extra sugar, but do add plenty of pure, nonsynthetic flavor.

Almost all the dessert mixes have one drawback in common— artificial flavoring. In the recipes that follow, this taste of synthetic vanillin is generally masked by the addition of pure extract, spices, wine, brandy, or rum.

Always follow exactly the directions on the package. You will be admonished to stir the pudding constantly. Do it faithfully and keep stirring for about half a minute after the custard or pudding is removed from the fire. Allow cooked puddings to cool at room temperature for a few minutes before placing them in the re- frigerator. Sudden changes from hot to cold may cause them to become watery.

RECIPES

Apple Pan Dowdy
Apple Snow with Cinnamon Sauce
Baked Alaska (Baked Ice Cream)
Baked Alaska Flambé
Baked Alaska Surprises
Light Blancmange
Butterscotch Blancmange
Mocha Blancmange
Cheese Blintzes
Cheese Blintzes with Cherry Preserves
Raspberry Bombe
Carolina Trifle
Chocolate Ice Cream Roll
Christmas Wreath Pudding Flambé
Coeur à la Crème
Coffee-Rum Jelly
Quick Crème Caramel
Cup Custard Caramel
Easy Crêpes Suzette
Italian Monte Bianco
Lemon Ice-Box Cake
Viennese Chocolate Mousse
Orange Omelet au Rhum
Pears with Eggnog Sauce
Glamorous Rice Pudding
Sfinge (St. Joseph's Cream Puffs)
Miracle Chocolate Soufflé
Berries Jubilee with Ice Cream
Raspberries Jubilee
Strawberries Romanoff
Tipsy Parson

Apple Pan Dowdy

In this version of the old-time apple pan dowdy, three short-cut foods are combined.

YOU WILL NEED:

canned sliced apples
white cake mix
whipped cream or ready-
   whipped cream

nutmeg
cinnamon
butter
molasses or brown sugar

In the bottom of a buttered baking dish, arrange 2 cups canned apple slices drained. Sprinkle with 1/4 cup molasses or brown sugar and 1/4 teaspoon each nutmeg, cinnamon, and salt.

Make up a package of white cake mix according to directions. Pour batter over apples. Bake in a moderate oven, 350° F., 20 to 25 minutes or until cake is done.

AT SERVING TIME:

Bring to the table in its own baking dish. Cut into squares and serve with sweetened whipped cream or ready-whipped cream. Serves 6.

Apple Snow with Cinnamon Sauce

An old-fashioned pudding, an old-fashioned sauce—both made without *any* cooking.

YOU WILL NEED:

canned applesauce
egg whites
lemon juice (optional)

instant pudding mix
cinnamon
milk

Beat 3 egg whites until stiff enough to stand in peaks after the beater is withdrawn. Fold in 2 cups canned applesauce. Flavor with 2 tablespoons lemon juice—a little more if you think it is needed. A drop or two of green pure-food coloring may be added, if desired. The applesauce should be very, very cold and so should the sauce.

Cinnamon Sauce

Make up a package of instant pudding mix—the kind that requires only beating, no cooking. Follow the package directions but increase the amount of milk by 1 cup and add 3/4 teaspoon cinnamon—enough to give the sauce a spicy flavor.

AT SERVING TIME:

Serve within a half hour after making the pudding. It is prettiest when piled in the center of a shallow glass or china serving bowl with the sauce poured around the edge and additional sauce passed in a pitcher or bowl. Serves 6.

Baked Alaska (Baked Ice Cream)

Formerly Baked Alaska was a dessert never attempted by the home cook but left to the restaurant—and the fancy restaurant chef. Today, with cake and ice cream, and even a meringue mix available, it is no trick to make. Remember only one thing—ice cream that goes into the oven must be carefully and completely insulated.

YOU WILL NEED:

    sponge cake   ice cream
        packaged meringue mix or egg whites, cream of
        tartar (optional), and confectioners' sugar

The trick is to protect the ice cream from the oven heat. This is done by means of a board, paper, and most important of all a thick layer of meringue. Cover a small board with brown paper cut to fit. On top of the paper place a layer of cake. Set 1 quart ice cream, which must be very hard frozen, on top of the cake. Cover cake and ice cream *completely* with a meringue made from a packaged mix, or make your own meringue of 6 stiffly beaten egg whites to which has been added 6 flat tablespoons confectioners' sugar and, if you have it, 1/4 teaspoon cream of tartar. *There must be no holes in the meringue.* Bake in a hot oven, 400° F., 4 or 5 minutes just long enough for the meringue to take on a golden tinge around the peaks.

AT SERVING TIME:

Lift the board onto a platter and hide the edges of the board with a garland of green leaves. Slice about an inch thick. Serves 8.

VARIATION:

Baked Alaska Flambé

This is the ultimate in blaze-of-glory desserts and not at all difficult. Proceed as above but before setting the meringue in the oven arrange in it like little cups 4 or 6 unbroken eggshell halves.

Fill each eggshell with slightly warmed rum, kirsch, or brandy. Set fire to the liquor and bring flaming to the table.

Baked Alaska Surprises

Prepare like large baked Alaska but instead of 1 layer of cake use 6 small thin rounds. Top with a scoop of ice cream. Make a hollow in the top of the ice cream and fill with cherry or strawberry preserve. Top with meringue and set in a hot oven 3 to 4 minutes. Watch carefully. Serve immediately.

Light Blancmange

The cookbooks of long ago called for "clarified isinglass" or "Irish moss" for the making of this pudding. Today we put it together with vanilla pudding mix.

YOU WILL NEED:

vanilla pudding mix	egg whites (optional)
milk	lemon
sherry or Madeira (optional)	canned peaches or apricots

Make up a package of vanilla pudding mix according to directions but use only 1 3/4 cups milk. Remove from the stove. Add 1/4 cup Madeira or sherry, 1 tablespoon grated lemon rind. Fold in stiffly beaten whites of 2 eggs for a very light and delicate pudding. Pour into a mold that has been previously rinsed in cold water. Chill several hours.

AT SERVING TIME:

Turn out on a plate or tray. Decorate with canned drained sliced peaches or apricots.

VARIATION:

Butterscotch Blancmange

Use butterscotch pudding mix and instead of lemon rind use grated orange rind.

Mocha Blancmange

Use chocolate pudding mix and add to the milk 2 teaspoons instant coffee. Decorate the mold with whipped cream instead of fruit.

Cheese Blintzes

There are as many recipes for cheese blintzes as there are for a true and proper fruit cake. Quick-frozen cheese blintzes taste very good, and may be stepped up with little effort.

YOU WILL NEED:

quick-frozen cheese blintzes	honey
sour cream	lemon and/or almond extract

Heat cheese blintzes according to package directions in the oven or on top of the stove.

AT SERVING TIME:

Serve on heated plate with a strip of thick sour cream down the center of the blintzes. Sweeten the cream slightly with honey and season it with grated lemon peel and/or a dash of almond extract.

VARIATION: Cheese Blintzes with Cherry Preserves

Instead of sour cream, or along with the cream, pass whole sour cherry preserves or cherry jam, with or without a scatter of chopped almonds.

Raspberry Bombe

In this day of frozen-food cabinets one needs no caterer to achieve that elegant combination called the "bombe." All that is needed is a mold, and some ice cream and sherbet, whether bought or made from a mix.

YOU WILL NEED:

sherbet	ice cream
sweet butter	brandy or kirsch (optional)

Lightly grease a mold with sweet butter. Then with a spoon, press into the mold and all around the crevices a thick layer of raspberry sherbet made according to package directions from a sherbet mix —or bought. Fill the center of the mold with ice cream—pistachio is particularly pretty if you are using raspberry sherbet. Set in the freezing compartment of your refrigerator for several hours. The bombe should be very hard frozen.

AT SERVING TIME:

Unmold on a chilled tray or serving dish. If you wish you may serve the bombe flambé. Pour 1/4 to 1/2 cup slightly warmed brandy or kirsch around the edge of the platter. Set ablaze and serve each portion with liqueur spooned over the ice cream. Since most mixes for ice cream and sherbet make about a pint, the combination of the two will fill a quart mold and should serve 6 to 8.

Carolina Trifle

There is no set recipe for this famous English dish. Much depends on the resources of the household at the moment.

YOU WILL NEED:

lady fingers or sponge cake	custard or vanilla pudding
jam	mix
sherry, Madeira, or port	whipped cream
almonds	egg whites
lemon (optional)	cinnamon
candied cherries, kumquats, or jelly	

Split lady fingers or use thin small slices of sponge cake. Spread with jam and arrange in the bottom of a glass bowl. Sprinkle with sherry (Madeira or port may be used). Then add 3 or 4 tablespoons canned shredded almonds and 1 tablespoon grated lemon peel if desired. Over all pour custard made according to package directions from custard-flavored mix or vanilla pudding mix. Let stand in the refrigerator several hours, or better still, overnight.

AT SERVING TIME:
Garnish with 1 cup sweetened whipped cream or ready-whipped cream to which has been added 1 stiffly beaten egg white, 1/4 teaspoon cinnamon. Garnish with candied cherries, drained preserved kumquats, or bits of bright jelly or preserves. Serves 8 to 10.

Chocolate Ice Cream Roll

A delicious chocolate ice cream roll is available in the frozen-food bins of even the least pretentious stores and delicatessens. Serve with a dressed-up prepared chocolate sauce—no one could ask for a finer dessert.

YOU WILL NEED:

quick-frozen chocolate ice cream roll	prepared chocolate sauce sherry and/or brandy nuts

The chocolate roll itself needs no preparation. Just place it on an attractive dish, preferably one deep enough for the sauce to be poured around it. For sauce—heat gently in the top of a double boiler, 1 cup prepared chocolate sauce with 1 tablespoon sherry or 1/2 tablespoon sherry and 1/2 tablespoon brandy.

AT SERVING TIME:
Sprinkle slivered canned almonds or other chopped nuts over the roll. Pistachio nuts are particularly attractive. Slice at the table. Additional sauce may be passed in a small pitcher or bowl. For a larger group set two or more rolls end to end and cover the separation with a piping of ready-whipped cream.

Christmas Wreath Pudding Flambé

Far more beautiful than a pudding for a holiday meal is a fruit cake heated in the top of a double boiler until fragrant and steamy, then served afire. This idea dates back many centuries to the days when Christmas and New Year's fruit cakes were "censed" for luck. Most effective for this purpose are the fruit cakes which are baked in a ring mold. There are several good brands.

YOU WILL NEED:

fruit cake
candied citron or maraschino cherries

brandy or rum

Steam fruit cake in top of a double boiler or in a covered pan set over hot water until thoroughly heated.

AT SERVING TIME:

Place on a heated platter or tray. Arrange around the edge strips of candied citron and maraschino cherries to form a berried wreath. In the inner circle of the ring, place a small custard cup or crock with 1/4 cup slightly warmed brandy or rum. Set the brandy ablaze and bring flaming to the table. Serve in slices with a bit of the burning brandy spooned over the portions. Pass separately hard sauce which can be bought in jars and is much better if slightly thinned with a little added rum, brandy, or fruit juice.

Coeur à La Crème

This is one of the classic desserts of spring in France. The original method requires something like a gallon of whole unpasteurized milk and a good many hours of souring and draining. Our reasonable facsimile is made from ordinary cream cheese.

YOU WILL NEED:

cream cheese
salt
light cream

confectioners' sugar (optional)
strawberries, raspberries, or preserves

To a 3-ounce package of cream cheese, add 2 tablespoons light cream, just enough to give the cheese a thick spreadable consistency. Mash the cheese well with a fork and blend thoroughly. Add a few grains of salt and, if desired, 1 teaspoon confectioners' sugar. Line a heart-shaped basket or a heart-shaped mold with a square of wet cheesecloth and press the cheese into it, folding the cloth over the top. Chill in the refrigerator several hours or overnight. Turn out on a dish (the cheese cloth corners make it particularly easy to do this). Remove the cloth of course.

AT SERVING TIME:

Surround with sliced sugared strawberries, raspberries, fresh or quick-frozen, red currant jam, or any other preserve which pleases you. One 3-ounce package of cheese makes dessert for 1 or 2, depending on appetite.

Coffee-Rum Jelly

YOU WILL NEED:

gelatin
sugar
quick-frozen concentrated
coffee or instant coffee

sour cream or whipped cream

Soak 1 tablespoon gelatin in 1/2 cup cold water. Dissolve in 1 1/2 cups strong hot coffee made by adding 2 teaspoons frozen coffee concentrate or 2 teaspoons instant coffee to 1 1/2 cups hot water. Add 1/4 cup sugar. Stir. Pour into glass or china serving bowl. Chill till firm.

AT SERVING TIME:

Spoon out of dish and pass sour cream or sweetened whipped cream. Some families insist upon custard sauce with this coffee jelly. Makes 4 portions.

Quick Crème Caramel

Famed not only in France but also in all the Latin world is a caramel custard. With a mix it is possible to make this classic dessert without baking, without eggs and in a very few minutes. With a bottled caramel syrup which can be found in many specialty shops or ordered by mail, this recipe is completely fail proof.

YOU WILL NEED:
   custard-flavored dessert mix   bottled caramel syrup

Into the bottom of a tin or aluminum mold, which holds one pint, pour about 4 tablespoons of bottled caramel syrup and place over a slow fire. Cook 2 or 3 minutes until it becomes bubbly and syrupy. Remove from fire. Tilt this way and that way so that the mold will be coated with the syrup. Let stand while you make up a package of custard-flavored dessert mix according to package directions. Pour into coated mold. Chill in the refrigerator several hours.

AT SERVING TIME:

Unmold on an attractive plate. This can be done very easily by running a knife blade around the edge of the mold. Place a plate over the mold and turn plate upside down quickly shaking the mold a little to loosen it. The rich golden syrup will pour around the mold. If syrup sticks inside the mold heat it for a moment or two and pour it out. Serves 4 to 5.

VARIATION: Cup Custard Caramel

If you have no bottled caramel syrup, it is not at all difficult to caramelize your own sugar—simply melt 1/2 cup sugar over medium heat, stirring constantly till nut-brown and pleasantly caramelish in fragrance. Pour sugar into 6 custard cups and swish the syrup around in order to coat the cups. Fill cups with custard flavor dessert mix made up according to package directions. Chill. Serve in cups or unmold on individual plates.

Easy Crêpes Suzette

Flaming Crêpes Suzette are one of the most dramatic of desserts. They are practical for the company dinner because the pancakes can be made several hours ahead of time and simply reheated in the orange-flavored brandied sauce. Classic recipes for the sauce include a variety of liqueurs. Here, orange marmalade takes the place of orange rind, orange juice, orange-flavored liqueur, and sugar.

YOU WILL NEED:

French pancakes (page 197)   butter
orange marmalade   brandy, curaçao, or Grand
lemon juice (optional)   Marnier

Make batter and fry pancakes as for French pancakes, using the smallest frying pan you can find—about 3 to 4 inches in diameter. Fold pancakes into quarters. If done ahead of time, place pancakes on a plate or a biscuit sheet so that they do not touch each other. Cover with a piece of waxed paper.

To make the sauce melt 1/2 cup butter (sweet butter is best but not absolutely necessary). Stir in 1/2 cup shredded orange marmalade.

AT SERVING TIME:

Heat the pancakes in a shallow frying pan, special Suzette pan or heat-proof platter over a flame at the table, turning them in the sauce. Add 1/2 cup brandy and set fire to the brandy. Curaçao or Grand Marnier may be used instead of brandy. Serve flaming on heated plates, 2 or 3 to a person. A few drops of lemon juice is usually sprinkled over each portion as it is served, but this is not absolutely necessary. If the flame dies down or is not high enough to suit you, pour on a little more brandy. This amount should make about 18 pancakes.

Italian Monte Bianco

Monte Bianco, Mont Blanc, or White Mountain—whichever name you use—is a classic Continental dessert that will be a source of pride to you when you serve it. The purée of chestnuts can be bought in cans at quality grocery stores and is worth keeping on hand for those times when you want a quick and glamorous dessert.

YOU WILL NEED:

canned puréed chestnuts   golden rum, vanilla, kirsch,
ready-whipped cream   or maraschino liqueur

Combine equal quantities sweetened whipped cream and canned purée of chestnuts. Flavor to taste with 1 or 2 tablespoons of golden rum, vanilla extract, kirsch, or maraschino liqueur. Add flavoring bit by bit to make certain that it does not overpower the taste of the chestnuts.

AT SERVING TIME:

Pile lightly in a pyramid on a serving dish. Decorate with ready-whipped cream so that it will look like a snow-capped mountain. If you like, you may buy from the bakeshop ready-baked meringues and set these in a circle around the mountain. Meringues usually come in pairs—get three pairs—set halves around pyramid. One cup or an 8-ounce can of chestnuts should make 6 servings, for it is very rich.

Lemon Ice-Box Cake

An ice-box cake is ideal for a company dinner or a buffet supper because it takes no last-minute preparation. This one made from lady fingers and a lemon pie mix is always good after a heavy dinner because the flavor is delicate and light.

YOU WILL NEED:

lady fingers	whipped cream
lemon pie filling	sugar
eggs	butter

Brush the inside of a large mold or bowl with melter butter. Line with 30 lady fingers. If they come in pairs, separate and use 30 halves, placing the rounded side against the bowl.

Make up a package of lemon pie filling according to pudding recipe on package. (Most require the addition of egg yolks and egg whites.) Fold in lightly 1/2 cup cream whipped. Place in center of mold. Cover with plate or waxed paper and chill 12 hours or longer.

AT SERVING TIME:

Loosen edges of mold with a knife blade. Place serving plate over mold. Turn upside down. Remove plate. Garnish pudding with swirls of ready-whipped cream. Serves 6 to 8.

Viennese Chocolate Mousse

YOU WILL NEED:

semi-sweet chocolate pieces	vanilla, or almond, extract,
eggs	rum or brandy
instant coffee	macaroon (optional)
	whipped cream

In a bowl, put 2 tablespoons water, 1/2 teaspoon instant coffee, a 6-ounce package of semi-sweet chocolate pieces. Place the bowl over hot water and stir until chocolate mixture is melted and blended. Add 1/4 teaspoon salt. Beat 4 egg yolks until thick and lemon colored. Add 1 teaspoon vanilla or almond extract or 2 teaspoons rum or brandy. Fold in lightly the whites of 4 eggs beaten until very stiff. Spoon into 6 tiny demitasse cups or small sherry or cocktail glasses. Chill.

AT SERVING TIME:

For the true Viennese touch top each portion with a small macaroon and pass a bowl of whipped cream well flavored with whatever flavoring was used in the pudding or best of all, with crème de cacao liqueur using 1 tablespoon liqueur to 1 cup whipped cream. Since this dessert is very rich it should serve 6.

Orange Omelet au Rhum

Very like a soufflé is a puffy omelet cooked on top of the stove, made with concentrated quick-frozen orange juice flamed with rum and sprinkled with powdered sugar. This is an inspired solution to the problem of—nothing-in-the-house-for dessert.

YOU WILL NEED:

eggs	concentrated quick-frozen
powdered sugar	orange juice
	rum

Beat separately yolks and whites of 4 eggs. The yolks should be beaten until thick and daffodil colored—the whites until stiff. To the yolks add 1/2 teaspoon salt, 1 tablespoon concentrated (un-diluted) quick-frozen orange juice. Gently fold in the stiffly beaten whites. Heat an omelet pan or heat-proof serving dish. Butter the sides as well as the bottom. Ladle the egg mixture into the pan, cook slowly but do not lift the edges as for a regular French ome-let. As soon as the omelet is puffy and a delicate brown around the edge place in 375° F. oven or 3 inches away from the broiler in order to brown the top. To judge if the omelet is sufficiently cooked touch it with your finger. If the finger stays clean it is done.

AT SERVING TIME:

You need not fold this type of omelet but merely sprinkle with powdered sugar. Slightly warm 4 tablespoons rum, set a match to the rum and pour blazing around the omelet. Serve immediately. Serves 4 to 6.

Pears with Eggnog Sauce

Bottled eggnog with or without spirits is available in all parts of the country—especially during the holiday season. It makes a simple dessert unusual and delicious.

YOU WILL NEED:

bottled eggnog	nutmeg (optional)
sherry or rum (optional)	canned pears
egg whites	

Flavor bottled eggnog with wine, rum, or brandy as desired. Gently fold 2 stiffly-beaten egg whites into 2 cups eggnog.

AT SERVING TIME:

Drain canned pears. Place in dessert dishes or sherbet glasses rounded side up and pour over eggnog sauce. Sprinkle with grated nutmeg. Serves 6 to 8.

Glamorous Rice Pudding

A prepared rice pudding takes on elegance when shaped in a mold and surrounded with big luscious quick-frozen or canned logan-berries. Inexpensive and unusual!

YOU WILL NEED:

packaged rice pudding   butter
canned or quick-frozen lo-
  ganberries

Make up a package of rice pudding mix according to directions. Brush with melted butter, a mold that holds 1 pint. Pour the rice pudding into the mold. Place in the refrigerator and chill several hours or overnight.

AT SERVING TIME:

Unmold on a shallow but not absolutely flat serving dish. This is done easily if you loosen the edges with a knife. Place the plate on top of the mold and turn the whole thing upside down, shaking gently to release the pudding. Garnish with quick-frozen or canned loganberries. If quick-frozen berries are used, they should be almost but not entirely thawed—a little iciness improves the shape as well as the taste. If canned, pour off about half the liquid or else you will have too much juice. Serves 6.

Sfinge (St. Joseph's Cream Puffs)

March 19 is St. Joseph's Day, and since the good saint is patron of home and family his has always been the day of great buffets and village feasting. The special dessert for the day is a cream puff filled with Italian cottage cheese. You can make cream puffs from a mix or order them from a bake shop. Fill them with the true St. Joseph mixture.

YOU WILL NEED:

cream puff shells   sugar
Italian ricotta or creamed   light cream
  cottage cheese   almond extract
chocolate pieces   maraschino cherries
orange   candied orange peel

Make a slit in cream puff shells and fill with a mixture of 1 pound ricotta or creamed cottage cheese, 2 tablespoons chocolate pieces, 1 tablespoon grated orange rind, 3 tablespoons light cream, 1 teaspoon almond extract, sugar to taste—all mixed together quite thoroughly.

AT SERVING TIME:

Sfinge should be garnished in the traditional way with a maraschino cherry on top and 2 thin strips of candied orange peel. A scatter of grated orange or lemon peel is good too. One pound of cottage cheese should provide enough filling for about 16 cream puffs, about 2 inches in diameter.

Miracle Chocolate Soufflé

A package of chocolate tapioca pudding mix can be transformed into soufflé. The tapioca helps to keep the soufflé high without interfering with its delicacy—the grains do not show or alter the taste. This recipe suggests a way to make the soufflé rise high in the center in the manner of the French restaurateurs. Really wonderful!

YOU WILL NEED:

chocolate tapioca pudding mix	eggs
milk	sherry or brandy (optional)
	confectioners' sugar

Make up a package of chocolate tapioca pudding mix according to directions. Add, 1 at a time, 6 egg yolks, beating well after each addition. Then fold in lightly 6 stiffly beaten egg whites. Flavor with 4 tablespoons sherry or 1 tablespoon brandy, if desired.

To bake, pour mixture into unbuttered straight-sided baking dish that can come to the table. Pottery is preferred. Fill 7/8 full and make a deep cut all around the soufflé mixture, an inch from the edge. Set in a very hot oven, 425° F., and bake 15 to 20 minutes. This method makes a soufflé with a crusty top and leaves the center soft enough to serve as a sauce.

AT SERVING TIME:

Shake a little confectioners' sugar over the top of the soufflé to give it a professional touch and serve instantly. Serves 6.

Berries Jubilee with Ice Cream

Any dinner no matter how simple takes on distinction when it comes with a flambé dessert. Cherries Jubilee are exceedingly well known—almost too well known to be exciting. Either fresh or quick-frozen strawberries however may be used in the same fashion.

YOU WILL NEED:

strawberries	lemon
concentrated quick-frozen orange juice	vanilla ice cream, lemon or orange sherbet
brandy	

Cut the peel from 1 lemon and leave it curled cork-screw style. Place in a shallow pan—a chafing dish if convenient. Add 2 tablespoons quick-frozen orange juice, undiluted. Heat gently about 3 minutes pressing the peel to get all the flavor. Add 1 pint fresh or quick-frozen whole strawberries and toss berries around in the hot juice. Pour on 1/4 cup brandy. Warm and light with a match.

AT SERVING TIME:

Do all this at the table if you can and serve the flaming berries over vanilla ice cream, lemon or orange sherbet.

VARIATION: Raspberries Jubilee

Raspberries can be done in the same fashion.

Strawberries Romanoff

In strawberry season all over the world the most famous restaurants feature—each with its own variation—this classic combination of fine strawberries, orange juice, curaçao, and cream. To achieve the most dramatic effect arrange the makings on a tray and put the dessert together at the table.

YOU WILL NEED:

fresh or whole frozen strawberries	curaçao
orange juice	vanilla ice cream

Arrange on a tray an attractive bowlful of strawberries. If you use quick-frozen berries, have them almost but not completely thawed. To 1 pint berries add 1 cup orange juice. Also have on hand a bowl of vanilla ice cream—about a pint—and a bottle of curaçao. Provide yourself also with a fork and a large spoon for serving.

AT SERVING TIME:

Stir and soften vanilla ice cream with a fork. Add 1/4 cup curaçao (Cointreau, Grand Marnier, or brandy may be used). Stir into the ice cream. Serve strawberries on chilled plates and top each portion with a couple of spoonfuls of the liqueur-flavored ice cream. Serves 6.

Tipsy Parson

This combination of sponge cake and wine-flavored sauce dates back to the English colonists. It is called tipsy because of the wine in the sauce—parson because it was so often served when the preacher came to Sunday dinner.

YOU WILL NEED:

sponge cake layers	vanilla-flavored pudding
jelly	mix
almonds	sherry or Madeira wine

Buy from the grocery store 2 sponge cake layers, the kind that are usually sold for shortcake. Place between the layers, currant, grape, or apple jelly. Sprinkle the jelly liberally with canned shredded almonds. Place the top layer over the jelly. Spread the top of the cake with a thin layer of jelly and sprinkle with almonds.

Tipsy Sauce

Prepare the sauce from a package of vanilla-flavored pudding mix by using 1 1/2 as much liquid as required for a regular pudding. Cook according to package directions. Add 1/2 cup sherry or Madeira. Stir and chill.

AT SERVING TIME:

Cut cake into regular servings and pass chilled sauce in a separate bowl. 6 to 8 servings.

❧ 16 ❧

~~~~~~~~~~~~~~~~~~~~~~~~~~~~~~~

Fruits

TO END THE MEAL

WHEN IN DOUBT, serve fruit. Fresh, quick-frozen, or canned—raw or cooked—plain or glamorized in any number of tempting ways—fruit is almost everybody's favorite dessert. So many different kinds of fruits and berries in so many different guises are now available, quick frozen or canned—it is sad to confine your attention entirely to old favorites. Have you, for instance, heard of the many forms in which the apple is being packed—in slices for pies and puddings, cubed and sweetened for compotes, in the form of applesauce sweetened or unsweetened—baked apples, too, in cans or quick frozen? Now all year round you can have your favorite fresh berry desserts with quick-frozen strawberries, blackberries, blueberries, boysenberries, cherries, loganberries, and youngberries too. Be sure to include them in your menu plans.

And when you serve the stand-bys, canned peaches, pears, cherries, and pineapple, present them imaginatively. A touch of vanilla or almond extract added to the syrup, a little brandy or wine—a frosty sauce made of whipped vanilla ice cream. All these can lend variety. Be wary though, do not overpower the delicate flavor of fruit with too much flavoring or trimming. The recipes that follow pursue a judicious middle course.

RECIPES

Apple Croutes

Baked Applesauce

Baked Apples Garni

Baked Apples with Orange

Baked Apples Porcupine

Caramel-Rum Sauced Pears

Whole Baked Bananas Flambé

Cerises au Claret

Stewed Figs à la Glace

Grapefruit à la Rector

Nectarines Melba

Mandarins à la Mexico

Peach Ambrosia

Baked Peaches Italienne

Baked Stuffed Peaches with Macaroons

Pineapple Royale

Pineapple Sauté with Lemon Sherbet

Hot Fruit Compote

Frozen Macédoine of Fruits

Apple Croutes

YOU WILL NEED:

sliced white bread or English muffins
butter or margarine
currant jelly

canned baked apples
vanilla, or almond, extract
heavy cream or sour cream

In butter or margarine brown 6 slices of thin white bread from
which the crusts have been removed. Or toast lightly and butter
generously 6 halves of English muffins. Cut down through the
center 3 canned baked apples. Set cut side down on the bread.
Melt 1/2 cup currant jelly and add 1/2 teaspoon vanilla, or almond, extract. Spoon carefully over the apples. Allow to stand
long enough for the jelly to thicken—about half an hour or less
in the refrigerator.

AT SERVING TIME:

Serve with plain cream, whipped cream, or slightly sweetened
sour cream. (Whole baked apples may be used but they make
rather a large dessert—too much for most people.) Serves 6.

Baked Applesauce

YOU WILL NEED:
unsweetened applesauce
brown sugar

flour
butter

Place in the bottom of a buttered baking dish 2 cups unsweetened
canned applesauce. Make a mixture of 1 cup dark brown sugar,
3/4 cup unsifted flour, 2 tablespoons butter broken up into little
dabs. Cover applesauce with this mixture. Bake in a hot oven,
375° F., until brown, about 20 minutes.

AT SERVING TIME:

Delicious warm or cold, with or without cream. Serves 4 to 6.

Baked Apples Garni

Baked apples can be bought either canned or quick frozen. Generally there are 3 or 4 apples in a can or carton. There are a number of ways to dress up these apples to make them look and taste homemade.

YOU WILL NEED:

baked apples	red cinnamon drops or red
lemon juice	pure-food coloring
heavy cream	cinnamon
	lemon (optional)

Place apples in a buttered heat-proof glass pie plate or other shallow serving dish. Drop into the center of each apple, 2 or 3 red cinnamon candies or lacking these, add to the syrup from the apples a few drops of red pure-food coloring and sprinkle apples with cinnamon and a few drops of lemon juice using about 1/2 teaspoon on each apple. A twist of lemon peel may be put in the center of the apples, too, or laid over the top. Pour about 1/2 inch of apple liquid into the bottom of the baking dish. Cover and allow to heat in a hot oven, 400° F., about 10 minutes or until warm.

AT SERVING TIME:

These are most delicious when served warm with a pitcher of plain heavy cream. However you may use whipped cream if you like. Serves 3 or 4.

VARIATIONS:

Baked Apples with Orange

Into the center of each apple, place 1 teaspoon undiluted quick-frozen concentrated orange juice.

Baked Apples Porcupine

Set 4 well-drained baked apples in the baking dish. Cover each apple completely with a stiff meringue made by beating the whites of 2 eggs with 2 tablespoons sugar. Meringue may be flavored with 1/2 teaspoon vanilla. Stick almond halves all over the meringue porcupine fashion. Sprinkle lightly with granulated sugar. Place in a moderate oven, 350° F., 5 minutes. Then increase the heat to 400° F. and bake 5 minutes longer or until delicately brown. *Do not put any liquid in the bottom of the pan.*

Caramel-Rum Sauced Pears

YOU WILL NEED:

canned whole or halved	rum
pears	butter
packaged caramel chips	cinnamon

Chill and drain canned pears. Meanwhile make a delightful rum-flavored caramel sauce by melting one 6-ounce package (1 cup) caramel chips along with 1/4 cup water, 1/4 cup rum, 2 tablespoons butter, 1/8 teaspoon cinnamon, stirring over low heat until smooth. Do not boil. Makes 1 1/2 cups sauce.

AT SERVING TIME:

Place chilled pears in individual dishes or champagne glasses. Cover with the sauce, which may be served warm or cold. One large can of pears and this sauce makes 6 generous servings.

VARIATION:

Place pears and caramel sauce over mounds of vanilla ice cream or vanilla pudding or on squares of white cake.

Whole Baked Bananas Flambé

YOU WILL NEED:

bananas	confectioners' sugar
golden rum	

Place whole not-too-ripe unpeeled bananas, 1 for each person in a shallow baking dish—preferably one that can be brought to the table. Bake 30 minutes in a moderate oven, 350° F.

AT SERVING TIME:

At the table or if you prefer before you bring the dish to the table, pull back one section of skin, sprinkle bananas with confectioners' sugar and pour over them slightly warmed golden rum which has been set ablaze with a match. Use for 4 bananas about 1/2 cup rum. The guests spoon the banana out of its shell just as one eats a baked potato.

Cerises au Claret

YOU WILL NEED:

canned cherries	cinnamon
claret	red currant jelly

Drain juice from a No. 1 can (about 2 cups) of cherries. Add to the juice a stick of cinnamon or a half teaspoon of powdered cinnamon and a half cup of claret. Cook until about 1/3 of the liquid has boiled away. Then add 4 tablespoons currant jelly. Put the cherries back into the juice. Chill very well.

AT SERVING TIME:

Serve from a cold glass bowl with lady fingers or a macaroon. Serves 4 to 6. Black cherries are often packed in a No. 2 1/2 can which contains about 3 1/4 cupfuls; if you use this size of can, double the amount of claret and currant jelly. Will serve 8.

Stewed Figs à la Glace

Canned figs deserve to be a lot more popular. They're particularly good with a pep-up of liquor or a bit of candied ginger.

YOU WILL NEED:

canned figs	rum or brandy (optional)
vanilla ice cream	

Thoroughly chill canned figs.

AT SERVING TIME:

Place a scoop of vanilla ice cream into individual dessert dishes, sherbet glasses, or champagne glasses of the saucer type. On top of the ice cream carefully place 2 or 3 figs together with a little of the syrup. Add a teaspoonful of rum or brandy to each portion.

Grapefruit à la Rector

When there is no fresh fruit on hand, you can create the effect of freshness with the combination suggested below.

YOU WILL NEED:
grapefruit sections   mint
orange juice

Drain liquid from a can of grapefruit sections and cover grapefruit with orange juice. If grapefruit is unsweetened add a little powdered sugar and a sprinkle of salt. Scatter over the grapefruit 2 tablespoons finely cut fresh mint or 2 teaspoons dried mint leaves. Cover and set in the refrigerator to chill about half an hour or longer.

AT SERVING TIME:
Serve well chilled either as a first course or for dessert. This combination is particularly good for a late Sunday breakfast. Some people will like it before the main course; others will prefer it afterward.

Nectarines Melba

When you want an unusual dessert, something different and delicious, serve nectarines. They are available in cans and are generally packed whole. The nectarine looks and tastes like a cross between a peach and a plum. Escoffier suggests that they "may be prepared after all the recipes given for peaches." They are particularly delicious when combined with red raspberries.

YOU WILL NEED:
nectarines   sherry
quick-frozen or **canned red**
   raspberries

Drain syrup from canned nectarines and also from canned or quick-frozen raspberries. Place nectarines on a shallow serving dish. Arrange the raspberries around the nectarines. Combine nectarine and raspberry syrups. Cook over brisk fire uncovered till reduced to half the volume. Flavor with 2 tablespoons sherry and pour syrup over fruit. Chill.

AT SERVING TIME:

Sprinkle if desired with slivered almonds and serve with or without vanilla ice cream. Nectarines usually are packed in No. 2 1/2 cans or glass jars holding about 3 cups. Serves 6.

Mandarins à la Mexico

YOU WILL NEED:

canned mandarin orange sections	rum
grated orange peel	mint (optional)

Turn the canned mandarin orange sections and their juice into a serving dish. Sprinkle generously with orange peel, either freshly grated or dried. Sprinkle lightly with golden rum. Cover and let stand at room temperature for about an hour or longer, so that the rum and orange flavors become deliciously blended.

AT SERVING TIME:

Sprinkle with fresh mint leaves. Or, lacking fresh mint leaves, use a scattering of dried mint leaves and add them before the mellowing.

Peach Ambrosia

The traditional ambrosia of the South is made of oranges, but this delightful variant uses canned or quick-frozen sliced peaches in place of them.

YOU WILL NEED:

peaches	sherry, white port, or lemon
coconut	juice

Drain canned peaches or quick-frozen sliced peaches. Save the juice. Arrange in a glass bowl suitable for serving. Alternate layers of peaches and shredded coconut. To 2 cups peaches, use about 1 cup shredded coconut. Add to the juice of the peaches, 1 tablespoon lemon juice or 2 tablespoons sherry or white port. Sprinkle over peaches and coconut.

AT SERVING TIME:

This dessert may be served as soon as it is made, an advantage over the old-fashioned ambrosia which had to stand for several hours at least in order to blend the flavors. Makes 4 servings.

VARIATION:

One cup sliced bananas, oranges, or diced pineapple may be added to the peaches. Increase coconut to 1 1/2 cups. Serves 6.

Baked Peaches Italienne

Pesche ripiene they are called in Italy. There, of course, they are always made with fresh, large peaches which are not too ripe. But our own canned peach halves make an excellent substitute.

YOU WILL NEED:

canned peach halves	lady fingers
nuts	almond extract
lemon or orange	white or brown sugar
white wine	

Drain a large can of peach halves. Place 6 on a buttered baking pan, preferably one that can come to the table. Make the stuffing for the peaches by mashing together 2 peach halves, 1/2 cup finely chopped toasted almonds or other nuts, 1/2 teaspoon almond extract, a bit of grated lemon or orange rind (about 1 teaspoon), and 4 lady fingers cut into very fine pieces. If the mixture is not moist enough to hold together, add a couple of teaspoons of peach syrup from the can. Form into balls about the size of a peach seed. Place in the peaches and cover with other peach halves so that the peaches look whole. Pour over them 1/4 cup white wine. Sprinkle with 1/4 cup white or brown sugar. Bake in a moderate oven about 10 minutes or until the sugar has formed a pretty crust.

AT SERVING TIME:
Serve warm or cold. 6 servings.

VARIATION: Baked Stuffed Peaches with Macaroons
In the above recipe use 8 macaroons instead of lady fingers and omit the almond extract.

Pineapple Royale

For a party nothing could be more impressive than this Escoffier dessert. You must choose a pretty pineapple with a well-shaped topknot of leaves.

YOU WILL NEED:

large pineapple with leaves	kirsch, brandy, Contreau,
canned or quick-frozen fruit	or Grand Marnier
salad or cocktail	canned peach halves
large strawberries or blue-	
berries	

Cut off the top of the pineapple with the bunch of leaves and set aside in a safe place. Scoop out the pineapple leaving a wall about half an inch thick all around and at the bottom. Cut fresh pineapple into small pieces and combine with 1 can (or 1 package frozen) fruit cocktail or fruit salad, drained. (The pieces of fruit are larger in fruit salad.) Sprinkle with 2 tablespoons kirsch, brandy, Cointreau, or Grand Marnier. Place fruit back into the pineapple. Set the top in place and if you wish to follow the great tradition surround the base of the pineapple with canned peach halves and large fresh or quick-frozen strawberries or blueberries.

AT SERVING TIME:
Decorate with shiny green leaves. (Violet or rose leaves are particularly appropriate.) If desired, a little liquor such as is used to flavor the fruits may be sprinkled lightly over the canned peaches. A slight frosting of confectioners' sugar over leaves and fruit is effective. (For looks only.) The number of servings depends upon the sizes of the cans and the number of fruits used.

Pineapple Sauté with Lemon Sherbet

The combination and contrast of flavors and textures as well as heat and cold makes this a novel dessert.

YOU WILL NEED:

canned pineapple slices
butter
lemon sherbet bought or
   made from a mix

pistachio nuts or rum (optional)

Drain canned sliced pineapple and brown lightly in a small amount of butter, first on one side then on the other.

AT SERVING TIME:

Bring the sautéed pineapple slices warm to the table and top each slice with two spoonfuls of lemon sherbet bought or made from a mix according to package directions. A sprinkle of finely chopped pistachio nuts or a spoonful of rum may be added to each portion.

Hot Fruit Compote

A combination of leftover canned fruits or several small picnic-size cans of fruits make the most interesting hot compotes. Particularly good combinations are apricots, pears, sour cherries or greengage plums, sweet black cherries and peaches or pineapple, purple plums or prunes and canned mandarin orange sections.

YOU WILL NEED:

canned fruits
sherry, port, brandy, rum,
   or Grand Marnier (op-
   tional)

vanilla, or almond, extract

Heat together fruits and juices. Flavor to taste with sherry, port, brandy, rum, or Grand Marnier. Or if you wish, omit wine and liquor and simply add to the fruits a little vanilla extract, or a few drops of almond extract—not enough, however, to overpower the fruit flavors. If the syrup looks pallid, add a few drops of pure-food coloring.

AT SERVING TIME:
Serve warm or chilled with cookies and/or ice cream.

Frozen Macédoine of Fruits

Fruit cocktail often is one of the least interesting of canned foods but this is an excellent way to lend distinction to this popular and economical dish.

YOU WILL NEED:

canned fruit cocktail	sour cream
nutmeg	sugar

Place a can of mixed fruit cocktail in the freezing compartment of your refrigerator, or open the can and pour it into a refrigerator tray. Freeze solid.

AT SERVING TIME:
If you have frozen the dessert in the can open the can at both ends and push the cylinder onto a chilled plate. Cut into slices and serve with a garnish or thick sour cream which has been lightly sweetened with a little sugar. Sprinkle cream with a few gratings of nutmeg. If you have used a refrigerator tray, cut the mixture into strips and serve with sour cream and nutmeg. Servings depend on size of can.

❧ 17 ❧

∿∿∿∿∿∿∿∿∿∿∿∿∿∿∿∿∿∿∿∿∿∿

Time-Saving Beverages

INSTANT TEA, coffee, and chocolate are certainly here to stay. So convenient and economical—in many busy households they have already become indispensable. Suggested in this chapter are a number of ways for serving instant beverages to the best advantage.

A number of party drinks—punches and nogs—are included. Each is a short-cut recipe using either canned, bottled, or quick-frozen fruit juices or, in some cases, sherbet or ice cream, bought or made from a mix.

One point cannot be overemphasized: Hot drinks should be hot, hot, hot. Whenever possible, demitasse cups should be heated. This is not difficult. You can put them into an oven set at *not more than 200° F.*

Cold drinks must be cold, cold, cold. If you are giving a party, you may find yourself faced with an ice-cube shortage. You can, of course, freeze ice cubes ahead of time emptying and saving the cubes in bowls in the refrigerator until needed but there is an easier way. In cities and in medium-sized towns you will find listed in classified section of your telephone directory one or more ice companies who will deliver to you in cartons—at no great expense—any quantity of ice cubes as well as shaved or finely crushed ice so necessary for juleps, frozen daiquiris, cobblers, and the like. They can also send you large chunks of ice for your punch bowl.

On the subject of punch bowl ice, those of you who are fortunate enough to have a freezing compartment in your refrigerator or a deep-freeze will find it a simple matter to make your own ice blocks by freezing water in a bowl, mold, or deep pan. If you wish, you may decorate the ice, by placing in the water to be frozen, flowers, leaves, or fruits. Imagine the drama provided by a bunch of grapes frozen into a block of ice!

RECIPES

Instant Demitasse

Demitasse with Cinnamon Stick

Café Royale

Viennese Coffee

Coffee Cobbler

Café Diable

Frosted Mocha

Frosted Mocha with Rum

Ice-Saving Iced Tea

Iced Tea Angostura

Iced Tea with Rum

Flaming Tea Bowl

Tea Punch

Holiday Nog

Punch Frappé

Peach Champagne

Quick Fish House Punch

Wassail

Wassail for the Young

Instant Demitasse

Some connoisseurs still object to instant coffee but because it is so easy, so quick, and so economical to use its use is becoming more and more widespread. There are a number of ways by which one may add a full body and a stronger flavor to an instant demitasse.

YOU WILL NEED:
instant coffee

By using standard measurements—a measuring cup and a measuring spoon, you can be assured of uniform quality in your demitasse. For instance, to make 6 servings pour 2 *measuring cups* of actively boiling water on 2 level *measuring* tablespoons of instant coffee. Stir to assure a brew of even strength. To make 12 servings use 4 measuring cups of water and 4 level measuring tablespoons of instant coffee. *Prize Hint:* Add instant coffee to *cold* water. Bring to a boil and boil for 30 seconds. Amazing—the difference.

AT SERVING TIME:
According to tradition, demitasse is generally served in the living room after dinner but since most of us do not have special dining rooms nowadays many hostesses prefer to bring the demitasse to the table and serve it along with the dessert. To keep the coffee piping hot, it is convenient to set the coffee pot over a candle-warmer. These are available at most department store houseware counters now and are quite inexpensive. The candle flame is not hot enough to harm even a thin china coffee pot.

VARIATION: Demitasse with Cinnamon Stick
Into each demitasse cup, place a stick of cinnamon which is to be used as a stirrer. The cinnamon stick looks attractive and adds a delicate flavor to the coffee.

Café Royale

This is a simple trick which will most certainly add a gala note to any occasion. Serve demitasse in the usual fashion and provide rum, brandy, or Grand Marnier. Each person flames his own coffee like this: The coffee spoon is dipped into the coffee to be warmed. Then the spoon is rested on the rim of the coffee cup. A lump of sugar goes into the spoon and over the sugar is poured a little liquor. If the liquor is slightly warmed beforehand you are certain to have a good blaze. Set a match to the liquor. Let it flame up for a minute or so and then drop the flaming sugar into the cup. For those who do not like sugar in their coffee the liquor may be flamed in the spoon without sugar. This ceremony is most effective if the room is darkened.

Viennese Coffee

It is traditional in Vienna and all through the Austrian Tyrol to serve strong, hot coffee topped with whipped cream not only after dinner but at any time during the day. Make up instant demitasse for 6. In an attractive chilled bowl, pass ready-whipped cream delicately flavored, if desired, with a little brandy or liqueur. Instead of whipped cream, vanilla ice cream may be passed in the bowl. This should be softened with a fork and flavored with brandy, rum, or liqueur. Use a tablespoon of liqueur to a cup of cream or ice cream.

Coffee Cobbler

In Europe many wines and liqueurs are served in small glasses over shaved or finely crushed ice. This is an attractive way to serve demitasse on a warm summer evening. Fill sherry or cocktail glasses with very finely crushed or shaved ice. Pour over the ice instant demitasse. Top with a swirl of ready-whipped cream and decorate with a bit of glazed fruit. Serve with short straws, which are made by cutting ordinary ice cream soda straws into 2 or 3 pieces.

Café Diable

Special pans, burners, and ladles are available for making and
serving this most dramatic of after-dinner coffees but it can be done
and very effectively with any chafing dish.

YOU WILL NEED:

instant demitassee (page 254)	lemon
orange	brandy
cloves	sugar
	cinnamon stick

Heat but do not boil in a chafing dish or Café Diable pan, 1 1/2
cups brandy along with the thin outer peel of 1/2 orange and 1/2
lemon, 8 lumps of sugar, 4 cloves, a stick of cinnamon. Warm a
small ladle by holding a match under it or hold it over the candle
flame. Dip up about 2 tablespoons of the spice-brandy mixture and
place 2 sugar lumps in the ladle. Set fire to the sugar. Lower the
blazing spiced brandy into the bowl which will blaze up in its
turn and while it is blazing pour in 2 measuring cups instant demitasse.

AT SERVING TIME:

All the above should, of course, be done with some ceremony at
the dinner table in a darkened room. Ladle the Café Diable into
tiny coffee cups after the flame has died down. 8 to 10 servings.

Frosted Mocha

One of the most delicious summertime beverages imaginable is
put together from ready-to-serve products—requires no cooking
whatsoever.

YOU WILL NEED:

canned chocolate syrup	vanilla ice cream or ready-whipped cream (optional)
milk	
quick-frozen coffee concentrate	nutmeg or cinnamon (optional)

Put into a bowl or into a cocktail shaker 5 tablespoons chocolate syrup, 3 teaspoons quick-frozen coffee concentrate, and 1 1/2 cups milk. Beat with a rotary egg beater or shake in cocktail shaker. Fill 3 or 4 tall glasses with ice cubes. Pour the mixture over the ice. Top with a spoonful of vanilla ice cream or ready-whipped cream.

AT SERVING TIME:

Serve immediately with a few gratings of nutmeg or a dash of cinnamon over the top. Serves 3 or 4.

VARIATION: Frosted Mocha with Rum

If desired, a jigger of rum may be poured into the bottom of each glass. In this case the drink should be stirred with a long-handled spoon and the cream or ice cream may be omitted.

Ice-Saving Iced Tea

During the iced-tea season, it is always difficult to keep a sufficient supply of ice cubes on hand especially when your refrigerator space is not unlimited. Here are two helpful suggestions.

YOU WILL NEED:

loose tea or tea balls   lemon, lime, or orange
mint

Tea intended for icing should be made double strength: Use 1 to 2 teaspoons tea for each glass or at least 1 tea ball. To make 6 servings, pour a small amount of boiling water—about 1 cup over 6 to 12 teaspoons tea or 6 tea balls. Cover and allow to steep about 5 minutes. Strain into a pitcher and add 3 cups cold water.

AT SERVING TIME:

Fill tall glasses with ice cubes. Pour tea over ice. Garnish with mint sprigs and sections of lemon, lime, or orange stuck with cloves if desired. Pass *powdered* sugar or sugar syrup in a small pitcher.

VARIATION: Iced Tea Angostura

A couple of drops of angostura bitters, such as are used for old-fashioned cocktails will add an interesting flavor and color to iced tea.

Iced Tea with Rum

Either golden rum or pungent dark Jamaica rum may be added to iced tea. For most people a tablespoonful is enough in a glass of tea as the effect desired is not that of an alcoholic beverage but merely a flavoring of rum.

Flaming Tea Bowl

On a cold winter evening after skiing or just walking, nothing could be more appropriate than this hot and spicy drink. It has the further virtue of being inexpensive and very easy.

YOU WILL NEED:

hot tea   golden rum
lemon   honey
cinnamon sticks (optional)

To a quart of hot tea made from your very best tea add 1 lemon thinly sliced, and 4 teaspoons honey. Stir well.

AT SERVING TIME:

Bring punch to the table in a chafing dish or a casserole which will fit over a candle-warmer so that it will keep blazing hot. Warm separately but do not boil 1 cup golden rum. Set rum ablaze with a match. Pour into the hot tea and ladle into cups or mugs. If you have them you may put cinnamon sticks in the cups for stirrers. Makes 6 or 8 servings.

Tea Punch

Quick-frozen concentrated lemonade takes all the work and fuss out of the making of a party punch. This one is decorated in the Continental fashion with thin strips of cucumber rind. In the watermelon season, green watermelon rind may be substituted for the cucumber. When borage grows in the garden this may be used too, or instead of the cucumber peel, because it has a cucumberlike flavor and fragrance.

YOU WILL NEED:

tea	cucumber rind
white wine	
quick-frozen, concentrated	
lemonade	

To a quart of hot tea, add 1 can quick-frozen concentrated lemonade, 3 cups white table wine, and 3 strips cucumber rind. Cover and let stand about 5 minutes. Don't let cucumber rind stay in too long for it may give a bitter flavor to the drink.

AT SERVING TIME:

Place a block of ice in a punch bowl—or any large and attractive mixing bowl will do. Pour the punch mixture over the ice. Stir 2 or 3 times to chill and ladle into small cups or glasses. How much punch you should make for a party depends, of course, on the kind of party and the kind of guests. Usually, however, you can count upon 2 to 4 cups per person, which means that a quart will serve 4. This recipe should serve 8.

Holiday Nog

Instead of going to all the bother of beating egg yolks, egg whites, and cream for an eggnog party try this very simple and most delicious recipe made with ice cream from the corner store.

YOU WILL NEED:

vanilla ice cream	whiskey
nutmeg	golden rum
milk	

Place 1 pint vanilla ice cream in a bowl. Pour over it 2 cups rye whiskey or bourbon whiskey, 1 cup golden rum, 1 cup milk. Beat with a rotary egg beater until the ice cream is almost melted and the nog is foamy.

AT SERVING TIME:

Ladle into small punch cups and sprinkle with grated nutmeg. Serves 6.

Punch Frappé

One of the prettiest and easiest refreshment beverages for any party is made of sherbet or water ice and ginger ale. Sherbet may be bought or made at home from a mix. In Atlanta, Georgia, it is the custom to serve this punch in glass bowls, and the hostess usually matches the color of the punch to the hue of the flowers in her centerpiece. Lemon, lime, orange, pineapple, or raspberry sherbet may be used.

YOU WILL NEED:

sherbet	ginger ale
white rum or brandy (optional)	

Place a pint of sherbet or water ice into a punch bowl.

AT SERVING TIME:

Add a quart of chilled ginger ale. Stir until sherbet is softened but not entirely melted. Ladle into small punch cups or glasses. Some people may wish to have demitasse or teaspoons handy so that they can eat some of the unmelted sherbet. This punch is generally non-alcoholic but if desired a cup of white rum or brandy may be added. Serves 6.

Peach Champagne

This might be considered a drink or a dessert—may be served for either. Special tall footed glasses are available in Europe for serving it, but any commodious wide-mouthed wine or beer goblet may be used.

YOU WILL NEED:

fresh and juicy small peaches or canned whole peaches plain or brandied	champagne brandy or peach brandy (optional)

Prick a small juicy peach all over with a fork to release the juices (or use a canned whole peach or a brandied whole peach). Place in a large glass. Add a tablespoon of brandy or peach brandy, if desired.

AT SERVING TIME:

Pour in enough very well chilled champagne to fill the glass just about half full. Provide teaspoons so that the peach can be eaten after the champagne has been consumed. One quart of champagne serves 6.

Quick Fish House Punch

Probably the most famous as well as one of the most potent punches in all the world was invented by America's oldest cooking and eating club called the State in Schuylkill. Their Fish House Punch is served in a special Lowestoft china bowl which was presented to the club in 1812. We have not tampered with the ancient recipe except to substitute bottled lemon juice for the fresh squeezed variety, and bottled sugar syrup instead of the loaf sugar. The only ingredient that might not be available is peach brandy. Peach liqueur or cordial may be used in its stead and in that case a little less sugar is needed.

YOU WILL NEED:

brandy	water
peach brandy or peach liqueur (optional)	golden rum
	sugar syrup
lemon juice	

Combine in a large bowl 1 cup sugar syrup, 3 cups bottled lemon juice, 2 bottles golden rum (or 1 bottle Jamaica rum and 1 bottle golden rum), 1 bottle brandy, 2 quarts water, 1/2 cup peach brandy or peach liqueur. If peach liqueur is used cut down the amount of sugar syrup to 3/4 cup. If desired, the peach liqueur may be omitted entirely. Stir well and allow to "ripen" in a cool place for 2 or 3 hours.

AT SERVING TIME:

Place a large block of ice in the bowl. Stir until liquid is chilled. Ladle into punch cups or glasses. Since this punch is very strong, this amount should be ample for 20 persons.

Wassail

On Christmas Eve, New Year's, or Twelfth Night, the Wassail
Bowl is traditional, for

> "When midnight bells are tolled, let's gather
>   'round the Wassail Bowl.
> Let the wealthy and great roll in
>   splendor and state
> I envy them not I declare it
> I eat my own lamb, my own chicken
>   and ham
> I shear my own fleece and I wear it."

So goes the inscription on a lordly eighteenth-century Wassail
Bowl of the same era as this recipe which we have adapted for
modern living.

YOU WILL NEED:

canned baked apples	bottled apple juice
cinnamon stick	cloves
lemon	honey or brown sugar (op-
brandy or apple jack	tional)
vanilla	nutmeg

Warm 12 canned baked apples in the oven providing 1 for each
guest. To 3 quarts apple juice add 1 teaspoon vanilla, stick of
cinnamon, 2 teaspoons whole cloves, a whole nutmeg cracked or
1/2 teaspoon nutmeg, and a little thin lemon rind. Also if desired,
add 2 tablespoons honey or brown sugar. Simmer for a few minutes. Pour while hot into punch bowl.

AT SERVING TIME:

Place a baked apple in each mug. Pour on 1 or 2 jiggers (3 tablespoons) of brandy or apple jack that has been slightly warmed. Set
aflame and ladle the spiced apple juice over the apple. Serve with
a spoon. Serves 12.

VARIATION: Wassail for the Young

Even without brandy or apple jack, Wassail can be a very festive
drink. Simply omit liquor.

❧18❧

〰〰〰〰〰〰〰〰〰〰〰〰〰〰〰〰〰〰

Can-Opener Parties

AMERICA TODAY is probably the most "entertaining" civiliza-
tion in all the world and in all history. But our entertainment
is our own. We specialize in help-yourself parties. Most of our
finest party menus require comparatively little effort. They are
simple and easy to achieve. Generally our party dishes can be
cooked ahead of time; and most of them—at least most of those
featured in this chapter—will wait obligingly, retaining their good
looks and good taste not only for minutes and hours, but even for
days in the refrigerator or weeks in the freezer.

These entertaining menus rely more or less upon processed
foods—canned, frozen, or dehydrated. In order to be truly successful they also require some sort of keep-warm equipment. There
are innumerable warming devices on the market, ranging all the
way from candles or alcohol lamps to electric chafing dishes and,
best of all, electrically heated, thermostatically controlled warming
trays.

All the recipes in this section are designed to serve a party of
twelve. All of them have something extra-special in the way of
flavor, drama, and enticement. In many of them wines or beer or
spirits are used, not only because they add so much to the taste,
but also because it has been discovered by great chefs that foods
so flavored tend to improve and mellow rather than deteriorate as
they stand.

RECIPES

Aspic of Beef à la Mode

For a buffet supper in summer time nothing could be more appealing than this simple-as-can-be version of one of the most delightful of Parisian specialties.

YOU WILL NEED:

roast beef or leftover pot roast	unflavored gelatine
fresh or dried tarragon	tarragon vinegar
olives, green and black	Tabasco sauce
carrots	canned consommé

You may start with cold roast beef from the delicatessen, or you could use leftover pot roast cut in slices about 1/4 inch thick. Arrange 16 slices of beef, overlapping slightly, in a shallow serving dish or a deep platter. Sprinkle with 2 tablespoons of fresh tarragon or 1 tablespoon dried tarragon. Garnish attractively with very thin slices of carrots and green and black olives.

Now make an aspic by softening 4 envelopes of unflavored gelatine in 1 cup cold water. Heat 2 cans consommé. Add the softened gelatine and stir until dissolved. Flavor with 2 tablespoons tarragon vinegar and 3 or 4 drops of Tabasco sauce. Cool until the aspic mixture is syrupy. This will take about 30 minutes in the refrigerator or about 10 minutes in the freezing compartment; but be sure to time yourself if you use the freezer, because the aspic will get grainy if it is kept too long in the freezing compartment.

Pour aspic over the beef slices, being careful not to disarrange the decoration. Chill until set. This will take about 2 hours in the refrigerator.

AT SERVING TIME:

Serve with heated crusty bread. Provide one hot vegetable and a salad. Serves 12.

Blanchette de Veau

This is one of the treasures of French cuisine, a dish with a delicate flavor and a silky smooth sauce. This recipe makes enough to serve

12 people. If there isn't a large party in the offing, you might make up the same quantity—some to eat at once and two or three portions to put into the freezer.

YOU WILL NEED:

veal	onions
cream of chicken soup	canned mushrooms
dry white table wine	egg yolks

Have 6 pounds of boneless veal cut into 1-inch cubes. Put the veal cubes into a large kettle with 3 cans of condensed cream of chicken soup and 3 cups very dry white table wine, like California Reisling. Add 1 1/2 cups water and 3 medium-size onions thinly sliced. Cover and cook slowly for 1 hour. Five minutes before the hour is up, add three 6-ounce cans of button mushrooms, sliced or whole.

AT SERVING TIME:

Place 3 slightly beaten egg yolks in a warm serving dish; slowly add the sauce from the kettle, stirring constantly. Then put the meat into the sauce. Keep warm but do not allow to boil after the eggs are in or the sauce will curdle.

Serve with rice and a tossed green salad.

In spring at violet time, you might want to serve a Parisian salad of fresh young greens and wild violets.

Brunswick Stew

You can buy an excellent Virginia-made Brunswick stew in cans but it is not widely distributed. Luckily, however, you can make one almost as fast by combining several products that are universally available.

A Brunswick stew is one of the many traditional dishes which are difficult to classify. Some call it a stew; others call it soup. Some people prefer the meats in very small pieces; others, in bigger chunks. Some like it hot with Worcestershire sauce and Tabasco. Others like it mild or winey. In this recipe you have room to express your own preferences. This recipe should provide sustenance for twelve.

YOU WILL NEED:

canned beef stew (prefer- ably without potatoes)	canned succotash sherry
canned chicken fricassee	Worcestershire sauce
canned tomatoes	Tabasco sauce

Heat together 3 cans each of the following: beef stew, chicken fricassee, tomatoes, succotash. Let simmer 5 minutes.

As for seasoning: In the Carolinas they would add 1 1/2 cups sherry and about a tablespoon of Worcestershire. In Georgia there would be no sherry but maybe 3 tablespoons of Worcestershire. In Virginia they might use the sherry and instead of Worcestershire several dashes of Tabasco sauce.

If you want a more liquid dish, add canned consommé or chicken broth. If you would rather have a thick stew, add about 1/2 cup packaged bread crumbs.

AT SERVING TIME:

Ladle into deep hot plates or shallow bowls. Serve with squares of hot corn pone or corn sticks and plenty of cole slaw.

Carbonade of Beef

Originally this dish came from Belgium. Essentially it is a beef stew, but it is made with beer.

YOU WILL NEED:

beef from rump	brown sugar
flour	tomato sauce
bacon fat or butter	celery flakes
malt vinegar	parsley flakes
beer	bay leaf
canned onion soup (with- out cheese)	thyme canned consommé (if neces- sary)
carrots	

Order 5 pounds of beef cut from the rump. Ask the butcher to slice the meat 1/2 inch thick. And when you get home, pound it thinner and cut the slices into 2-inch squares.

Place the meat in a plastic bag along with 1/2 cup flour. After the meat has been well floured, brown the pieces in 1/2 cup bacon fat or butter. Remove the meat from the pan and add to the rich brown glaze that the meat has left 3 tablespoons malt vinegar, 2 cups beer, 3 cans onion soup (the kind that does not contain cheese), 1 can sliced carrots, 2 teaspoons brown sugar, 1/2 cup tomato sauce, 2 teaspoons dehydrated celery flakes, 2 teaspoons parsley flakes, 1 bay leaf, 1/2 teaspoon dried thyme. Bring to a boil, then lower the heat and simmer about 5 minutes.

Now place the meat and the gravy in layers in a casserole that can come to the table. The gravy should cover the meat. If you haven't enough gravy, add condensed canned consommé. Cover the dish tightly with its own lid or aluminum foil and cook about 1 hour or until the meat is very tender.

AT SERVING TIME:

Bring to the table in its own baking dish and serve with fluffy boiled potatoes or, if you prefer, with rice, hominy grits, or polenta. Beer, of course, is the ideal accompaniment, and dill pickles have an especial affinity. Serves 12.

Cassoulet of Beans

In almost every country in the world you will find interesting bean dishes. Among the most noted are the various cassoulets of France. In the old days such dishes required days of preparation, soaking, simmering, baking. Now all that is necessary is to combine canned beans with different kinds of meat. The popular baked beans in tomato sauce give an authentic look and flavor. Or those smoky beans known as "Campside" may be used.

We think that a cassoulet is more interesting if the meat is in good-sized pieces. If, however, your party is to be a buffet, you can of course use cubes of pork instead of pork chops. Leftover meats can be used also, but they should not be browned.

YOU WILL NEED:

pork chops or pork
bacon or other drippings
onion
garlic
rosemary
powdered ginger

tomato-sauced beans
red or white table wine or
    dry vermouth or sherry
packaged bread crumbs
parsley

Brown 12 small pork chops or 4 pounds of cooked, diced pork in bacon fat or drippings. Place in a well-buttered casserole along with a large onion cut into quarters and 2 cloves garlic that have been put through the press or 1/2 teaspoon instant garlic. Sprinkle both sides of the browned meat with salt, pepper, a little rosemary, and a touch of powdered ginger.

Open 4 cans (1 pound 5 ounces each, about 10 cups) tomato-sauced beans. Arrange in the buttered baking dish with pork chops. The chops should be half hidden, half showing.

Pour on 1 to 2 cups red or white table wine or dry vermouth or 1/2 cup sherry. Sprinkle with packaged bread crumbs. This recipe is particularly good if put together the day before, refrigerated overnight, and put in oven before the party.

About 2 hours before the party, place the refrigerated cassoulet in a moderately hot oven 375° F. for 1 hour or until bubbling hot and golden brown.

AT SERVING TIME:

Sprinkle generously with fresh parsley. Serve with heated crusty rolls and a green salad. Serves 12.

Chicken Tetrazzini

This delightful combination has the advantage of being very simple and easy to prepare—and economical, too. Can be baked in individual casseroles or in large shallow baking dishes, whichever is most convenient.

YOU WILL NEED:

thin spaghetti	white wine (optional)
butter or olive oil	Cheddar cheese
onion	canned boned chicken
garlic	pimientos
condensed cream of mush-	parsley
room soup	paprika

Cook 1 pound thin spaghetti or vermicelli in boiling salted water until just tender but not soft. Drain and mix thoroughly with a little melted butter or olive oil.

Cook 1/2 cup chopped onion and 1 clove garlic (crushed) in

2 tablespoons butter or olive oil until tender. Blend in 4 cans condensed cream of mushroom soup and 2 cups water or 1 cup water and 1 cup dry white wine. Stir until smooth. Add 2 cups (1/2 pound) shredded sharp Cheddar cheese (preferably not processed). Save remaining cheese to use later. Cook over low heat until cheese is melted. Stir occasionally. Fold in 4 (6-ounce) cans of boned chicken, diced or broken into pieces; add 1/4 cup drained chopped canned pimientos and 1/4 cup chopped fresh parsley or 2 tablespoons parsley flakes.

Butter baking dishes lavishly. Place the cooked spaghetti on the bottom of the baking dish. Cover with the chicken mixture, sprinkle with 2 cups grated cheese and fleck lightly with paprika. Bake in hot oven, 425° F., until the sauce bubbles and the top browns: about 20 minutes for a large casserole, or 10 minutes if you use individual casseroles.

AT SERVING TIME:

Serve in the original baking dish garnished with bouquets of parsley. A wonderfully good and complete meal when served with assorted relishes. Serves 12.

English Steak and Kidney Pie

Canned beef and kidney stew and oven-ready biscuits combine to make a miraculously speedy but extraordinarily tasty version of an ancient British dish.

YOU WILL NEED:

canned beef and kidney stew	Worcestershire sauce
	ready-to-bake biscuits
canned silver-skin onions	Kitchen Bouquet
whiskey	butter

Count on 1 can of beef and kidney stew to make 2 servings. So for a dozen servings provide 6 cans and drain off about half the gravy to be heated and served separately. Turn the stew into a large but shallow baking dish. Add 2 cans silver-skin onions well drained. Sprinkle with 4 tablespoons whiskey and 1 tablespoon Worcestershire sauce. Set ready-to-bake biscuits on top of the stew. You can pat them a little thinner if your dish is very large and you feel the need of more cover-up. Usually there are a dozen biscuits in each package. Brush the biscuits with melted butter to give them a beautiful glaze and extra flavor.

Bake in a hot oven, 425° F., about 15 minutes or until the stew is bubbling hot and the biscuits are baked.

Meanwhile heat the extra gravy, seasoning it with a little whiskey, Worcestershire and adding a few drops of Kitchen Bouquet.

AT SERVING TIME:

Bring the steak and kidney pie to the table in its own dish. If you like, you may pin a napkin around the dish in the English manner. Have the extra gravy piping hot alongside with its own ladle. Provide traditional British accompaniments such as mustard, chow chow pickle, Worcestershire or A-1 Sauce, Walnut Catsup, or pickled walnuts. Serves 12.

Filet of Sole with Vermouth

This is an elegant Friday feast, wonderfully easy to do.

In this dish the vermouth is the same kind that you use for making a dry Martini. It imparts to the dish not only the quality of a dry white wine and a brandy but also the flavor of many delicate herbs.

YOU WILL NEED:

frozen fillets of flounder or red perch	instant onion
butter	dry vermouth
salt	packaged bread crumbs
white pepper	chives or parsley

Thaw 3 packages frozen fillets of flounder or red perch just enough to separate them. Cut crosswise in halves. Place in a well-buttered shallow baking dish and sprinkle with 3 teaspoons salt, 3/4 teaspoon white pepper, and 1 teaspoon instant onion. Combine 2 cups dry vermouth with 1 cup water and pour over the fish. Cover with 1 cup packaged bread crumbs; dot with 3 tablespoons butter.

Bake in a moderate oven, 350° F., 25 minutes or until the fish is cooked and the top lightly brown.

AT SERVING TIME:

Strew generously with chopped chives or parsley, and serve with new potatoes boiled in their jackets, peas or asparagus, and a cucumber and tomato salad. Serves 12.

Hungarian Beef Paprika

This is an unusually savory goulash. Made with canned onion soup in a pressure cooker, it is practically workless and ever so swift.

YOU WILL NEED:

butter or chicken fat	capers
beef for stew	bay leaves
flour	parsley flakes
canned onion soup	dry sherry wine
Hungarian paprika	broad noodles
vinegar	poppy seeds, almonds, or
caraway seeds	bread crumbs
fresh or dried marjoram	

Heat 3 tablespoons butter or chicken fat in a heavy kettle, a Dutch oven, or a big pressure cooker.

Have ready 6 pounds of beef for stew cut into inch cubes. Put the meat into a bag with a cup of flour and shake until the meat is evenly covered. Brown in hot fat, turning occasionally.

Add 3 cans condensed onion soup, the kind that does not have cheese in it. (To be sure, look at the list of ingredients on the label.) Add 3 tablespoons sweet Hungarian paprika. The better and fresher the paprika, the better the stew. Add also 3 tablespoons vinegar, 3 tablespoons caraway seeds, 1 tablespoon dried marjoram or twice that amount of fresh marjoram, 2 tablespoons capers, 3 bay leaves, a couple of tablespoons of parsley flakes and 1 cup dry sherry wine. Cook in a pressure cooker at 15 pounds pressure 15 minutes. Allow to cool, open the cooker, remove bay leaves.

Or you may cover the kettle and cook at a slow simmer about 2 hours or until the meat is tender.

AT SERVING TIME:

Serve with broad noodles well buttered and sprinkled with poppy seeds, almonds, or bread crumbs. Canned Blue Lake Green Beans make a delightful accompaniment. Serves 12.

Hunter's Stew

Now that quick-frozen rabbits, cut up for stew, are available at any time of the year in all sections of the country via the frozen food bins, even the hunter who comes home emptyhanded can celebrate. Or if you like, you may substitute beef for rabbit. For a party of 12, home from the hills and hungry, these proportions should be ample.

YOU WILL NEED:

canned sauerkraut
canned sliced mushrooms
bacon
frozen rabbit (or beef stew meat)

dehydrated onion soup
canned beef gravy
sugar
whiskey

Drain 2 cans sauerkraut; add 2 (6-ounce) cans sliced mushrooms complete with their liquid. Cover and simmer gently about 20 minutes. While they are simmering, cut 6 strips of bacon into small pieces and fry in a heavy frying pan. Remove the bacon from the pan and add 4 pounds cut-up rabbit or beef stew meat and brown in the bacon fat.

To the browned meat add the sauerkraut and mushrooms along with 1 package dehydrated onion soup, 2 cans beef gravy, 1 cup hot water, 1 tablespoon sugar, bacon bits, 1/2 cup whiskey (any good whiskey will do). Place in a large casserole; cover and bake in a slow oven, 325° F., about 2 hours or until the meat is tender.

Many of the older recipes for this type of stew suggest that it should be set aside in a cool place for 24 hours to mellow.

AT SERVING TIME:

Reheat. Serve with potatoes boiled in their jackets or baked stuffed potatoes. Regular baked potatoes are good too but they are not recommended for a party for they need to be served the instant they are ready. Baked stuffed potatoes, on the other hand, can be kept on the buffet table for a good long time and can even be frozen and reheated.

Whole small tomatoes are often served as an accompaniment to a hunter's stew and all kinds of raw vegetables are appropriate, too.

Instead of French bread, you might brush a loaf of caraway-seeded rye bread with butter and heat in aluminum foil in the oven.

Kentucky Burgoo

Traditionally burgoo is an outdoor dish of heroic proportions. It was, in the old days, prepared always in great iron cauldrons. Some of the ancient recipes demand a dozen "squirrels" for each 100 gallons. Many of Kentucky's most vivid political campaigns have originated or ended around the burgoo kettle.

At the present time burgoos are becoming popular again, but now they are being made in and served from electric kettles, or they can just as well be cooked in the kitchen even a day or so ahead of time and heated and kept hot in one of those ever-useful thermos jugs.

YOU WILL NEED:

bacon drippings or butter	medium-size potatoes
stew meat (pork, lamb, beef and/or veal)	carrots
	rice
frozen fricassee chickens	quick-frozen succotash
Bourbon whiskey	quick-frozen okra
dehydrated onion soup	black pepper
bay leaves	Tabasco sauce
canned stewed tomatoes	salt

Brown slowly in 4 tablespoons bacon drippings or butter 3 pounds cubed stew meat (pork, lamb, beef and/or veal) along with 2 quick-frozen fricassee chickens cut in pieces as for fricassee. When the meat has taken on a pale gold tinge, add to the skillet 1 cup Bourbon whiskey. Set the liquor aflame with a match and allow to blaze for about 1 minute. Then cover the meat with boiling water and add 1 package dehydrated onion soup, 2 bay leaves, 1 large can of stewed tomatoes—the kind that contain green peppers, etc. Simmer slowly about 1 1/2 hours until meat is almost tender.

One half hour before serving time add 6 medium-size potatoes cut into quarters, 6 carrots cut into 1-inch pieces, and 1 cup rice. After 15 minutes, add 2 packages quick-frozen succotash, 2 pack-ages quick-frozen okra, 1 tablespoon salt or enough to suit your taste, 1 teaspoon black pepper, and enough Tabasco to give a slight but authentic tingle. Cook 15 minutes longer. Burgoo is all the better for being made ahead of time and reheated.

AT SERVING TIME:
Ladle burgoo into shallow bowls or soup plates and serve with hot rolls or corn sticks and cole slaw. Serves 12.

Lazy-Luscious Lasagna

No one, not even an Italian connoisseur, would ever guess that any corners are cut in the preparation of this specialty. Classical recipes call for the widest kind of ribbon pasta with many layers of sauce, several kinds of cheese, chopped meats and meatballs. But here we use quick-frozen lasagna. When combined with cottage cheese or Italian ricotta 1 package quick-frozen lasagna can be counted on to serve 2 guests generously. This recipe serves 12.

YOU WILL NEED:

garlic	Creamed cottage cheese or
olive oil	ricotta
canned marinara sauce	Quick-frozen lasagna
	Parmesan cheese

Rub a large shallow baking dish or pan (which can come to the table) with a cut clove of garlic and brush with olive oil. Open 2 cans of marinara sauce. Cover bottom of baking dish or pan with marinara sauce and save a little for the top. Then spread a layer of creamed cottage cheese or ricotta about 1 inch thick. You will need about 2 pounds of ricotta or 4 of the usual containers of creamed cottage cheese for this. On top of the cottage cheese or ricotta place 6 packages quick-frozen lasagna and spread the rest of marinara sauce. Bake in a moderate oven, 350° F., about 30 minutes or until the sauce bubbles.

AT SERVING TIME:
Sprinkle generously with 2 cups Parmesan cheese and serve with a salad of hearts of escarole or dandelion greens.

To complete the meal, have a large platter of antipasto made up of celery, salami, radishes, olives, canned pickled Italian peppers, pickled eggplant (which is called caponata), canned pimientoes, sardines, anchovies, and tuna fish sprinkled with capers. For dessert: fresh fruit or berries, and/or raspberry, lemon or orange sherbet.

Navarin of Lamb

Call it lamb stew, if you like, but be assured this is a most glamorous French version.

YOU WILL NEED:

boned shoulder of lamb	bay leaf
butter	Blue Lake green beans
onions	canned carrots
allspice	dry white table wine

Have 5 pounds boned shoulder of lamb cut into pieces for stew. Melt and allow to brown slightly 1/4 pound butter in a heavy kettle or Dutch oven. Place the meat and 3 sliced onions in the butter and cook until the meat is browned on all sides. Season with 1 tablespoon salt, 1 teaspoon pepper, 1/2 teaspoon allspice, and 1 bay leaf.

Drain the juice from 3 cans Blue Lake green beans and 2 cans (or jars) baby carrots or sliced carrots. There should be about 2 cups of juice. If there isn't, add a little water. Pour this liquid onto the meat, add the same amount (2 cups) of dry white table wine.

Cover the kettle and stew gently on top of the stove or in a moderate oven, about 350° F., about 1 1/2 hours or until meat is tender. Or, if you are in a hurry, cook 15 minutes at 15 pounds pressure in the pressure cooker.

AT SERVING TIME:

Add the canned green beans and the carrots. Heat momentarily and serve with fluffy boiled potatoes. Serves 12.

Old Charleston Chicken and Oyster Fricassee

If you wish you could, of course, omit the oysters and you would still have one of the most interesting chicken fricassees that anyone has ever tasted.

YOU WILL NEED:

canned chicken fricassee	canned broiled-in-butter
nutmeg	mushrooms
anchovy paste	lemons
pale dry sherry	capers
egg yolks	toasted almonds
oysters	

To serve 12 generously, use 6 cans chicken fricassee. Add 3/4 teaspoon nutmeg, 2 teaspoons anchovy paste, and 1 cup pale dry sherry. Cover and heat, but do not boil or the chicken will fall apart and become shreddy.

In a bowl, beat 3 egg yolks lightly; add to the egg yolks a little of the sauce from the chicken, stirring until smooth. Then little by little add more of the hot sauce to the egg mixture and finally turn the mixture into the kettle.

Heat 3 dozen fresh or frozen oysters in their own juice until the edges begin to curl—about 2 minutes. Combine with the oysters 3 cans sliced broiled-in-butter mushrooms drained, 1/2 cup lemon juice, 3 tablespoons capers.

Put everything together and heat but, once again, do not boil. Keep hot over hot water in a warming oven set about 180° F. or on an electric hot tray set at low heat.

AT SERVING TIME:

Garnish with the thinnest possible slivers of lemon peel and toasted almonds. Serve with rice.

Pasta with Clams in Bianco

For those who have true appreciation of the full glories of Italian pastas, *in bianco* represents the zenith. It is a white sauce guiltless of flour or any thickening and guiltless also of tomato.

All sorts and shapes of pasta may be used in this recipe—exceedingly thin spaghetti, vermicelli, linguini, or fettucini, all of which are of varying thicknesses.

You can also add drama and interest to the dish by using pasta in the shape of shells or quills, bow knots, wheels or corkscrews. (Not only Italian shops but even supermarkets now carry a wide variety of shapes and sizes.)

Count on 4 pounds of pasta for 12 people and you'll *surely* have enough. A giant-size kettle or two large ones are required.

YOU WILL NEED:

pasta	parsley
canned minced clams	olive oil
garlic	

Crush or finely mince 6 cloves of garlic and cook them in 1 1/2 cups olive oil. Add liquid from six 10 1/2-ounce cans of minced clams and save the clams to add later. Add 1/2 cup chopped fresh parsley, 1 tablespoon salt, and 1/2 teaspoon pepper. Simmer sauce for 10 minutes. Then add clams and simmer exactly 2 minutes longer—no longer.

About 15 minutes before serving time, cook 4 pounds of pasta according to package directions. Be sure not to overcook. Each type of pasta requires a different cooking time.

AT SERVING TIME:

Drain the water from the pasta. Add the sauce, mixing it gently but well. Turn onto well-heated platters or bowls and serve immediately.

Serve with a green salad made up of escarole, cooked cauliflower flowerlets, black olives, cut-up celery, and tomatoes, mixed with a dressing of olive oil and lemon.

Shrimps Armenonville

One of the most beautiful restaurants in the world is the Café Armenonville set in the fairylike gardens off the Bois de Boulogne in Paris. It was here that we got their original recipe for their renowned chafing dish specialty. Years later we evolved a quick version made with canned quick-frozen cream of shrimp soup and quick-frozen shrimp. Canned shrimp could be used, but at the present writing they are not as good as the frozen. The best of frozen shrimp are individually quick-frozen and will rattle when you shake the package. This type is all deveined and shelled, too.

YOU WILL NEED:

quick-frozen cream of shrimp soup	pale dry sherry
milk	Tabasco sauce
curry powder or paste	nutmeg
prepared mustard	quick-frozen shrimp
Worcestershire sauce	eggs

To make 12 generous servings, use 4 cans quick-frozen cream of shrimp soup and 2 soup cans of milk. Heat along with 2 tablespoons curry powder or paste, 1 tablespoon prepared mustard, 1 tablespoon Worcestershire sauce, 3/4 cup pale dry sherry, a few drops of Tabasco sauce, and 1/4 teaspoon nutmeg. When the sauce is thoroughly hot but not boiling, add 4 packages of quick-frozen shrimp. Bring to a boil and cook slowly until the shrimps are pinkish and done. This will take only about 2 minutes. Remove from the stove.

Beat 2 whole eggs or 4 egg yolks slightly along with 2 tablespoons sherry. Stir a couple of spoonfuls of the hot sauce from the shrimp into the eggs and then turn the whole thing into the sauce. Keep hot but do not boil.

AT SERVING TIME:

Present in a chafing dish along with heated wild rice or parsleyed rice and canned stewed tomatoes sprinkled with garlic-flavored croutons. (You can buy croutons in jars, too.)

Sukiyaki, Chain-Store Style

This special party dish is *not* one that waits. An adaptation from the Japanese, it uses only products available at any grocery store.

Quick and dramatic, sukiyaki should be prepared at the table in full view of your admiring guests—not at all difficult to do in this day of supremely portable electric units and electric skillets.

YOU WILL NEED:

beef suet or peanut oil	spring onions
Bermuda onions	chicken broth or consommé
celery	frozen chip steaks or fresh
canned sliced mushrooms	rump steak
frozen leaf spinach	sugar
canned bean sprouts	soy sauce
	raw eggs (optional)

Arrange all the ingredients attractively on one or two large platters.

Rub a heated frying pan with pieces of beef suet, using about
4 pieces 1 by 2 inches, and after you have rubbed the pan leave the
suet in the pan. Or, in place of suet, use 3 tablespoons peanut oil.
Add 3 large sliced Bermuda onions; cook till onions are golden.
Now add 3 cups thinly sliced celery, three 6-ounce cans drained
sliced mushrooms, 3 packages frozen leaf spinach, 6 cups canned
drained bean sprouts (three 16-ounce cans), and 3 bunches spring
onions with 3 inches of tops left on (cut these into 1-inch pieces).
Cook only until vegetables are thoroughly heated, about 3 minutes.

Now add 1 can (1 1/3 cup) condensed chicken broth or bouillon. There should be just enough liquid to cover bottom of pan.
Over the top of the vegetables place 3 packages (about 3 dozen)
very thin quick-frozen chip steaks or 3 pounds rump steak sliced
paper thin. Cover and allow to steam about 5 minutes. Then add
3/4 cup soy sauce. Sprinkle with 3 tablespoons sugar and simmer
until the vegetables are done but still on the crisp side. A little
more broth or soy sauce may be added, if you wish.

AT SERVING TIME (*which means immediately*):

Spoon the sukiyaki onto steamed rice. For interesting authenticity,
provide each guest with a tiny bowl in which there is a raw egg.
Each person breaks the egg and dips morsels of his sukiyaki into
the egg. It gives a delicious flavor. Have on hand extra soy sauce
for those who want it. A light beer is an excellent accompaniment.

Always there must be tea. Try Japanese tea if you can get it,
Chinese tea, or any green tea.

Trout in Champagne

As prepared in Paris this dish is an intricate work of art. There,
the trout is skinned and boned but the head and tail are left on.
Often the fish are stuffed with chopped trout. But we have simplified the method enormously without altering the essential char-
acter of the dish. The sauce, even though it is made with canned
cream of mushroom soup, is still rich with butter and eggs inef-
fably blessed with champagne. Quick-frozen trout from Iceland

are available in many parts of the United States, but if your shop is out of trout you may use fillets of any other delicate fish like flounder or perch.

YOU WILL NEED:

trout or fillets	*For sauce*
canned whole mushrooms	cream of mushroom soup
carrots	egg yolks
shallots, optional	champagne
garlic, optional	lemon juice
onion	cayenne pepper or Tabasco
bay leaf	sauce
thyme	
champagne	
butter	

Provide 1 small trout or 1 small whole fillet for each person. For 12, place a dozen fish or fillets in a long shallow baking dish which has been lavishly buttered.

Drain three 4-ounce cans of whole mushroom caps and place them around the fish, along with 3 thinly sliced carrots, 1/2 dozen shallots put through a garlic press, 2 cloves of garlic also put through the press, and 1 medium-size onion finely chopped or 1 tablespoon instant onion. Add 1 bay leaf and sprinkle lightly with the merest pinch of thyme and a little salt and pepper. Moisten with 2 cups champagne. Cover the dish with a lid or with buttered aluminum foil and set in a moderate oven, 350° F., 20 to 30 minutes.

When the fish is opaque and flakes off easily at the touch of the fork, remove it from the oven. Drain or dip the juices out of the baking dish and combine with 1 cup champagne, 1 can condensed cream of mushroom soup, 4 slightly beaten egg yolks, and 3 tablespoons lemon juice. Do the combining off the stove. Then place the sauce over low heat and heat slowly while beating continuously until the sauce is well combined and very smooth. Be careful not to allow the sauce to boil. Add a mere mite of cayenne pepper or a couple of drops of Tabasco sauce.

AT SERVING TIME:

Place the fish in a large warm platter. pour the sauce over it, and arrange the mushrooms around the edge.

West African Chicken and Peanut Stew

This is one of the great specialties of West Africa. Like all of its kin, it is part stew, part soup, and has many variants. The salient characteristics in Ghana and Nigeria are peanuts (called ground-nuts in Africa), tomatoes, onions, okra. Always there is the hot glow of pepper and often, eggplant.

Traditionally, whole hard-cooked eggs are added to the stew at serving time along with boiled rice, hominy grits or mashed yams, or cornmeal mush similar to Italian polenta.

This type of stew nowadays is often accompanied by a wide variety of delicacies rather like the sambals served with curry.

YOU WILL NEED:

For the Stew:
frying chickens
peanut oil
onion soup
tomato sauce
peanut butter
okra
eggplant (optional)
chili powder
anchovy paste (optional)
liquid smoke (optional)

Accompaniments:
rice, hominy grits, mashed
   yams or mush
coconut, fresh or toasted,
   or both
canned roasted salted
   peanuts
anchovies
cayenne pepper smoothed
   into a paste with little
   water
sliced bananas and oranges
canned drained mangoes,
   papayas and/or peaches
diced or sliced tomatoes
chopped or sliced peppers,
   green or red
crisp crumbled bacon
canned French fried onions
hard-cooked eggs

Thaw 2 packages chicken cut up for frying. Season with salt and pepper. Sauté chicken in 4 tablespoons peanut oil or any other light salad oil.

Measure 2 quarts boiling water into a large pot. Add 2 packages dehydrated onion soup or use enough canned onion soup to make 2 quarts. Add two 8-ounce tins of American-style tomato sauce, then the sautéed chicken. Simmer about 10 minutes.

Wash and dice 1 medium-size eggplant. Peel or not as you wish, and sauté in the same oil that you have used for the chicken. You may need to add a little extra oil.

To 2 cups peanut butter, preferably the kind that comes with little chunks in it, add a little of the broth from the soup pot and stir until smooth, then add the stew. Season to taste with 1 to 2 teaspoons chili powder and about 2 teaspoons anchovy paste or salt. If you like, add a few drops of liquid smoke. Add 2 packages quick-frozen sliced okra or tiny whole baby okras, then the sautéed eggplant, if used. Heat slowly about 10 minutes longer.

Meanwhile, hard-cook a dozen eggs and shell them.

Have ready 6 cups cooked rice, mashed pale yams very lightly seasoned and lightly buttered, mush made from white or yellow cornmeal or hominy grits.

AT SERVING TIME:

Ladle stew into heated shallow bowls or soup dishes and spoon over it the rice, mashed yams, mush or grits. Put 1 hard-cooked egg in each soup bowl.

On a tray or Lazy Susan arrange all the accompaniments in small bowls. Be sure to provide each bowl with a tiny serving spoon. Each person adds to his plate of stew the preferred tidbits of spice and tang.

There is so much flavor in this dish that you may not feel the need of a real salad with dressing. Instead, why not have a bowl of crisp, cold raw vegetables (what the French call crudités): celery (hearts or sticks); finocchio—or do you call it fennel?—cut into wedges; radishes, white and/or red; hearts of lettuce, water cress; cucumber fingers; fresh cauliflowerlets or fresh broccoli; carrot curls or sticks or fresh young asparagus; spring onions.

For dessert, you might serve fresh fruits or a sherbet. And pralines, perhaps.

VARIATION:

Six pounds of stew beef may be substituted for the chicken. Here, too, eggplant may be omitted, but it does add interesting taste and smoothness.

❧ 19 ❧

〰〰〰〰〰〰〰〰〰〰〰〰〰

How to Open . . .

As any vaudevillian will tell you, the opener is crucial. First step toward becoming an impresario with a can opener is obviously getting the contents out of the can, the jar, or the bottle. Even in this day of technological miracles this process can range from easy and instantaneous to annoying, exasperating, and sometimes impossible.

Have you ever tried to cope with an imported ham? A sardine can that has lost its key? Jars with twist-off tops that refuse to twist off? Lids that will not flip? If you have ever had your temper frayed as you wrestled with a blunt old-fashioned can opener or your fingers snagged on jagged edges, you must certainly realize that in order to savor fully the ease and convenience of can-opener living you must consider the opener.

It pays to put some thought into choosing a can opener. The most expensive is not necessarily the best, nor is the cheapest always a bargain. Never buy a can opener unless you have an opportunity to try it first. A good can opener should be easy to use. It should not require too much pressure to puncture the can, and the opener should not be difficult to turn. The cut should be smooth, never jagged. Blades should be easy to clean and easy to keep clean. There is probably no more germ-laden area in the kitchen than a wall-type can opener that has become crusted with food particles. When a can opener cannot be immersed in water it should be cleaned with a brush and detergent.

Good quality hard steel is necessary for a can opener that is to be given constant use, for if the steel is not as hard as the can the blades become blunt and dulled. For occasional use a light, inexpensive, well-designed can opener will prove useful. For constant service it is usually better to pay more and get one that is durable and sturdy.

Every home should have at least one can opener that is equipped with a magnet that automatically lifts and holds the lid. The magnet not only will protect your fingers, but it will also keep the sterile contents of the can from becoming contaminated. This feature is especially important when you are opening baby foods, especially fruits that are served without additional heating.

PARADE OF OPENERS

Just as there are dozens of receptacles, dozens of different kinds of cans, jars and bottles, all sorts of different shapes and different closures, there are also dozens of tools for opening.

For the can there are openers that range in size from 1 1/2 inches to 15 inches, ranging in price from ten cents to over thirty dollars. There are some that are gilded and so small that they can hang from a charm bracelet or a watch fob. Many are attached to the wall. Quite a few plug into electricity. At least one electric can opener is portable—or, at least, portable to the length of the cord.

In addition to equipment designed specifically to open cans, there are numerous devices that flip up lids, take off tops, puncture beer cans, and whirl surely, neatly, and swiftly around a vacuum can.

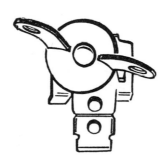

Small but mighty is a self-adjusting disc cutter that sells for about 29 cents. The flexible disc cutter adjusts automatically to any variations in the thickness of the rim, opens cans of all sizes and shapes. Operates with only one hand.

The littlest can opener is only 1 1/2 inches long. Originally designed by the military for K rations, it is constructed on a simple but sound engineering principle. The blade folds back so that it can be carried in the pocket or purse. It is ideal for the traveler. Available at shops that sell sporting equipment, it costs only 10 cents. Gilded to wear on your charm bracelet or key ring, the price is a little more.

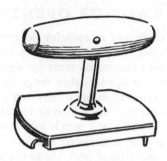

For all jars and bottles with screw tops, this opener is indispensable. It adjusts to lids from 1 to 3 inches in diameter. Costs about 50 cents.

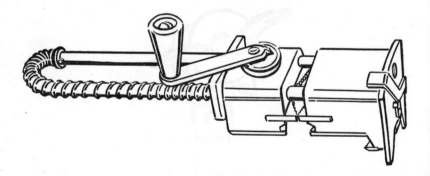

This excellent model opens all cans as well as beverage bottles and friction tops—ketchup bottles, pickles, olives, sardines, mushrooms, jams and jellies.

A tiny gadget, worth its weight in coin of the realm, this two-inch vacuum can opener takes the place of the key that comes with vacuum cans (constantly getting lost in our household). This

works much better than a key for it allows you to open the can hurriedly and even carelessly. The strip never breaks or gets off the track.

Jams, jellies, mayonnaise, all sorts of foods that come with lids, can be opened effortlessly with a lid flipper. A treasure for 15 cents.

Cap removers come in all sizes and in all types of metal from giveaways of plated steel to "gifts" of brass, copper, silver, and even gold. It's wise to have plenty of them in the kitchen, also at the dining table, the drink-mixing center, and in the picnic hamper.

For the well appointed table you should have an attractive beer and fruit juice opener. These come with many different kinds of handles, plastics, wood, even silver and gold.

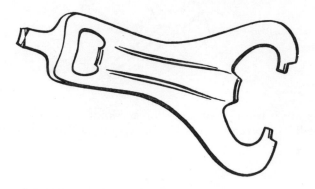

Utility combination can opener will not only open cans but also bottles. Punches beer cans and pulls corks.

This plier-type hand can opener is a de luxe version of a sturdy and highly versatile opener first developed for civil defense. With

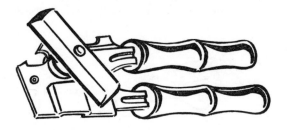

Tahitian wood handles, it is particularly handy as well as beautiful. Will not split, burn, stain, can be put in the automatic dish washer.

The can opener on the wall has been called the hub of the home in America. The best of them have excellent features including one-hand operation; a grease-sealed cutting wheel; powerful, long-lasting magnet to lift lids and hold tight; heavy plating of chrome or copper; enamel that is baked and will not chip; and cutting surfaces that are super-honed to keep their edges for a long time.

With such automatic can openers, lids are completely severed,

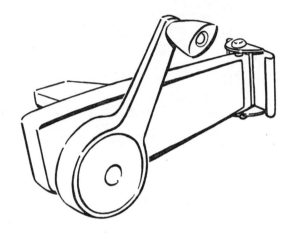

leaving a clean smooth edge. A built-in click tells you when to stop turning the handle after the lid is severed. A quarter turn backward releases the can.

Extremely useful in kitchens where there is no space to attach a wall bracket is an opener attached to a bracket, which stands on a table top.

Another table-top can opener, also for kitchens with limited wall space, comes equipped with a large and ever-clinging vacuum cup that will hold fast to any nonporous horizontal surface. Can be set up or put away in seconds.

ELECTRIC CAN OPENERS

Opening a can by hand is no great labor. Nevertheless, electric can openers have achieved considerable popularity in the last few years.

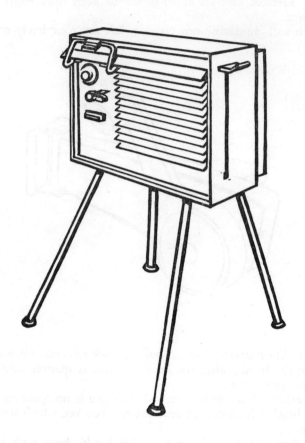

This electric automatic can opener looks as sleek and slim as a transistor radio. Can be mounted on the wall or used on its own rubber-footed stand. Opens cans any size in seconds. Even a heavy or dented can presents no problem.

Several companies that make blenders and mixers also have can-opening attachments.

Outstanding in this group is a portable electric can opener that has many fine features. It is compact, easy to handle, easy to clean;

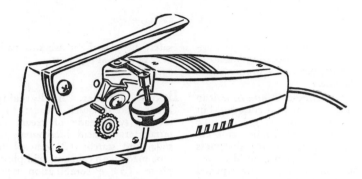

it has a folding magnetic lid lifter and is so light and small that it fits in the palm of your hand. It can be mounted on the wall or kept on the shelf. A six-foot cord makes it easy to use wherever you stand. Most modestly priced.

~~~~~~

Ac-cent. Brand name for a popular product containing monosodium glutamate. (See Monosodium Glutamate.)

American Cheese. White American Cheddar contains no coloring, but the usual yellow or golden type generally is artificially colored. Cheddar increases in sharpness with age. The young, mild cheese is best for slicing. Older ripened cheese becomes crumbly but has a finer flavor.

Anchovy (Fillets). There are two types of anchovies, Spanish (or Italian) and Norwegian (or Swedish). The former are the true anchovies, while the second are made from tiny fish called sprat.

Anchovy Paste. Comes in tubes and is made of finely crushed or ground anchovies. Used in canapés and salad dressing.

Anise. Sweet, spicy, licoricelike flavor; anise flavoring or seeds are used in baked goods, pickles, and candy.

Apple Brandy or Apple Jack. A true brandy distilled from apple cider. In France it is known as Calvados.

Asbestos Pad. A piece of asbestos material usually sold with a metal rim and handle. Can be obtained at most five-and-ten-cent stores, hardware or department stores. Useful for slow simmering or warming of foods at low heat. Baking dishes and Pyrex pans may safely be placed on asbestos pads over burners at low heat.

Baking Powder. A leavening agent used in quick breads: (1) tartrate type made of cream of tartar, tartaric acid, bicarbonate of soda, and starch; (2) phosphate type made with calcium, acid phosphate; (3) a combination type, generally referred to as double acting. It is not advisable to substitute one for another.

Basil or Sweet Basil. An annual herb of the mint family. Fresh or dried, the savory leaves are used in spaghetti sauces or in tomato dishes.

Bay Leaves. Aromatic leaves of the laurel tree, dried and used for flavoring pot roasts, stews, pickles, vinegar, soups, and fish—especially good with any tomato mixture.

Benedictine. A sweet liqueur, often served instead of dessert; very good over ice cream.

Blue or Bleu Cheese. A Roquefort-type cheese made in this country or in Argentina. In the United States, blue cheese is made with the same type of mold as French Roquefort, but generally of cow's milk rather than ewe's milk.

Camembert. A famous French cheese with a soft, mottled rind, which can be eaten. The inside is soft and creamy. American Camembert is now being made.

Can Sizes. Approximate contents in the most popular sizes of cans and jars:

6 oz: contains 1/2 cup, used generally for mushrooms, infant foods, tomato paste, tomato sauce, and meat spreads.

No. 1: Picnic, contains 1 1/4 cups. A small can used for vegetables, fruit juices, individual soups, a few meats, and fish products.

No. 303: contains about 2 cups and is used for vegetables, fruits, juices, and soup specialties.

No. 2: this is the most commonly used size—for fruits, vegetables, juices, ready-to-serve soups, and many specialties.

No. 2 1/2: contains about 3 1/4 cups. A large can in which many fruits and some vegetables, juices, and meat products are packed.

No. 10: a very large can holding 3 quarts or 12 cups. Fruit and vegetable juices are often sold in these large cans, and baked beans, soups, and other specialties in this size for the use of restaurants and hotels. If you want these cans for a large gathering, any grocer can order them for you.

Catchup. Popular condiment sauce containing tomatoes, vinegar, spices.

Caviar. Any fish roe preserved by salting is a caviar, but the word was originally applied only to sturgeon roe. An economical caviar is prepared commercially from the roe of the white fish.

Caviar (red). The roe of salmon.

Cayenne Pepper. Similar to red pepper, but made from small red pods of tropical peppers. It is dull red and very hot, and is used for catchups, relishes, fish, stews.

Celery Salt. Made by grinding celery seeds and salt together. Good with fish, boiled or fried eggs, potato salad, salad dressings, tomato dishes, and Irish stew.

Celery Seed. Seeds of celery used for flavoring.

Chablis. A white table wine.

Chafing Dish. Usually consists of two pans that fit into each other— a hot water pan on the bottom and a "blazer," which is the top, or cooking, pan. When hot water is placed underneath the "blazer," foods can be kept warm for a long time. Most chafing dishes are equipped with a heating element —alcohol lamp, sterno, or electric.

Chapon. The heel of a loaf of French bread or crusty roll into which a peeled halved clove of garlic has been pressed (may be held in place with a toothpick). This is usually tossed with a salad to impart a garlic flavor.

Chartreuse (yellow and green). Famous cordials made only by monks in the French Alps.

Cheddar. (See American Cheese.)

Cheese (How to Keep). Cut portions of cheese can be kept moist if they are wrapped in a cloth, dampened in a weak salt solution, about 1 tablespoon of salt to 1 pint of water.

Chervil. A parsleylike herb with a flavor reminiscent of parsley and basil. Can be bought dried.

Chili Powder. Main ingredient is chili pepper. Mexican pod peppers are ground and blended with various spices. It is used for making chili con carne and as a seasoning.

Chili Sauce. A condiment made of tomatoes, green peppers, and onions, with some sweetening spices and vinegar. Useful in salad dressings, sauces, stews, or casserole dishes.

Chives. One of the most useful of cooking herbs. Chives belong to the onion family, have very thin, threadlike green stems which are cut into fine bits and used in cooking and as a garnish.

Chutney. An East Indian relish, made of sliced mango, ginger, raw sugar, spices, and herbs. American versions combine chopped dry fruits. Home-type chutneys are made from apples or pears, chopped beets, horse-radish, or pickle. Chutney is served with curried dishes.

Citron. The fruit of the citron tree usually put up in two forms; "glacé," which means covered with a light coat of sugar; and "drained," which has all surplus sugar removed. Glacéed citron is usually diced, ready to use.

Cointreau. Clear, pale, orange-flavored liqueur. It imparts a subtle flavor to many desserts.

Coloring. (See Vegetable Coloring.)

Coriander. Small, light brown seeds used in making curry powder and in cakes, also for flavoring pickles, sausages, and mixed green salads.

Cottage Cheese. A soft, unripened, fresh cheese with a white color and a mild taste. Highly perishable. Does not freeze well.

Cream Cheese. A soft, unripened cheese akin to cottage cheese, but of a finer texture, made from cow's milk enriched with cream.

Crème de Cacao. A cordial that has a strong chocolate flavor; excellent for flavoring whipped cream or frozen desserts.

Crème de Menthe. A green or white, peppermint-flavored liqueur.

Cumin. Seeds something like caraway, used in making curry powder and seasoning sausage, rice dishes, soups, cheese, and canapés.

Curaçao. A cordial made of orange peel and spices.

Curry Powder. A mixture of herbs and spices. The various brands differ somewhat in proportion of ingredients.

Dill. Seeds of an herb of the parsley family. Widely used for pickling. Good for flavoring sauerkraut, salads, and soups.

Dubonnet. A French wine fortified with herbs and flowers. There are two kinds, regular red Dubonnet and white or blond Dubonnet, which is used as a flavoring for chicken and fish dishes.

Edam Cheese. A hard, Dutch-type cheese, often packed in a ball shape with a bright red paraffin coating.

Endive. A salad green, served either raw or cooked.

English Muffins. A raised yeast muffin which must be split and toasted before it is served.

Escarole. A lettucelike salad green with a delicious, bitter tang.

Extracts. Made, in most instances, from the essential oils of the items that give the extracts their names. These oils are generally dissolved with alcohol. The oil gives the extract its flavor. When the juices of fresh fruit, such as pineapples, raspberries, and strawberries are used, the flavor may be fortified.

Such fortified extracts must be labeled "imitation."

Fennel. The feathery leaves of this plant are used as a flavoring or garnish. The fleshy bulb, which has an anise flavor, is cut into sections and served like celery.

Fillets. Strips of meat or fish. Fish fillets are usually cut off the backbone. The skin is removed and there are few, if any, bones. A filet mignon is the eye of a sirloin steak, usually cut into individual slices.

Fines Herbes. A combination of herbs, usually parsley, water cress, chives, tarragon, chervil. Any two or three of these may be used in equal proportions to make a dish "aux fines herbes."

Finnan Haddie. Lightly smoked haddock. Available loose in dry form, but for timesaving it is best to buy it in cans or jars, for this type of finnan haddie can usually be used immediately without soaking or cooking.

Finnochio. The Italian name for fennel.

Flags. For the International Cheese Board see page 34. Can be secured from stationery stores or from the United Nations Information Office, UN Secretariat, New York. A complete set of paper flags for all the United Nations sells for about one dollar.

French Bread. A long, crusty loaf, the longest and thinnest of which are often known as flutes. Rolls made of the same dough are generally referred to as French, club, or hard rolls.

Garlic. A bulb that is divided into sections, popularly known as cloves or buds. Instead of fresh garlic, you may use garlic essence, powder, or salt. Since most garlic salt includes only about 30 per cent garlic in pure form and 70 per cent salt, the potency is limited. A good garlic powder is more satisfactory. A clove of prime raw garlic is equal to 1/6 of a level teaspoon of the best garlic powder.

Garlic Essence. Made from the garlic cloves, a powerful extract. A few drops of extract are equal to 1 clove garlic.

Garlic Salt. A combination of garlic and dairy or table salt, used for seasoning soups, salads, and spaghetti.

Gherkins. Tiny, pickled cucumbers available either sweet or sour.

Grade Labeling. Is the summary of many quality factors, indicated on the package "A," "B," "C," and "D" or "Fancy," "Choice," or "Extra-Standard," "Standard," and "Sub-Standard." The use of the letters *A, B, C,* and *D* is based on U. S. standards: *Grade A* or *Fancy:* the finest and most uniform vegetables or fruits obtainable; *Grade B, Choice,* or *Extra-Standard:* excellent product, but not quite as perfect or as uniform in color and size; *Grade C* or *Standard:* all sound and good, but the average run of the crop—may be slightly irregular in color and size, *Grade C* may not be so tender or as mature as the two top grades; *Grade D* or *Sub-Standard:* wholesome, but lacking in uniformity—some of it may be tough and may contain defects.

Grand Marnier. A clear, white, orange-flavored liqueur, similar in flavor to curaçao or Cointreau.

Green Chartreuse. There are two kinds of Chartreuse: green, which is most pungent and expensive; and yellow, which is almost as aromatic and much less expensive.

Gruyère Cheese. As sold in America, this is generally a processed Swiss cheese, most often cut into 1-ounce wedges and put up in six- or eight-ounce packages.

Hearth Bread. A round, crusty loaf, generally of the Italian or French variety.

Herb Specialists. For herb plants, unusual herb seeds, and information about growing herbs, write to Herb Garden, Inc., Huntington Station, Long Island, New York, or Spice Islands (Frederick Johnson), 70 Pine Street, San Francisco, California.

Hock. A dry, white German table wine. Excellent with fish. Should be served chilled.

Horse-Radish. A highly pungent root which is always shaved or grated. In all grocery stores, grated horse-radish can be found in bottles put up in vinegar. Sometimes beet juice is added to the vinegar. There is also dehydrated horse-radish which should be soaked for a few minutes in water or milk before using.

Ketchup. (See Catchup.)

Kippers or Kippered Herring. Sea herrings, slightly salted and smoked, available in quick-frozen form or in cans. Kippers require only heating before they are ready to serve. Canned kippers are packed plain or in tomato sauce.

Kirsch or Kirschwasser. Made in Germany, France, and Switzerland, from small black wild cherries. Popular with fruits. Use with discretion, as too much gives a medicinal flavor.

Kitchen Bouquet. A bottled, trademarked coloring and flavor that adds a rich brown color to gravy, sauces, etc. Useful for giving color to meats roasted at low temperatures. Contains onions, carrots, parsnips, turnips, celery, parsley, and spices as well as caramelized sugar. Use very little, for it can impart a bitter flavor.

Lingonberry. A small, cranberry type of berry about the size of a red currant, popular in Scandinavia, and generally available in this country in a preserve. Also known as preiselberry.

Mace. The dried outer coating of the nutmeg seed. It is sold ground or in blade form and is used to flavor soups, sauces, cakes, and puddings.

Madeira. A fortified dessert wine used for flavoring desserts and cakes. Dry Madeira is used to flavor soups.

Mail Order. All kinds of specialty foods, flavorings, herbs, and spices, as well as unusual canned and prepared products, can be ordered by mail. Many of these shops have catalogs free on request. All are equipped to handle orders quickly and efficiently. Listing is alphabetical by states.

Albert Steinfeld and Co., Tucson, Arizona

Pfeifer's Home Center, Little Rock, Arkansas

E. Gottschalk and Co., Inc., Fresno, California

Baltzer, Los Angeles, California

Bullock's, Los Angeles, California

The Farmer's Market, Los Angeles, California

Holman's Department Store, Pacific Grove, California

City of Paris, San Francisco, California

The Emporium, San Francisco, California

D. F. May Company, Denver, Colorado

G. Fox and Company, Hartford, Connecticut

Edward Malley Co., New Haven, Connecticut

Shartenberg's, Inc., New Haven, Connecticut

W. W. Mertz Co., Torrington, Connecticut

The Epicure, Wilmington, Delaware

Karl the Caterer, Washington, D. C.

Magruder, Inc., Washington, D. C.

The Hecht Co., Washington, D. C.

The Little Caledonia Shop, Washington, D. C. (Georgetown)

Woodward and Lothrop, Washington, D. C.

Burdine's, Miami, Florida

Maas Brothers, St. Petersburg, Florida

Maas Brothers, Tampa, Florida

Davison-Paxon, Atlanta, Georgia

Rich's, Atlanta, Georgia

Carson Pirie Scott and Co., Chicago, Illinois

Marshall Field and Co., Chicago, Illinois

The Wm. H. Block Co., Indianapolis, Indiana

George Wyman and Co., South Bend, Indiana

The Killian Co., Cedar Rapids, Iowa

Younker-Davidson's, Sioux City, Iowa

The Stewart Dry Goods Co., Louisville, Kentucky

Baker and Hickman, Madisonville, Kentucky

D. H. Holmes Co., Ltd., New Orleans, Louisiana

Solari's, New Orleans, Louisiana

The Cuban Liquor Co., Inc., Shreveport, Louisiana

Freese, Inc., Bangor, Maine

The Senter Co., Bangor, Maine

Porteous, Mitchell and Braun Co., Portland, Maine

William Bouchee, Baltimore, Maryland

Jordan Marsh Co., Boston, Massachusetts

S. S. Pierce, Boston, Massachusetts

Newton House, % McAuslan and Wakelin Co., Holyoke, Massachusetts

Forbes and Wallace, Inc., Springfield, Massachusetts

J. L. Hudson Co., Detroit, Michigan

Paul Steketee and Sons, Grand Rapids, Michigan

Gilmore Brothers, Kalamazoo, Michigan

Hardy-Herpolsheimer's, Muskegon, Michigan

J. B. Sperry Co., Port Huron, Michigan

Dayton's, Minneapolis, Minnesota

Donaldson's, Minneapolis, Minnesota

Golden Rule, St. Paul, Minnesota

Natchez Department Store, Natchez, Mississippi

European Import Corporation, St. Louis, Missouri

Scruggs, Vandervoort, & Barney, St. Louis, Missouri

Miller and Paine, Lincoln, Nebraska

Bamberger's, Newark, New Jersey

H. M. Voorhees and Bros., Trenton, New Jersey

Arnold Constable, Trenton, New Jersey

McLean's, Binghamton, New York

Abraham and Straus, Brooklyn, New York

Weed and Co., Buffalo, New York

H. G. Munger and Co., Inc., Herkimer, New York

B. Gertz, Jamaica, New York

B. Altman and Co., New York, New York

Bloomingdale's, New York, New York

Charles and Co., New York, New York

Fraser & Morris, New York, New York

The Vendome, New York, New York

Joseph Victori & Co., Inc., New York, New York

Beir Bros., Inc., Niagara Falls, New York

Bresee's Oneonta Dept. Store, Oneonta, New York

Sibley, Lindsay and Curr Co., Rochester, New York

Dey Brothers, Syracuse, New York

J. B. Wells and Son Company, Utica, New York

J. B. Ivey and Co., Charlotte, North Carolina

Ivey-Taylor, Raleigh, North Carolina

A. Polsky Co., Akron, Ohio

Canton Hardware Co., Canton, Ohio

H. S. Pogue, Cincinnati, Ohio

Halle Brothers, Cleveland, Ohio

Henry Taylor and Son, Cleveland, Ohio

Wm. Taylor Son and Co., Cleveland, Ohio

Rike-Kumler, Dayton, Ohio

LaSalle and Koch Co., Toledo, Ohio

Strouss-Hirshberg's, Youngstown, Ohio

Carl H. Meiser, Erie, Pennsylvania

Darmstaetter's, Lancaster, Pennsylvania

New Hope Craft Shop, New Hope, Pennsylvania

Gimbels, Philadelphia, Pennsylvania

Wm. Penn Fruit Shop, Philadelphia, Pennsylvania

C. A. Rowell's (Germantown), Philadelphia, Pennsylvania

John Wanamaker, Philadelphia, Pennsylvania

Joseph Horne Co., Pittsburgh, Pennsylvania

Kaufmann's Department Store, Pittsburgh, Pennsylvania

The Shepard Co., Providence, Rhode Island

The White House Dry Goods Co., Beaumont, Texas

Lichtenstein's Inc., Corpus Christi, Texas

Titche-Goettinger, Dallas, Texas

Frost Brothers, San Antonio, Texas

Zion's Cooperative Mercantile Inst., Salt Lake City, Utah

Charles Sterns and Co., Rutland, Vermont

Globman's, Inc., Martinsville, Virginia

W. G. Swartz Co., Inc., Norfolk, Virginia

Thalheimer's, Richmond, Virginia

The Anderson-Newcomb Co., Huntington, West Virginia

The Surprise Store, Parkersburg, West Virginia

Baron Brothers, Madison, Wisconsin

Malden Salt. (See Salt.)

Maple Flavoring. Usually, maple syrup fortified with lovage, fenugreek, and similar herbs. Maple extract can be used with sugar and water to make a maple-flavored syrup.

Maraschino. Originally, maraschino referred to a cherry liqueur richly flavored by the bruised cherry stones. Now the word usually refers to preserved cherries, brightly colored and flavored with coal tar derivative.

Marron. A large French- or Italian-type chestnut bottled with syrup and used principally for frozen desserts.

Marrons Glacés. A confection made from dried French marrons, cooked in sugar.

Meat Extract or Glaze. Concentrated meat juices available in the form of paste. Usually contain a sizable proportion of salt, some spices, and coloring. May be used instead of bouillon cubes. One teaspoon makes a cup of broth.

Monosodium Glutamate. A chemical generally known as MSG or by a number of trade names, it has no taste of its own, but seems to stimulate the taste buds and so accentuate flavors. Some brands contain salt, spices, and garlic; and this is stated on the label.

Mustard. There are two principal kinds of mustard seed: yellow or white, which is comparatively mild; and brown, which is pungent. Yellow or white mustard seed is sometimes sold in small packages for use in mustard pickles and other products. Dry mustard is the powder obtained by bolting the mustard flour through silk cloth after removal of the outer hull. *Prepared mustard* is the paste made by grinding mustard seeds and blending with salt, vinegar, and spices. The most popular prepared mustard is made from yellow mustard seeds; it is a mild mustard, often called *salad mustard*. Prepared mustard made from the brown seeds is sharper and is often described as Dijon-, French-, or German-type mustard because it is the color of the mustard prepared in European countries. *Horse-radish mustard* is a typical American mustard; it is a coarse-ground hot mustard with grated fresh horseradish. In some sections sharp mustard is known as *English mustard.* This is usually bought in powder form and mixed.

Nectarines. A fruit that combines the flavors of plum and peach.

Nutmeg. The dried seed kernel of the fruit of the nutmeg tree, ground or whole. Used for flavoring milk drinks, custards, puddings, cakes, and mincemeat.

Onion Extract. Made from the concentrated juice of onions.

Onion Flakes. Prepared by controlled drying of selected onions, flakes have natural flavor and can be used in place of chopped fresh onions. One teaspoon equals one medium-sized onion for cooking purposes.

Onion Salt. Combination of dehydrated onion powder, rice flour, and salt, used for flavoring soups, meats, and dressings.

Oka. A Canadian cheese similar to French Port du Salut. It is a semihard variety with a delicate, spongy texture.

Orange Extract. Made from the oil pressed from fresh orange peels. A few drops of extract may be used to give the flavor of orange peel.

Orégano. An herb that imparts some of the flavor of marjoram and thyme as well as sage.

Paprika. The dried and ground fruit of capsicum plants used for enriching gravies, sauces, sausages, etc.

Peach Brandy. A distilled liqueur with a strong flavor of the peach, as well as the peach kernel.

Pepper. Black and white pepper comes from the same plant. The black is picked green and dries black. When left on the vine until mature, pepper turns white. Red peppers are from another plant. All pepper should be protected from moisture and sunlight.

Peppercorns. The whole berry of the pepper vine. Peppercorns are used in pepper grinders. Freshly ground, black pepper has more flavor than commercially ground pepper.

Peppermint. Extract, or oil of peppermint, obtained by distilling leaves of the plant. A different extract from mint, for which the spearmint plant is used.

Pernod. An anise-flavored liqueur similar in taste to absinthe, but containing none of the harmful wormwood.

Pilot Crackers. Large crackers, very lightly salted, or unsalted, and traditionally used to thicken New England-type chowder or to serve as an accompaniment to chowder.

Pimiento. Sweet red peppers, seeded, flattened, and canned. Widely used as a flavoring in salads and sauces. To keep pimiento that has been opened, cover with olive or salad oil, place a lid on the dish and store in the refrigerator.

Pistachio. Small, oval nut with a thin, rosy-brown shell. Meat has characteristic pistachio-green color.

Pistachio Flavoring. An imitation flavor which also colors food pale green.

Poppy Seed. Very small seeds of the poppy plant, dark blue in color and used for garnishing bread and buns.

Port Wine. A full-bodied, fortified, dessert wine, particularly good with fruits and nuts. There are three kinds: ruby port, tawny port, and white port. White port is wonderful poured over peaches or grapes.

Processed Cheese. Natural, or bulk, cheese that has been heated, pasteurized, blended, and packaged for uniformity of flavor, texture and to provide better keeping qualities. Further ripening is impossible after a cheese has been processed. All cheeses of this type are marked as such.

Provolone. A smoked, Italian-type cheese. Widely used either sliced or grated in Italian dishes.

Pumpernickel. A bread made of coarse rye flour that is neither bolted nor screened. Has a distinctive flavor, a dark color. Russian pumpernickel is softer and more porous than the German pumpernickel, which is black-brown, and very moist.

Red Table Wine. Dry, nonsweet wine made of red grapes, traditionally served at room temperature, with red meat, game, goose, duck, or turkey.

Rhine Wine. Dry, white table wine which should be served chilled, usually with white meats, cheese dishes, or fish.

Rice. *Brown rice:* This is not a special variety, but is any rice from which the hull has been shelled, but the kernel left unpolished. *Parboiled rice:* partially cooked before milling, also known as *processed rice. White rice:* milled or polished rice of any variety. *Precooked packaged rice:* does not require any washing or draining. It is merely brought to a boil and allowed to stand, covered, in a warm place for 10 or 11 minutes. *Canned, cooked rice:* both white rice and wild rice are available already cooked in cans and need nothing but heating. *Wild rice:* is not a rice at all, technically speaking. It is greenish-gray in color, has a distinctive flavor and texture.

Romaine. A leafy vegetable of the lettuce family with long, pointed leaves. Delicious in salads.

Romano. A hard, salty, grating cheese.

Roquefort. A French cheese made of ewe's milk with a mottled appearance and a greenish-blue mold. Roquefort-type cheeses made in U. S. A., Denmark, and Argentina are generally called "blue" or "bleu" cheese.

Rose Extract. Prepared from the oil or attar of rose by distilling the petals of the flower. This is a highly concentrated, powerful essence requiring three thousand pounds of petals for the production of one pound of oil.

Rose Water. A dilute extract of roses, used for flavoring cakes, frostings, and beverages.

Rosemary. An herb that looks like a curved pine needle and has a sweetish taste. Rosemary is used for soups, stews, roasts.

Rum. A distillate of sugar cane. The light, brandy-type rums usually called white or white label rum; the darker, medium type referred to as golden or gold label rum; and the very dark, almost black, richly flavored type known as Jamaica or dark rum.

Saffron. Dried stamens of the purple crocus so concentrated that one ounce represents five thousand flowers. Used for coloring and flavoring foods.

Sage. The pleasantly bitter leaves of a shrub, used for flavoring soups, sausages, poultry stuffing, cheese.

Salad Oil. Oils, other than olive, widely used for making salad dressings: corn, peanut, soy bean, walnut, and coconut oils.

Salt. *Free-running salt*—harmless chemicals are added to keep the salt from caking; *iodized salt* to aid in the prevention of goiter; *Malden (or crystal) salt,* to be used in salt grinders. *Rock salt* is for killing weeds and freezing ice cream, also it is used as a bed for Oysters Rockefeller and other foods, which should be held and served at a very high temperature.

Sauterne. A white wine. Dry types are used as table wines and are particularly good with chicken or other white meat. Sweet sauternes are best served with dessert.

Savory. An annual herb, the leaves of which are used for seasoning meats, poultry, stews, and salads.

Sesame. Small seeds that vary from grayish-white to black when unhulled. When hulled, the seeds are pearly white with a flavor that resembles toasted almonds. In the south these are called benne seeds, and are widely used in Charleston recipes.

Shallot. A small, bulbous plant, reddish in color. Since a shallot combines the flavor of onion and garlic, these two ingredients may be substituted, though the resultant flavor is not exactly the same.

Sherry Wine. The most popular wine for flavoring. Use the dry sherry to flavor soups and sauces; sweet, dark sherries for the flavoring of desserts and fruit.

Soy Sauce. A condiment of Oriental origin made from the soy bean and containing herbs, spices, and salt.

Sugar. (1) *granulated,* white sugar, the most widely used; (2) *superfine, or powdered,* a granulated sugar that is especially good for fruits or sweetening cold drinks; (3) *confectioner's,* a pulverized sugar for uncooked frostings, icings, fondants, or candy; (4) *loaf, tablet, lump, or cube sugar*—principally used for sweetening hot tea or coffee; (5) *old-fashioned, dark brown sugar,* a moist, refined cane sugar in which some molasses has been allowed to remain. *Light brown sugar* or yellow sugar, lighter in color than the old-fashioned brown sugar, has a less-pronounced molasses flavor. Good in butterscotch or caramel puddings, sauces, or frostings.

Swiss Cheese. A mild, nutty cheese, having eyes or holes formed by gas-producing bacteria. The true Swiss product has the word "Switzerland" imprinted on the rind.

Tabasco Sauce. Trade name for a hot, red-pepper sauce. Only a drop or two should be used.

Table Wines. Dry, or nonsweet wines of the type usually served with the meal—not as a cocktail or dessert wine. There are three principal types of table wines: red, white, and an in-between wine known as rose or pink.

Tarragon. An herb, whose leaves are used for flavoring vinegar, mustard, etc. Available in dried leaves, sometimes put up with peanut oil. Leaves are also preserved in vinegar. Tarragon vinegar can often be substituted for tarragon when vinegar flavor is not objectionable.

Truffles. A fungus that grows under the earth. Imported from France and Italy, the truffle is glossy black, has a distinctive flavor rather like that of a musty, wild mushroom. Truffle peelings, or a combination of mushroom and truffles, are available in jars. These impart some truffle flavor at much less expense.

Turmeric. A dried and ground root that combines well with mustard; an important ingredient in curry powder.

Vacuum Packing. Means that the can has been sealed in the absence of air to prevent deterioration or staling.

Vanilla. The most important of the extracts is prepared from vanilla beans, the seed pods of a climbing plant belonging to the orchid family and growing in tropical countries. *Vanillin* is the most prevalent of the imitation extracts. Its base is vanillin, which sometimes appears on vanilla beans in the form of frost-like crystals; it is also made synthetically from oil of cloves and from lignin (obtained from wood).

Vegetable Colorings. Available in liquid, paste, or pellets.

Vinegar. An acid obtained by the fermentation of cider, wine, or beer: (1) *cider vinegar,* made from apple juice; (2) *malt, or beer vinegar,* made from malted grain, principally barley; (3) *tarragon vinegar,* cider, malt, or wine vinegar in which the leaves of the tarragon plant are infused; (4) *white (or distilled white) vinegar,* used in pickling, cooking, or for salads; because it is exceptionally strong, a lesser amount should be used; (5) *wine vinegar,* made from dry wines. Vinegar made from red table wine is red, while white wine vinegar has a light, golden color. Wine vinegars are often seasoned with basil, tarragon, garlic, shallots, or herbs.

Water Cress. A pungent salad green, delightful for garnishing, to use in salads, in soup, or in sandwiches.

Wine. Used in cooking to accent and balance the flavors already present and to supply aroma, acidity, and smoothness. Properly used, the flavor of the wine in a cooked dish cannot be readily identified and the alcohol passes off as soon as the food is heated.

Wintergreen Flavoring. Made from oil of wintergreen, distilled from leaves of the checkerberry plant, and from the bark of the black birch.

Worcestershire Sauce. In addition to soy sauce, made from soy beans, Worcestershire sauce contains vinegar, lime juice, tamarinds, onions, red chili peppers, and garlic. Some types are flavored with anchovy or pickled herring.

Yogurt. A cultured milk product, yogurt is infant cheese. It is generally packed in individual jars or cartons.

Zeste Morestin. A bottled caramel syrup, used to flavor desserts and fruits.

Index